The
COACHING
MANAGER

2
EDITION

To Our Coaches

The COACHING MANAGER

DEVELOPING TOP TALENT IN BUSINESS

2 EDITION

JAMES M. HUNT
Babson College

JOSEPH R. WEINTRAUB
Babson College

Los Angeles | London | New Delhi
Singapore | Washington DC

For information:

SAGE Publications, Inc.
2455 Teller Road
Thousand Oaks,
  California 91320
E-mail: order@sagepub.com

SAGE Publications India Pvt. Ltd.
B 1/I 1 Mohan Cooperative
  Industrial Area
Mathura Road, New Delhi 110 044
India

SAGE Publications Ltd.
1 Oliver's Yard
55 City Road
London EC1Y 1SP
United Kingdom

SAGE Publications Asia-Pacific Pte. Ltd.
33 Pekin Street #02-01
Far East Square
Singapore 048763

Printed in the United States of America

Library of Congress Cataloging-in-Publication Data

The coaching manager: developing top talent in business/editors, James M. Hunt, Joseph R. Weintraub.—2nd ed.
    p. cm.
Includes bibliographical references and index.
ISBN 978-1-4129-7776-0 (pbk.)
    1. Mentoring in business. 2. Executives—Training of. 3. Leadership. 4. Management. I. Hunt, James M. (James Michael) II. Weintraub, Joseph R.

HF5385.H86 2011
658.3'124—dc22   2009051846

This book is printed on acid-free paper.

10   11   12   13   14   10   9   8   7   6   5   4   3   2   1

Acquisitions Editor:	Lisa Cuevas Shaw
Editorial Assistant:	MaryAnn Vail
Production Editor:	Carla Freeman
Copy Editor:	Melinda Masson
Typesetter:	C&M Digitals (P) Ltd.
Proofreader:	Scott Oney
Indexer:	Diggs Publication Service
Cover Designer:	Bryan Fishman
Marketing Manager:	Helen Salmon

Contents

Preface

This is a book for those who want to be better managers. Most specifically, it is for those who want to become more effective at building organizational capability by actually developing the talent of those with whom they work. The basic idea is simple. Take the time to hire properly. Look for those who would want to contribute to the kinds of work your team or organization is charged with completing. Look for some foundational strengths. Help those who join the organization grow by offering them challenging job assignments when you can. Then—and this is the step that is too often overlooked by practicing managers—help them learn from their experience when confronting the aforesaid challenges. Help them learn to reflect on their efforts in a way that will help them improve their performance, yes, but more important grow as workers and as individuals. They will thank you for it, and your organization will more likely be successful. If you're in a business, to put it bluntly, you just might make more money. If you're part of a mission-driven organization, such as a hospital, your people will do a better job of providing service. You'll all feel better about your work, at least in most cases. That's really the message of this book.

Of course, it isn't quite that easy. If it were, then we'd have lots more managers who behave as we've just described. We can't say this for certain, but our hunch is that there are more "coaching managers" than there were a decade ago when we began writing the first edition. We don't take credit for any improvements noted, but maybe we helped a bit. We now find that, for whatever reason, we get very little "push back" from audiences in most industries when we talk about the value of building relationships that help people learn from experience. So perhaps things are a bit better in that regard, but our guess is that the practice of management has not improved to nearly the degree that would result in the average worker feeling fully engaged in his or her work.

The conditions necessary to support improvements in the practice of management have not improved, we fear. Massive economic disruption and a seemingly never-ending preoccupation with short-term results at any and all costs don't help people think about how to create better organizations. At the same time and for related reasons, the need for effective leadership has grown exponentially. It's not clear that we're going to be able to meet those needs. The problem isn't the next generation; it's the current generation. The next generation understands full well that you have to keep learning to stay on top of your job, particularly if you hope to move ahead. I feel zero disappointment in my students as a group, and there are lots of them. Sure, the occasional individual doesn't take responsibility for his or her growth, but most do. The next generation of leaders is there and ready to step up, but they need help to do so.

We've come to understand that being a coaching manager is far more than demonstrating a few specific abilities. Coaching managers demonstrate a bit of good old-fashioned maturity as well. They are able to look beyond their individual needs and think about the good of the larger organization and those who work in the organization. They find the time to develop their people, even though time is probably their most precious resource. They do it because they know that it is their job, it's the right thing to do, and it will help (much like effective parenting and effective citizenship).

Leaders who are preoccupied solely with their own individual needs and stresses (or lusts as the case may be) are not likely to have the time to help their people grow. They are too busy trying to survive. In the coaching manager business, jokes about bad managers are not hard to come by. The most common form, one that we used to tell regularly, is a variation on "I got my review when I saw my paycheck," the implication being that zero performance appraisal was actually done. We used to think such jokes were actually quite funny, until it happened to one of us a few years ago. There's nothing funny about it.

Good managers create (or maintain) organizations that make people feel valued. Anything less than that is not sufficient. Poor managers rob organizations of their vitality and sense of personal integrity. They may be able to squeak by for a time, but over the long haul, they will create conditions that cause the performance of their people to deteriorate, along with their morale. Organizational failure, or a "meltdown" of some sort, is typically the result. Clearly we need more people to step up and serve as effective leaders and managers. So after 14 years of work, the task before us is more clear than ever. Our sense of urgency as to the importance of this work is even greater. In this second edition, we hope to serve those individuals who wish to engage with this challenge. We thank you for your interest in doing so and hope that we can help.

In this second edition of *The Coaching Manager*, we've tried to keep what worked, remove some material that has not been found to be useful, and add some material that we think warrants your consideration. (Notice that this follows the time-honored schema for continuous improvement: What should you keep doing, start doing, and stop doing?) In this effort, we've been aided not only by the many individuals who participate in Babson College's Coaching for Leadership and Teamwork Program (www.babson.edu/coach) but also by readers, educators who have made use of the book in course work, consultants, and MBA students. In particular, we've been helped by our Fast Track MBA students at Babson. Fast Track is an accelerated MBA program for more experienced working professionals who are capable of self-guided learning and development. We teach them the tools of talent management so that they will be better able to develop the talent in their organizations as well as their own talent. In the process of doing so, we've come up with what we think is a slightly more effective way to organize our presentation of the material.

The basic tactical tools of developmental coaching are described, in a fashion similar to that utilized in the first edition. We provide you with a quick overview and a somewhat expanded case example in Chapter 2. For those of you with no time to lose, we recommend going to Chapter 2 first. You can then utilize the outline of the developmental coaching model to choose areas on which to focus from the subsequent chapters.

We describe the coaching setup in Chapters 3 through 6. Here we talk about what a manager needs to do to create an environment in which coaching can take place. Chapter 3 represents a major reorganization of our presentation. In Chapter 3 we talk in detail about how you can define what you are hoping to achieve through the use of developmental coaching. We strongly recommend that the reader not overlook this chapter. Coaching is merely one tool among many that the manager has at his or her disposal. It should fit in with the other tools, but more important, the manager should be clear about what he or she is trying to accomplish. The manager also needs to communicate this clearly to those in his or her organization. If you can do this effectively, you'll provide a road map that is of enormous help to those hoping to learn from their experiences in working with you. If you can't, things may get muddled.

You also need to take the time necessary to coordinate your hiring activities with your goals and with your talent development work. It makes no sense to spend a lot of valuable time and effort trying to develop talent unsuited to the opportunities you have before you. As such, we have added a discussion about how the selection process fits into your overall talent management efforts. This is not a book on selection, so in case you need additional help in this area, we've provided several references that we, and others, have found useful.

Even having defined success and tried to staff your organization with those who are interested in learning and who are good fits for their roles, it is so important to create a context in which developmental coaching discussions can flourish. In Chapter 4, we discuss what we call the coaching-friendly context. If you can create a good context—some might call it a positive working climate or culture—we believe you're likely to find that coaching will break out even if you don't push it. Coaching conversations are naturally occurring, when they are not blocked by fear. Again, we encourage you to think about this strategically. Create a work environment in which people help each other, and your own responsibilities for helping them will be shared.

In Chapter 5, we discuss the thorny question of what it takes to be a good coaching manager. So much of it is still about your own intent. You have to be a good listener, yes. However, you don't have to be perfect. You have to demonstrate a consistent interest in your people and a desire to help them succeed. We discuss the road to becoming a coaching manager here.

We continue to stress in Chapter 6 the importance of deploying your coaching efforts carefully. Developmental coaching isn't remedial coaching. Chapter 6 will help you consider who can benefit the most from the developmental coaching process.

Get the coaching setup right, and the tactics of holding developmental coaching conversations, the skills required to be an effective coaching manager, can, we believe, be developed by most. We discuss those tactical issues in Chapters 7 through 11. Most important here, we believe, is the ability to create an effective coaching dialogue. Coaching is not feedback. In fact, as you'll see when you read Chapter 9, feedback as a learning tool is severely hampered in the absence of self-reflection on the part of the learner. Feedback is only one small part of the coaching process. We hope that from these chapters you'll develop a more confident ability to listen and ask useful questions and understand how such a conversation can result in real growth. However, as we indicate in Chapter 11, as a manager you're also in a good position to promote learning by holding people accountable for their efforts. This is another very thorny problem. How do you hold people accountable and yet help them feel a sense of safety at the same time? Much of this has to do with how you help your people define goals. Clear goals facilitate accountability. Chapter 11 will, we hope, help you help your coachee define those learning goals more clearly.

Chapter 12 builds on Chapter 11 and represents a significant expansion of our thinking about development. Learning goals are often linked in the minds of the coachee with career goals. This makes sense even though it brings with it some built-in challenges. We have come to believe that the relationship between career development and on-the-job learning has become almost hopelessly confusing. Almost hopelessly, but not quite. Chapter 12 presents a new schema for understanding career development that has been quite heavily field-tested. We put forth the notion that a career is, in part, a negotiated outcome between individuals and their organizations. Career development and planned development then should be understood as, in part, an ongoing negotiation. Managers and their organizations have needs, and so do individuals. We suggest that it is possible to factor into that relationship options that help both parties. However, the employee has to be an effective negotiating partner. Many are not. We suggest that this chapter be read carefully by any manager who is called upon, or would like, to talk with employees about their careers. Perhaps just as important, share this chapter with your employees to help them become better at working with you in support of their development. We have found that the more informed and prepared the employee, the better the outcome of career development discussions.

Finally, in Chapters 13 and 14, we discuss two issues that remain challenging for most managers. In Chapter 13, we discuss working with employees who have severe performance issues and for whom developmental coaching has not seemed to work. No tool works for everyone. We want to indicate what we believe to be some of the other options you may need to consider. In Chapter 14, we end on a more positive note. If you or your organization are funding classroom training for employees, we suggest you consider how you can maximize the positive impact of your investment by linking classroom and on-the-job learning.

Acknowledgments

This effort began with the Coaching for Leadership and Teamwork Program. These individuals are interested in developing talent. They come largely from the community of Babson College: the alumni, MBA students, staff, and friends of the college. The Babson College Coaching for Leadership and Teamwork Program has provided an ongoing laboratory in which we have been able to deepen our understanding of helping, coaching, and learning from experience. More than 4,000 Babson alumni and MBA students have participated in the coaching program since its inception, and we wish to thank them all. There are so many people to thank from the ranks of those participants that it's hard to know where to begin.

The alumni who have provided significant leadership and support for the Coaching Program include, but aren't limited to, Amy Weil, Doug Adams, Steve Gaklis, Lisa Mandel, Dan Riley, and Patrick McGonagle. These individuals are all current or former leaders of the Babson College Alumni Association, which we also need to thank as a group. Bob Bonnevie, faculty member of the Management Division and president of the Palmer Group, has been our partner in developing and teaching our coach training programs over the past 14 years. We greatly appreciate his wisdom and friendship. The Coaching Program is a major operational undertaking (some might say nightmare), and we've been blessed with two outstanding operations managers since the first edition was released: Kristen Shulman and Jackie Harris, who currently runs the ship. Rob Major has also provided enormous managerial, moral, IT, and "roll up the sleeves" support as well.

In addition, we've had significant support from the college faculty and leadership, including Dennis Hanno, the dean of the Undergraduate Program, who has funded this program and whose sponsorship, through material and emotional support, has been terrific. Anne Heller from the Babson Alumni Office has provided advice, coaching, and collaboration throughout for which we are grateful. In our broader coaching-related research and consulting activities we've had help from Dean Elaine Eisenman of Babson Executive Education. Elaine sponsored the creation of, and now teaches in, Coaching Inside the Organization at Babson Executive Education. This is an in-depth program for individuals from human resource management and organizational development (typically) who are interested in gaining greater experience in the formal uses of developmental coaching. As always, I would like to give a personal thanks to Allan Cohen, Edward A. Madden Distinguished Professor of Global Leadership, whose comprehensive support and friendship have made so much of this possible. Mark Rice, formerly the Murata Dean of the F. W. Olin Graduate School of Business at Babson and currently professor of entrepreneurship, provided a key opportunity for the continued evolution of our efforts by bringing the concepts of developmental coaching into Babson's new Fast Track MBA Program. In making that leap a reality, we also had incredible help from our colleagues Keith Rollag, Nan Langowitz, and Susan Alvey from the Babson faculty. Keith is our current division chair and has been steadfast in his support of this effort. We also want to thank the faculty of Babson's first-year course, Foundations of Management and Entrepreneurship. They have been among our biggest supports by bringing the Coaching for Leadership and Teamwork Program into so many classrooms. There have been so many faculty involved in that effort that we can't list them all, but we have to offer a special thanks to professors Dawna Dewire and Richard Mandel, who are the current leaders of that effort.

We've had significant support from a number of businesses since we launched the first edition. In particular, I would like to thank John Ferrie, Donna Conlin, and Cindy Stulac from the Bose Corporation. I would also like to thank Nina Mickelson of the World Bank, Patricia Hickey of Children's Hospital Boston and her colleagues, and Suzanne Levin Glazer, now of Harvard Business School. These are individuals who have in a variety of ways endeavored to promote the kind of management that has inspired the writing of this book.

We would be remiss if we didn't thank all of those readers who purchased and hopefully read the first edition! Without them, the second edition would surely not have seen the light of day, for very good reasons. We've had a great deal of support from our readers over the past years. We have been honored to hear phrases like "That was actually useful." There can be no higher compliment for an academic effort. In that regard then we also owe a debt of gratitude to Lisa Cuevas Shaw and MaryAnn Vail from Sage Publications. Their interest in promoting this project represents a vote of confidence that we hope we have earned. I want to thank Lisa in particular for pushing to make this happen, and I say "pushing" in the best possible sense. In addition, I'd like to personally thank Melinda Masson and Carla Freeman who worked with me in the actual editing of the text. They are terrific partners, and I'd wish that every author should find themselves in such capable and understanding hands.

We and SAGE would also like to thank the following reviewers for their critique and suggestions throughout the writing of this second edition:

Deborah Butler, *Georgia State University*

James Milojkovic, *Stanford University*

Margaret New, *The George Washington University*

Charles Vance, *Loyola Marymount University*

Mara H. Wasburn, *Purdue University*

I would like to personally thank Joe Weintraub, whose vision for the creation of the Coaching for Leadership and Teamwork Program led to so much, including the first edition of this book; our second book, *The Coaching Organization: A Strategy for Developing Leaders;* Coaching Inside the Organization; and countless executive education programs, all in the service of promoting more effective management through the use of developmental coaching. All that and his work supported the development of a generation of Babson undergraduate students who actually have had a good coaching experience or two.

Finally, I would like to thank my loving wife Chris. This is it, promise!

James Hunt
Babson College

Introduction

1

The Coaching Manager

"**I** was dreading the next meeting. I knew that there was going to be a real problem. I knew this one particular guy in the meeting was going to challenge the results of my analysis. He had made that clear. He's a more senior guy too. I was very angry, feeling like he was just doing this to put me in my place. I couldn't figure out what to say, how to turn this conversation into something productive for the group. I just wanted to blast the guy. I've always had trouble with people like this. My boss has told me that I really need to be able to handle tough political problems if I'm going to be ready for a program manager role I'm hoping to move to.

"I was mulling all this over while I was walking down to the cafeteria and happened to bump into my boss. We chatted for a minute. He noticed that I wasn't being myself. He made a small comment: 'What's going on? You look worried.' I trust him, so I thought I'd tell him. I told him about the meeting tomorrow and the confrontation that seemed inevitable. Gave him some background on the situation. He didn't seem annoyed. He asked me a few more questions. One question in particular got me thinking. He asked me if my critical view of this more senior colleague was the whole story. Was this guy a consistent problem, or did he become more confrontational when he really was worried about something? He didn't say it like he was cross-examining me. He just wanted to know. (He's never worked with the guy.) I thought about it for a second and said, 'No. Actually this is a pretty complex situation.' I explained that this gentleman (notice how I was changing my description) had actually done some good work for us in the past, and though his style was a bit harsh at times, he often did make some useful points.

1

My boss then simply said, 'Is there any way that you can take that track record of his into account here?' I began to see the big picture as we talked. I needed to get beyond my own reactions and my own view of things. The words started to come to me, and I actually felt calmer. I knew what to say to the guy tomorrow. I knew how not to get defensive. Even though his style was very challenging, I could just let him speak and try to really listen to him. I could defuse the situation rather than making it worse. If I didn't attack him, we could keep the conflict where it belonged, on issues rather than on his style or mine. We could both come out of this in decent shape. I thanked my boss. He said, 'For what?' That's why I like working for him."

You probably know someone like our friend's "boss." (Hopefully, you work for someone like this, but the odds are that you don't.) When you think about a manager like this, you probably feel admiration and maybe even a bit of jealousy. If you know any coaching managers well, you have probably gotten a sense of the impact of their styles on their work and on others around them (Goleman, 2000). Everyone seems to want to work for them. Perhaps managers like this seem too "touchy-feely" for you. Even so, you may still wonder: How do they do it? How do they get their jobs done and still find time to talk with their people like that?

This is a portrait of the coaching manager, someone who uses coaching to develop talent in his or her business unit, *in order to achieve business or organizational results*. We have talked with people like our friend's boss, and we know they are out there. We also know that they can play critical roles in addressing some of the most important concerns in business today. Regardless of the state of the economy, if you are in business, you need talented people to do their best. In a down market, it may be easier to fill jobs, but it is probably not easier to fill those jobs with the right people and to keep the right people moving ahead, with commitment.

Furthermore, hiring—one of the most if not the most important decisions a manager can make (Collins, 2001)—is expensive and can't solve all your talent management needs. So, do we send people off to school? Even though we're teachers, we have to stress that sending people to the classroom doesn't constitute a talent development strategy. Classrooms don't ensure that individuals develop. Actual work-related development takes place largely on the job. This is particularly true when it comes to the skills associated with leadership, teamwork, and management. (Our friends from other disciplines would actually disagree with the latter statement. Current research now tells us that expertise in nearly every field of endeavor from the arts to writing software code is built through a process of learning from experience, involving on-the-job practice and coaching [Ericsson, Prietula, & Cokely, 2007].)

Many organizations are beginning to understand how development really works. "We're good at making the numbers, and we're good at telling people what to do. But we're not developing leaders. Telling people what to do, if that's all we do, is just going to make them more dependent on the top. We can't keep doing that. We've got to get them to think." These are just a few of the comments we've heard over the past decade from talent managers and human resource leaders. The next generation of talent can't develop unless its members are given the chance to learn, to think, and to grow. If we focus solely on making the numbers today, we'll lose tomorrow. Our next set of questions typically includes the following: Does your CEO really want to prioritize talent development? In the past, the answers varied but were often more negative than positive. Now, the pendulum seems to have swung. Changing demographics, the upcoming baby boomer retirement boom (we think!), an increasingly diverse workforce, and the need to manage new technologies and new ways of doing business all require ongoing learning and talent development.

Coaching Can Help, for Employees Who Want to Learn

Over the past 10 years, we have talked with more than 4,000 practicing managers and entrepreneurs about coaching and talent development. (We've worked with an additional 2,000 ͡ so since the first edition.) In addition, we've had extensive opportunities to talk with business leaders, human resource professionals, and learning and development specialists in some of our best business and not-for-profit organizations. (Some of those conversations, which are beyond the scope of this book, are described in Hunt & Weintraub, 2007.) We have continued to learn from them about learning from experience and how managers can build organizational capability by encouraging a coaching-friendly culture in their teams and units.

At the core of this capability is the conversation, what we describe as the *coaching dialogue*. The coaching dialogue is far more than just an occasion for feedback for an employee. Feedback, as we will describe later in this book, is really only one step in the process of learning from experience. In the coaching dialogue, two individuals, for our purposes a coaching manager and one of his or her reports, meet formally or informally to discuss a challenge/problem/task on which the employee is working. Rather than meeting only to discuss business *results*, the participants also talk about *how* the employee is going about trying to achieve those results. They talk about the process of getting there, as well as the ultimate goal. It is those conversations about process, actions, and decisions that the employee makes while trying to deal with the challenge from which the employee can draw the lessons of experience.

We'll provide an overview of the developmental coaching model in Chapter 2 and then provide detailed discussions of its various components in subsequent chapters. For the purposes of this chapter, however, let's describe it as follows. In a coaching dialogue, the manager seeks, often through the use of questions, to encourage the employee to reflect on his or her actions—to examine his or her actions critically with an eye toward understanding the gaps between actual and desired performance. While individuals can critically reflect on their performance in isolation, reflection in the company of another interested party is more powerful, as we'll describe in some detail. Reflection by itself, however, may not be enough to give the employee a full understanding of his or her actions and their role in achieving the desired outcomes.

It may be necessary for the coaching manager to provide feedback to help the employee get a clearer sense of his or her actions, and at times, it may be helpful to provide some needed advice. The latter tactic, however, is used carefully so as not to undermine the employee's sense of ownership for next steps and further improvements. You can see immediately that there is some art to this on the part of the manager. A good coaching manager develops a sense of when to jump in and provide feedback and advice and when to step back and let his or her employees think things through. (This dilemma will seem very familiar to parents, teachers, and athletic coaches.) In most instances, one might think that the manager's own style and timing will dictate a response to that question. A skilled coaching manager, though, tries to make that judgment call based on the employee's needs, not the manager's predilections.

We are acutely aware that the preceding paragraph might already scare off some folks who are interested in improving their ability to coach their people. Please don't be frightened! You don't have to be perfect at this stuff to be effective. You have to be OK. Intent does matter here, along with your ability to receive feedback from those you coach. If you are genuinely trying to help and you occasionally jump in too quickly, and if you've let your people know that you need their help to help them, you'll do just fine. Yes, practice does help. Perfection, though, is not what you're trying to achieve.

As such, in addition to some basic skills, trust between the parties here is obviously a critically important enabling factor. That's why intent is so important. If you are really trying to help, not to punish, if you really do want to know what is happening with your people and their work, and if you behave accordingly (we'll talk about this in great detail), sufficient trust will materialize in your relationships with your people for coaching to take place. (Of course, intent by itself will not be enough if you are inadvertently undermining your efforts to build trust by behaving in a fashion that contradicts that intent. This can happen without your awareness. We'll explore this problem in some detail later.)

The best way to learn to coach, and to build trust in your relationships with your people, is to try coaching. Acquaint yourself with the basics of the developmental coaching model; let your people know what you're trying to do, assuming you're clear about what that is, and ask for their feedback.

But here's where the anxiety begins to build. Why? Managers have the wrong mental models about coaching from years of being taught that coaching is a tool for dealing with serious performance problems. When an employee has a severe, persistent performance problem, the model of coaching we have described may not work. The employee may be more motivated to cover up problems than talk about them. Trust may be minimal or even absent, since the manager naturally will have to represent the interests of the organization, not the employee. The employee would prefer otherwise. Tension builds. Communication breaks down. This is what most managers associate with coaching. Sounds like fun, right?

Here's what the managers we've talked with, those who use coaching on a daily basis, tell us: Don't devote your precious time just to coaching individuals with performance problems. How much attention do your good and best employees receive? Probably they receive very little, far less than they deserve. But they don't cause any trouble. And you're busy. But—and this is the key part—those good and great employees are the ones most likely to help your business. They are probably the most engaged in the work. They probably have good ideas or have a good idea of where the problems lie. They are also the ones who are most likely to *want* to engage in the kind of developmental work described in this book. But they don't get that kind of attention. Coaching these people, the people who can help your business and who want to learn, is a very different experience from coaching someone who is unhappy with the job, with you, with the company, with his or her performance, with your performance, or with all of the above. (We are very aware that you may at times *have* to coach employees who are experiencing severe performance problems. This is tough going. There are no magical answers. We will, however, try to address this difficult area later in the book.)

Coaching Is Good for You

The managers we interviewed also told us that coaching has helped them do a better job as managers and has helped them evolve as leaders. Consider briefly what happens if you have honest and open discussions with your employees about their work. What will *you* learn in the process? You'll learn lots more about each individual employee, to be sure. You'll learn about employees' strengths and weaknesses. You'll learn what really motivates them.

In addition, however, you'll also learn about the business. You'll learn more about what is working and what isn't. You'll learn more about customers, processes, and opportunities. You can't be everywhere. Coaching is a vehicle for accessing the eyes, ears, and brains of your team members, without micromanaging them. Coaching helps you stay on top of your business without staying on top of your people.

Data from studies such as the Gallup Organization suggest that *organizational,* not just personal, productivity will improve as a result of manager-facilitated learning (Buckingham & Coffman, 1999). The U.S. Army, for example, has made a significant effort to leverage this opportunity (Garvin, 2000). After any military action around the world, involved army units conduct an "after-action review" (AAR). The AAR uses a coaching methodology very similar to the one described here, in a team context. In the smallest appropriate unit, the unit commander and his or her direct reports "stop the action" by meeting and talking about what happened. Following a highly structured procedure, team members reflect on what they did well, what they did not so well, and what they need to do better next time. Later in the book, we describe how the army makes this coaching process work. The point we're trying to make is that coaching represents two-way communications about the employees' efforts and about the challenges facing the business. You'll note as we report on coaching conversations through the mini cases such as the one opening this chapter that the conversations actually sound more like problem-solving discussions than developmental discussions. In reality, they are both.

The AAR illustrates a formalization of this kind of thinking. The officer or facilitator leading the dialogue gathers data from an AAR. (The data do not include "who said what"; they include only key learning points. The air force calls this a "nameless, rankless debrief.") Data on what has been learned are pooled to help larger units within the army adapt to new demands and challenges. The army's ability to use a coaching-like intervention to learn on the fly (even under combat conditions) has been a key factor in helping the organization deal with change. Some of the most common duties for the U.S. Army over the past decade, after all, have been peacekeeping, peacemaking, and disaster relief. These dangerous duties may fall outside the traditional training given to soldiers until very recently.

When a manager creates a coaching dialogue with an individual or a team, he or she is creating an opportunity for everyone, including the firm, to learn. Organizational learning coupled with the growth and development of the best employees can represent a significant competitive advantage for a firm. The cost is not high. It takes only a bit of time and thought to capture what has been learned and to circulate the insights to the rest of a team or firm.

But coaching has much more to offer you than business intelligence. As we've already said, coaching involves addressing that timeless dilemma of when to direct someone who works for you (or who is growing up under your care) versus when to coach, which involves the act of letting go, at least to an extent. Coaching teaches you the competence of working through others, not doing it yourself. That of course is not how you became a manager. You became a manager not by working through others but by being an effective individual contributor. If you are to be a really good manager—and, some would say, a more mature individual—you must learn how to bring out the best in others, in the service of your team and business. This is a substantial developmental leap (Drath, 1993). If you can make that leap, you'll be better positioned to think about your business strategically and step back from the tendency to engage in "firefighting" that can consume your time and rob your career of meaning. By talking with their employees through coaching, coaching managers have a different view of how their teams are functioning and, rather than trying to fix every problem themselves, spend more time building an organization capable of adapting and competing in challenging times. We concur with other writers, such as Bradford and Cohen (1998), who propose that the most effective leader for our time is *not* the hero who leads the charge up the hill, but the one who promotes shared effort toward and responsibility for achieving a goal and also builds organizational capability along the way. Our approach to coaching is consistent with that model.

Finally, coaching can actually be good for you on a personal level. As a manager, you're asked to take 24/7/365 responsibility for something important and for a group of people who are tasked with accomplishing something important. You can't turn it off, particularly in an age of instant and unrelenting communications. Yes, leadership and management roles can be exciting, but they can also be quite stressful.

Research suggests that coaching others can help in several ways (Boyatzis, Smith, & Blaize, 2006). More than technique, coaching, particularly developmental coaching, is related to the quality of the relationship between manager and employee. A high-quality relationship, characterized by trust and mutual support, can be a significant buffer against the impact of stress, including the physiological impacts. Developmental coaching can also help mitigate the isolation associated with leadership roles and the potential damage that such isolation can cause to the leader's psyche and ability to function on a sustainable basis. It is indeed lonely at the top (of a team or a conglomerate). While coaching cannot alleviate all of the problems associated with the assumption of a leadership role, it can help. But we emphasize that we're talking here about developmental coaching—coaching between a leader and a follower who wants to learn. If the only coaching you do is aimed at dealing with serious performance problems, we do not predict that your stress level will decrease!

Why Don't More Managers Coach?

We have shared these ideas with many managers. Few have objected to our hypotheses. Most employees, particularly the strong contributors, would like more support with their development, and coaching from the manager is a logical tactic for addressing that need. Unfortunately, it doesn't seem to happen to nearly the degree that it should. Interestingly, despite the fact that employees are interested in coaching, few are clamoring for it. Something is missing.

Although most managers agree with our point, there is nevertheless a great deal of confusion in the business world about the role that organizations and their managers can and should play in the development of their employees. This confusion has led to inactivity. Managers don't coach, and employees don't ask for coaching. In the world of business, we have created a stigma against learning and against coaching for both the manager and the employee.

We have asked the following question in our coach training sessions since 1996: "How many of you have had your manager devote 100% of a 60-minute (or even a 30-minute) block of time to observing you work on some task and then spend an additional 30 minutes or so talking with you about what he or she saw, in a way you really felt promoted your growth?" Although we occasionally do see a hand go up, most of the time, we do not. We're more likely to hear snickers.

Then, we hear the gamut of "anti–coaching manager stories": "I found out I'd gotten my raise when it came in my check. I have no idea what I did to deserve that." (We have heard that story from participants in our leadership programs. Little did we know that it would in fact happen to one of us in 2007. No one is immune to poor management, not even the authors of this book.) "I haven't seen or talked to my manager in 6 months. I guess that means I'm doing OK." "I had my performance appraisal over the phone." Our personal favorite: "Coaching is for wimps." Such stories have forced us to ponder the obvious question: Is this any way to treat talented employees? We should add that the sample of companies from which participants in our training programs are drawn includes some of the best on the planet. If you're a CEO reading this book and you think your managers are coaching, you might want to back up that assumption with some hard data. These anecdotal observations that developmental coaching, at least as we define it below, is rarely practiced are supported by a substantial body of research (Lombardo & Eichinger, 2001).

If the boss, the person with formal power, signals that she or he isn't interested in employees' development, and if this is a pretty common observation, what's the logical response on the part of employees? Most will lower their expectations. A self-fulfilling prophecy is the result. Little coaching takes place, so people don't expect to be coached even though they may wish otherwise. They don't expect coaching, so they don't ask for it—and not surprisingly, because they don't ask, they don't get it. To close the loop, if they don't ask for it, their managers will think they don't want it.

Furthermore, if they were to request coaching from their managers, they would quite likely be talking with people who don't really know how to coach or are afraid to coach. The mental models that both parties are likely to hold of coaching—that it is reserved for poor performers, not for good ones, as we discussed above—don't help. And so it goes. (Of course, if people work for a manager who believes that coaching is for wimps, they'll rightly be afraid to ask.)

Contrast this view with an earlier and more progressive vision put forth by management authors Evered and Selman (1989). They speculated that (a) if managers and organizations actually encouraged people to ask for coaching, (b) if managers made them feel safe in doing so, and (c) if managers could get used to coaching, a potent internal market for coaching would emerge. Employees would start to expect and even demand to be coached, and the stigma, the fear of retribution for admitting that they don't know something, would disappear rather quickly. Our experience tends to support this perspective.

We should note of course that in some organizations, performance appraisal and compensation systems, as well as the attitudes of some misguided senior managers, can actively discourage coaching. We've heard participants in our programs quote the jab they may have received from a senior organizational leader to the effect of "Why are you spending all that time talking with your people?" more than once. The best possible comeback is "because it gets results." So, while we admit that various human resource practices can discourage coaching, we believe that it is too easy to blame the entire problem on such antiquated policies and attitudes. Even in companies that actively encourage coaching, you can find many managers who don't explore its possibilities.

We know that most people want to learn (McGregor, 1985; Senge, 1990). Study after study shows that meaningful work, challenge, learning, and career development are high on the list of factors that workers look for in their relationships with employers. The coaching managers we have talked to tell us that it is indeed possible to tap all that pent-up motivation. They strive to create conditions under which their employees feel relatively comfortable asking for coaching. Some coaching managers have been able to achieve this even while working in companies not necessarily known for promoting the development of employees. The important question here is *Why?* What's your motivation, on a personal level but perhaps most important on a business level? At the close of this chapter, we will challenge you to consider what it would mean for you, and for your team/organization, if you were to more actively involve yourself in support of talent development, through talking with your direct reports. That's our sales pitch. But it's not all on your shoulders. Note we're saying that coaching—developmental coaching—is a cocreated activity. You have to make it possible, but it's not solely up to you.

Coaching and Learning

Developmental coaching has two goals then: first to help the team, organization, or business achieve results and second to help the people in the team, organization, or business grow from their work. *Growth,* as we refer to it here, means learning from experience, the development of expertise, and (one might say) wisdom. Before proceeding, then, we would like to say a bit more about what we mean by learning and how it occurs in this context.

The underlying theory behind how adults learn and adapt and how they can in turn help organizations learn and adapt is well understood. Learning is more than just action, though action is part of learning. Wolfe and Kolb (1984) have described a useful way to understand learning as requiring four interrelated steps. To learn, the individual must act and then make sense of the action and its implications with an eye toward developing increased competence. Action, Step 1 in the learning process, creates experience that registers with the actor in Step 2. This is where development stops in most organizations (Hicks & Peterson, 1997). Unfortunately, there is no guarantee that anything has been learned up to this point in the process.

If the experience of an action is subject to self-reflection, discussion, and external feedback, in Step 3 in the process, it is possible for the individual to then draw new conclusions about the nature and effect of that action. The learner generates a new set of ideas, a new theory if you will, regarding the action. The learner thinks about what worked and what didn't work, why, and what might be tried differently. The new theory is subject to experimental testing, in Step 4, as the individual strives to improve his or her performance.

Say that you are trying to help a new product development team get its meeting habits started in the right way. Based on your previous experience, you start with the assumption that a tightly structured agenda can help a group stick to its task. You bring in such an agenda to the first meeting and find that a number of the more creative members of this new team seem to just want to chat with each other. Frustrated, you get angry and become more directive. Your manager, a gifted coach, happens to be observing you. After the meeting, he takes a few minutes to ask you for your thoughts about how it went. You express frustration at your inability to get the crazy creative types to stay on track. He asks you whether you've ever worked with people like this before, and you say no. You then wonder aloud whether your approach to the creative types was perhaps not all that helpful. Your boss, agreeing with you, gives you some feedback to the effect that the creative types seemed to stop paying attention when you became more forceful and directive. A new theory about what is going on occurs to you. Your previous model of effective team leadership, a model that had always worked in the past, may need to be modified. Maybe you need to encourage a team like this to be a little more social with one another as a way of getting started. You resolve to try this next time. You leave this coaching interaction feeling as though you have gained a useful insight into how different kinds of teams run. You feel as though you're learning something and even feel a little more confident in your ability.

In this example, you have learned to expand your own set of assumptions about how to be an effective team leader. You don't just keep doing more of what you normally do. Such automatic behavior, continuing to do what we know even when it doesn't work, seems to reflect human nature to a degree, but it is also a hallmark of a failure to learn (Argyris & Schon, 1978). Not surprisingly, perhaps, it is all too common in the workplace. We do the same thing over and over again, hoping that this time it will work but ready to blame someone else if it doesn't. (Or we tell someone who has failed to try again, without talking about what he or she might do differently next time.)

What coaching can do is help people, both managers and employees, stop and think about what they are doing in the here and now, on their current jobs. Coaching helps people extract knowledge from readily available learning opportunities, think about what is novel or important (and, in most businesses these days, there is plenty of that), and grow "in place." When coaching occurs as we have described it here, the employees feel they are learning, and they are. Employees are also being directly challenged to keep improving their performance, and in that sense, they are being challenged to work at even higher levels of effectiveness. Their performance, and ultimately the firm's competitiveness, can improve in the process.

The Coaching Manager and Emotional Intelligence (EQ)

Some managers believe that providing feedback is all there is to coaching. We struggled for years, with the help of the coaching managers in our programs, to gain a clearer understanding of what was so special about what they were doing. Ultimately, it became obvious that they were promoting self-reflection in others. Effective coaching managers were successful because they not only gave feedback but gave feedback to people they had *helped make ready for feedback* through the process of reflection. *Reflection* is the step too often missing in employee development. Reflection allows individual learners to pursue what is significant or important to them, not just what is important to the manager. Reflection helps people learn to challenge their own assumptions, to push their thinking further. Reflection allows people to take ownership of their own problems and their choices. Learner ownership of the learning process drives development because it fosters and validates the importance of self-directed learning as an important aspect of successful job performance. Isaac Stern, the great violinist who died in 2001, captured the power of this concept when he described the outcome of his work with his own mentor: "He taught me to teach myself, which is the greatest thing a teacher can do" (Steinberg, 2001).

Readers familiar with the concept of emotional intelligence (EQ; Goleman, 1998) will see important parallels with the work we are describing here. Emotional intelligence represents a useful and often ignored perspective on the factors that lead to superior performance. Individuals with high levels of emotional intelligence have a clearer sense of who they are, are better able to manage their own feelings, have relatively high levels of personal motivation, are able to empathize with others, and are socially skillful.

The research to date indicates that employees who score high on measures of emotional intelligence are likely to be much more effective at their work, regardless of their jobs. Engineers with high levels of emotional intelligence are more likely to end up with more patents. Salespeople with high levels of emotional intelligence are more likely to be superior salespeople. Leaders with high levels of emotional intelligence are more likely to be superior leaders.

Note that there is a link between emotional intelligence and job performance even for those in areas that require highly technical skills. There are two reasons for this link. First, the ability to see yourself clearly helps you comprehend and adjust for your own strengths and weaknesses. For example, a great engineer who knows he's lousy at designing a certain kind of manufacturing process is able to admit that to himself and find someone else who can do the job effectively. Second, the interpersonal aspects of emotional intelligence relate directly to the ability to take even a highly technical idea and bring others to the task of working on that idea. Fortunately, it appears that one's emotional intelligence can improve under the right circumstances.

Developmental coaching relies heavily on the idea that learning requires a healthy dose of reflection and self-assessment on the part of the learner.

Self-assessment, particularly when coupled with feedback, is very likely to improve self-awareness. Suppose someone, say your boss, asks you to stop and think about your role on a team that produced a new marketing brochure and asks you to talk about your strengths and weaknesses on the project: You are being offered an opportunity to build your capacity for self-awareness. You don't have to talk about emotional intelligence, per se, to promote its development. (In fact, in most environments, you would not use language such as "emotional intelligence" as it would likely be a distraction.)

The benefits of helping any employee build self-awareness are significant. Most of us have a tendency to believe our skills are superior. Many of us learn, painfully, that not all of our skills are so superior. Miscalculations of this kind can wreck a project or a career. Coaching may not always be able to provide an avenue of rehabilitation for those already in performance trouble. However, a heightened sense of self-awareness, developed in a context of coaching, may help prevent performance problems in the first place.

Coaching Isn't the Same as Mentoring

Many managers are concerned that coaching, like mentoring, will take a great deal of time and emotional energy. The thought of having to participate in a long-term emotional relationship is anxiety provoking. We do believe that coaching can create better relationships between employees and managers. However, coaching relationships don't have to be emotionally intense to create an effective context for learning and development.

Coaching is not the same as mentoring (Kram, 1985; Ragins & Kram, 2007). Mentoring typically involves a more ongoing relationship, one with a significant emotional component to it. We talked above about the importance of high-quality, trusting relationships between manager and employee. Affection and emotional intimacy, however, are not required. Yes, it can be very valuable to like the people with whom you spend your working days and nights. It is very important to think of the people who work for you as humans, not as cogs in the wheel of industry. It is, however, a matter of degree. We would stress that it is possible to engage in helpful developmental coaching with someone who works for you, even though you don't know much about his or her personal life and may only see him or her at work. It is possible to utilize the techniques and strategies of developmental coaching with someone with whom you may work for only a short period of time, if you create the proper expectations and context.

Effective mentors do use some of the same coaching practices we discuss in this book. (They also do much more and engage in activities that at times are quite different from those of a manager. Perhaps most important, they are usually not "in the trenches" with their protégés. The manager may well be.) Our research suggests that coaching can take place in a rather brief episode, sometimes as short as a few minutes, between relative strangers. Undoubtedly, good chemistry between the manager and the employee can promote coaching and also make the experience of coaching even more satisfying. However, if the manager makes it "psychologically safe" for the employee to openly talk about what he or she wants or needs to learn, that is often enough to create learning.

Why Think About Becoming a Coaching Manager?

We've done a bit of a sales job here in our efforts to encourage you to build your coaching capabilities. In Chapter 2, we'll try to create a clearer picture of the actual behavior of a coaching manager. Before moving ahead, we want to challenge you to think about coaching in two ways. First, in this section, we'll ask you to think about how coaching can help your business. In the next, we'll ask you to consider the mental models you hold of coaching.

Putting business first, we are absolutely convinced that if you can't make a connection between developmental coaching and your business and personal needs or goals, you won't find the time to make it happen. That's understandable. Time is a working manager's most precious resource.

In order to help you articulate the business case or cases, we developed what we call the "coaching value proposition" (Hunt & Weintraub, 2007). This is a simple tool for helping organizations and individual managers ponder the issue of *why*. It consists of a series of questions. Thinking through these questions can help you create an understanding of the business value that can result from your coaching efforts:

1. To what business or organizational goals does your team or organization aspire? These are the business results or organizational/team outcomes you're responsible for achieving.

2. What skills or capabilities do your people need in order to be able to achieve those goals? What talents are required? One of the most common responses we receive to this question is "We need leadership." That's only one example. Needed skills may be drawn from the technical, cognitive (skills such as prioritization, organization, planning, etc.), or interpersonal realms. We'll discuss this issue in much more depth in Chapter 3, "Defining Success as a Coaching Manager."

3. What is the best way to attain that talent for your organization? You've got four options:

    a. You can hire the talent. You should certainly consider this option whenever you can, obviously. However, as we've said, conditions can change. The talent you had at your disposal that was helpful last week may not have the skills required to help you next week.

    b. You can teach the skills in the classroom. This is very helpful for developing a foundational set of skills. If you're doing challenging work, then the classroom by itself won't be enough. People will need to learn to apply those skills on the job.

    c. You can build those skills through coaching and aid in the process of learning from experience. This is particularly useful as a supplement to the classroom, when the classroom is unavailable, or when, as is often the case, there is no classroom available to jump-start a learning process.

    d. You can do nothing. We don't mean to be sarcastic here. You may believe that telling people what to do will mean that they'll do it. In some cases, if they have the skills, they'll get it done. If they don't have the skills, they won't, even if they want to. You do need to provide direction to help your team clarify goals, and you need to delegate tasks appropriately, appraise performance, and manage reward distribution. None of that, however, ensures that people will develop the skill set required to execute those tasks effectively.

4. What supports do your people need to sustain their effort over the long term? We're talking here about the challenge of keeping people engaged. This requires that talented people feel valued and feel like they have the opportunity to work with a purpose toward something that matters. Coaching can help, along with a range of other team maintenance activities such as communications about the purpose of the work and the long-term vision of the team or organization.

If you've got some coaching-oriented answers, particularly to Questions 3 and 4, then you have a rationale for moving ahead. You'll note that there's much more to being an effective manager than just coaching. Coaching can be one of your tools—an important one, yes, but not the only one. There's business to be done. So remember as we move through the model in more detail, coaching managers aren't coaching to be nice. They are interested in helping others be successful, yes, but they also want to be successful themselves. They coach to a significant degree because it helps the business. So let's assume that you want to move ahead. Before leaving the introduction, we want you to just spend a bit of time reflecting on what you already know about coaching.

Your Approach to Coaching
Determines the Outcome of Your Effort

Coaching is a very old form of human activity. It has been a fixture of athletics for centuries. You have almost certainly had occasion to interact with a coach. Take a minute and jot down some notes in response to the following self-assessment questions.

SELF-ASSESSMENT 1.1: Your Existing Mental Models of Coaching

As may not be the case in your studies of other subjects, you already know a great deal about coaching. You have probably worked with a coach. You have seen coaches on TV. You have read about them. You may have received coaching from managers or other individuals over the course of your career. These experiences will shape your approach to coaching. You will see how those models compare with the model presented in the remainder of this book.

Think about the best coaches you have known or have some familiarity with:

- What did they do that was most useful?
- In what ways have they influenced your thinking about what coaching really means?

Think about the worst coaches you have known or have some familiarity with:

- What did they do that was not useful?
- In what ways have they influenced your thinking about what coaching really means?

If you were honest with yourself about the influence these models have had on you and your beliefs about coaching:

- What beliefs do you bring to the task of coaching in business that you probably need to stick with?
- What beliefs do you bring to the task of coaching in business that you may need to change?

In evaluating your responses, consider the following question: Did the best coaches push for compliance, or did they push for growth and learning? In other words, did the best coaches do nothing more than make sure you did your job? Alternatively, did the best coaches make sure that you learned something while you were doing your job? We suspect that most of you, when thinking about good versus not-so-good coaches, will see the difference.

To clarify this point further, we'll speak more directly to the kinds of learning outcomes you might think about while considering what you learned along the way. D. Tim Hall (1986) has proposed four different kinds of learning outcomes to consider when assessing one's development. Two of those outcomes are short-term: We may learn to perform our current jobs more effectively, or we may feel differently about our current jobs. These are valuable goals directly relevant to coaching, but there is more. A manager who insists on compliance or only offers feedback may well see at least temporary improvements in performance.

Two of the outcomes are more long-term in nature. We come to see ourselves differently (our identities evolve), and we become more adaptable and more able to deal with change. Just a bit of prodding can usually help individuals learn to perform their work more effectively, which will make them feel better about what they are doing. We would guess that the learning outcomes you experienced from coaches you found particularly effective left you feeling even more strongly about the experience. Perhaps you felt more confident or had a clearer sense of your strengths, weaknesses, likes, and dislikes. We would also guess that you left the experience feeling more capable of dealing with the world and interested in taking on new challenges. It is our hope that the model of developmental coaching we present in overview form in the next chapter will give you the tools that can help create both the short-term and the long-term gains just described. We predict, based on what we've learned from the managers we've worked with, that you will accrue some of the same results yourself.

An Overview of Developmental Coaching

2

In this chapter, you'll learn about the basic model of developmental coaching, which includes the following elements:

- Defining success
- A coaching-friendly context
- A "coachable" coachee
- A challenge that can provoke learning
- A helpful mind-set
- Stopping the action and starting the coaching dialogue
- Providing balanced and useful feedback
- Collaboratively interpreting performance gaps
- Setting a plan for change and following up

Developmental Coaching: An Example

It had been a pretty anxiety-provoking day for George. He had completed his update on the status of his company's work with Building Co., one of its most important customers. His manager, Samantha, thought he was well prepared and did a credible job, though he seemed a bit unsure of himself. Samantha knew that George was working outside his comfort zone here, but she trusted him. She also knew that while the senior management team could be difficult, in that its members had a tendency to spar with anyone who presented at a staff meeting, they were in reality pretty open-minded. She didn't think she was "throwing George to the wolves."

In fact, George had done a number of major presentations recently, and they seemed to have gone well. Samantha reflected on how much progress George had made over the past year. George was a brilliant engineer, but his influence skills had varied considerably depending on the situation. He was also shy and not particularly adept at thinking on his feet in front of a group, managing the unexpected, and keeping things moving in the right direction. He was liked by most of his colleagues, but his reputation was that of a great technical, not commercial, engineer. In front of senior managers, from inside or outside the company, he seemed to talk past them and spent too much time on technical minutiae. He didn't seem to understand how to relate to them effectively when talking about key business issues.

About 6 months before, it had become evident to Samantha that this combination of his awkwardness in leadership contexts, his apparent (though she didn't think real) lack of business acumen, and his ability to make anything sound far more complicated than necessary was a real liability. The word from senior management was that George shouldn't expect much more in the way of upward mobility at the company. Yes, the senior managers valued his engineering expertise and his loyalty to the company, and they wanted him to stay. But to move up, he would have to have a greater impact on the business, not just on its products. He would have to become a spokesperson for his ideas and influence others to buy in to his technical vision, by connecting with the business issues that the company faced. He also had to deal with high-level customers and do so effectively.

The human resources vice president explained to Samantha that George too often came across in senior staff meetings as though the engineering in the product was the only thing that mattered, which of course was not the whole story. When challenged around the business aspects of his ideas, he tended to become defensive or pull back from the point he was trying to make instead of engaging in the debate.

George had indicated in the past that he assumed he'd move into management. The human resources vice president, though, wasn't sure that George wanted to do the things he'd have to do in a management role, and he wasn't sure that George had the interpersonal talent required to make that leap work.

Samantha and George had a heart-to-heart talk. Samantha had known George for quite a few years, but he had only worked for her for a few months. She liked George and really appreciated what he could do. She told him, though, that his career at the company might be limited. She tried to give him the message in a reasonable but direct tone. She brought up the examples raised by the human resources vice president. She wanted to be sure that George understood his situation. But she also wanted to challenge him, give him a "nudge" to see if he would rise to the occasion.

George did indeed respond. He could see that Samantha and her colleagues in senior management had a point. He understood his strengths, and he was very aware of his weaknesses. He knew that he could be awkward, a bit of a "geek" at times, but he also revealed a real passion for having a greater impact than was possible in a purely technical role. "We're doing great work here, and we can do a better job of getting the word out and producing results for our customers, and I want to be a part of making that happen." Samantha was not completely surprised. In past conversations, she had come to know that George had a broader vision, though he wasn't always good at explaining it. Now she heard frustration in his voice, not so much with her or senior management, but with himself. That's what she wanted to hear.

He went on to say that he thought he could learn to connect with customers and with the business side of things. After all, he wasn't that bad at it even now. Samantha agreed. She actually thought George displayed very solid business knowledge in one-on-one meetings. Overall, though, he had made engineering a priority. He could change that. His own team would help him. He knew that several of the customers valued his expertise and, even more, valued his commitment to his work and to them. The tougher part in his view was dealing with his own senior managers. He knew that he wasn't connecting with them, but he wasn't sure what he needed to do differently. Obviously, he was going to have to change how they perceived him, something he really hadn't considered before. He had been afraid of overstepping his bounds by talking too much about the business issues, but now he could see the error in his assumptions. Samantha suggested that maybe this was symptomatic of his not really understanding the senior management team, not knowing them well enough as individuals. George agreed. He wasn't very attracted to the idea of socializing with people at work for fun. He knew he didn't do enough of that sort of thing.

Samantha listened intently. She tested George a bit. This wasn't going to be easy. Yes, she would help, but it was really up to him. He insisted that he understood. He asked for her support, to which she agreed. What was the next step? She also had to ask herself whether or not supporting George in going down this road made sense, to her and to the business.

Samantha, taking the advice of the human resources vice president, suggested that George participate in one of the company's executive development programs, "Building Influence and Executive Presence." This was a one-week immersion program that involved classroom activities and practice, through role-playing and video-based exercises. George was surprised, but open-minded. "What is 'executive presence'?" was his first comment.

Samantha responded, "That's the issue, George. I think you first need to define the changes you'll have to make." Samantha hated the term *executive presence*. It was like trying to define "art." You know it when you see it. But of course one person's art can be another person's "trash." Nevertheless, she felt the term was a place for them to begin. She talked of things like being direct when speaking to senior management, using body language that conveyed confidence, and looking others in the eye. They probably couldn't find a "cookbook" recipe for executive presence, and George would also have to be able to pick up cues that would help him be seen as credible by top-level customers and his own vice presidents. He needed to be able to sell his ideas to the senior managers by talking about factors such as market share and return on investment, and not just expect that they'd be impressed by the engineering specifications of the product. He needed to sense when he was losing them and be able to change course. Samantha hoped that an intensive course work experience would help him understand better what it meant to look and act the part of a leader at the company.

But she knew that a course was only a course. One week in the classroom won't change a person's behavior that much on a sustainable basis once he is back on the job, no matter how effective the instruction. The challenge would be for George to translate what he learned in the course to action, on the job. She suggested to George that upon his return they spot opportunities for him to use what he'd learned about in real-life situations.

George did indeed return with some ideas. In their first meeting after the course, he identified a key customer account and a key individual in that account, with whom he wanted to work in a leadership capacity. His goal was to achieve successful implementation of the company's new robotic inspection system at Building Co.'s (the customer) manufacturing plant over the next year. In order to make that happen, he'd have to do more than just demonstrate his technical knowledge. He'd have to exercise significant influence with Building Co. leadership around both the business and the technical issues associated with implementation. If he could make that happen, it might help build his credibility with his own senior managers, in whose eyes this was a high-priority project.

It was, of course, also an opportunity to fail, for both George and Samantha. She had to think long and hard about one fundamental question: Did George stand a chance of being successful? She knew she was taking a risk. From a talent management standpoint, though, she could see that George was probably hitting his own ceiling as a technical specialist and project lead. If she stood in his way now, she'd probably lose him. Did he have the fundamentals necessary to become more influential? She thought so, but she couldn't be sure.

She tried not to be sentimental. She liked George, but she had to be objective. She thought about other contexts in which she had seen George in action. Yes, at times, he could be quite persuasive, even in working with a high-ranking group. She also reasoned that there was some trust in their relationship. She felt that George would come to her if he ran into serious trouble and that he understood what was at stake. Plus, it wasn't like she was delegating the work with Building Co. into deep space. She was going to stay on top of things through regularly scheduled conversations with George, even though George would actually be doing most of the work. If things started to go sour, she felt that she'd be able to catch it in time. George, with Samantha's support, assumed the project leadership role and began to work with Howard Smith, vice president of operations at Building Co.

Many issues emerged over the course of the program there, and George faced considerable personal challenge throughout. Yet, he also usually seemed to enjoy the challenge, particularly as he began to speak more often in what to him was the uncomfortable language of business. He had thought he could be effective, but he also had some serious doubts. Over time, he began to feel more confident. The process of coaching supported his development.

Several months into the work George found himself struggling to convince Howard of the need to move ahead with implementation of the first phase of the inspection process as quickly as possible so that Building Co. could begin to gain some return on its investment and also so that Building Co. could learn more about how to get the most out of the robot-based inspection process. Howard wasn't budging. He wanted to do a thorough analysis of all phases of the project before committing to any initial implementation, even of a pilot experiment. Right after returning from one particularly frustrating meeting at Building Co., George met with Samantha at one of their regularly scheduled updates. The discussion went something like this:

Samantha: So, how did it go with Howard this morning?

George: I'm not sure. He's very stubborn. He wants to do all the analysis up front, even though he's got the budget to move ahead at least with a pilot project. They really don't understand just how much the robotic inspection process can help them.

Samantha: (with a smile) Surely, George, you're not going to condemn him for being too technical.

George: Right, I've been known to overdo the analysis myself, I realize. And I do understand that he doesn't want any surprises. The reality is that the robotic inspection process isn't going to cost Building Co. all that much initially. It's not a huge risk for them. I'm not sure what Howard's really concerned about. When I happened to bump into Howard's boss, the first thing he said to me was "So, are we going to try a pilot demonstration of the robots? That might be helpful internally here."

Samantha: So it's not about his boss . . .

George: I don't think so.

Samantha: So what kind of a guy is Howard? I've only met him in meetings.

George: Good question. I've been so focused on the politics and of course the technical stuff over there, maybe that isn't the real issue with Howard. I really can't tell you what makes Howard react the way he does. I guess I don't know him that well.

Samantha: Well, how important is Howard to the process of getting things going there [at Building Co.]? I mean, is there a work-around here?

George: I don't think so; he's key. He's got lots of support, and he's really the decision maker. There's no working around him.

Samantha: So, what do you think you should do?

George: I'm thinking about your question here, and I don't really know this guy, after 2 months of working with him. He isn't all that open. I feel like I should probably ask him to go have a beer after Friday afternoon's meeting, just to get him out of the office, and talk. I suspect he's actually a good guy. Likes science and appreciates the elegance of what we're offering here. Maybe I just don't know him yet.

Samantha: Interesting idea. Might work.

George: I hate that kind of thing, though. More politics. It's just not my style.

Samantha: I don't know if I'd call it politics, but regardless, it makes sense to find out what's important to him. Something seems to be bothering him, and it's not coming out in the team meetings. If he's as important as you say, how are we going to know that this is taking us in the right direction? We are going to run into some deadline problems soon, if we can't get some sort of pilot operation up and running. I like what you're trying to do here, but we have to put our own deadline on this approach, I think, just so we can consider other alternatives.

George: I would hope that by the end of next week. I actually am going to ask him if he can meet me for dinner. I should be able to give you a more formal plan for launching a demo at Building Co., or at least tell you why we aren't moving ahead with the demo. I don't think we should drag this on much longer.

Samantha: Well, enjoy the dinner. Let's see what you find out. Let's set up a meeting for next Thursday. Good luck with this.

There were many such discussions over the year, as George became more comfortable with the idea that he had to build relationships with those whom he was trying to influence, and as he became more aware of the limitations of a purely technical argument. There were times when he would fall back into his old habits, insisting that the technological superiority of the product was such that people just "had to listen." Samantha could be pretty direct with her feedback on such occasions, but George rarely felt attacked. He typically felt a sense of *mea culpa*—that she was right.

In George's case, there were no earthshaking insights, no changes in personality. His tool kit grew. He spent more time getting to know people, including some of his own senior managers. He was still more comfortable making a technical argument, but he was also more aware of what those on the other side of the table wanted, or needed. So when George presented his update on the status of Building Co. to his top management, he was able to understand their concerns about some slips in the overall project schedule. But he also was aware that they would be very reassured by reports on the growing level of investment that Building Co. was making in the robotic inspection process. That's really what they wanted to hear.

Some of these managers also began to rethink their previously held perceptions about George and think more broadly about his future with the company. Changing the perceptions of other stakeholders, though, would probably take more time. Unfortunately, once you've been "typecast," as Samantha would say to George, it's hard to convince people that their perceptions need to change. You have to "get it right" several times, she warned him, before people begin to think, "Maybe I was wrong about this person" or "Maybe this person can change his behavior."

Does this all sound like a fairy tale? Perhaps, but we hope not. As we have said in different ways before and will repeat at various points throughout this book, we know that many of you have not experienced a manager like Samantha. But what did she do here? She helped a motivated employee stretch himself. She gave him an opportunity to take on a tough, challenging assignment. She didn't do so blindly. She really considered (a) whether or not he was motivated and (b) whether or not he had some foundational skill set on which he could build. She didn't have to be a psychologist to determine the latter. She just had to think a little bit about what she'd seen him do in the past. But she did more than that.

We've done an interesting exercise with all sorts of groups over the years. We ask them to think about a manager for whom they have worked who helped them develop, really develop—someone about whom, when they look back on their time working for that person, they are likely to say, "I am a better [worker, professional, or even person] for having worked for that individual." We ask the group, "What did he or she do to make that happen?" (The good news is that most people can point to at least one example in their careers. The bad news is that it's often only one example, even from folks who are in their 50s.) What do people say their "coaching manager" did?

- Gave them a challenge
- Believed in them
- Was a good role model
- Trusted them, even when involved in a stretch assignment
- Made time to meet and talk, formally or informally
- Didn't just "tell them" the right answer, but asked useful questions and provoked them to think
- Gave them feedback, even when it was critical feedback, but did so in a respectful fashion
- Backed them up from time to time and stood by them when they made some mistakes
- Seemed to be interested in them as human beings, not just workers

It's an interesting list, isn't it? There is nothing particularly surprising here. Consider, however, what would have happened here under a "non-coaching" manager. There are a few possible scenarios. George might have felt very limited and left, as Samantha feared. The company then would have lost his technical expertise and his loyalty. George might have been thrown into the work with Building Co. with no support, which could have been disastrous for everyone. George could have been given the work but had a micromanaging boss who might have made sure the project was completed on time but would have left him feeling as though he had learned nothing (and his confidence would not have been enhanced as a result). The business case is clear. Samantha was pursuing a desired result, building organizational capability by helping George expand his tool kit, and keeping a good employee engaged in the work.

A Simple Model of Developmental Coaching

Coaching from a conceptual standpoint is really pretty simple. Thankfully. Coaching is not the primary task of most managers. Managers have a variety of things to worry about (too many things in most cases). The number-one reason we still find that managers give for not coaching is "lack of time." As we discussed in Chapter 1, the situation is actually a bit more complicated. It may be lack of skill as well as the failure of these managers' organizations to reward them for developing talent. The skill issue and the time issue, though, go hand in hand. Keeping things simple makes sense.

A simple approach to coaching helps the coaching manager prioritize other business demands, while at the same time paying attention to employee development and organization building. Coaching managers don't want to imply to employees that they will help them develop—and then not follow through. They need a model that can be "slipped into" their daily routine. In fact, we've talked with managers who integrate coaching into their routines with such ease that their associates don't even label it "coaching." As you review Samantha's conversation with George above, you may say to yourself, "Is that coaching?" Yes, it is. (Some of you, we hope, are actually thinking, "Hey, I could do that.")

It is easy to spot what she did in what we'll call the "coaching dialogue." She responded to George's concerns through the use of helpful questions. Those questions encouraged him to think and come up with some ideas about how to proceed. In the process, George described more about some of the issues he had with "organizational politics." But in some ways, that dialogue was the outcome of a series of other actions that Samantha, and to a significant extent George, took to make such conversations possible. After all, coaching as we see here takes place in a context. There is business to be done, corporate politics, corporate culture, reward systems, and many other factors that ultimately impact whether or not conversations like this are going to take place. So the coaching model is hopefully simple enough to be actionable but at the same time to help you take into account the variety of factors that determine whether or not it will be successful.

Having said all this, we must emphasize again that although the model is simple and flexible, using it does take practice. The best way to learn to coach is to coach. The more you coach, particularly the more you create a demand for coaching among your employees, the more likely you are to become comfortable seizing small coaching moments, as well as using coaching to address major challenges. In addition, the more you create a demand for coaching, the more you can expect your employees to put themselves in the coachee role and generate their own opportunities to create a "coaching dialogue," not only with their manager but also with their peers. The model is presented in graphic form in Figure 2.1.

Figure 2.1   The Developmental Coaching Model

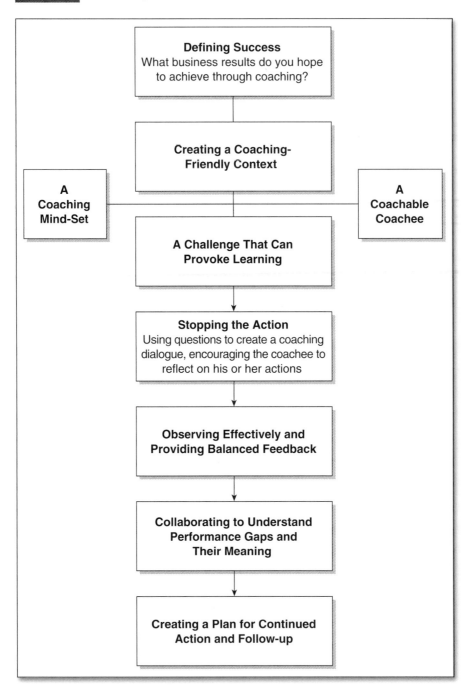

Defining Success

Several years back one of us was asked to consult with a senior sales manager about a possible coaching program for his sales team. He was asked what skills he was hoping to build among his team members as a result of the coaching. He couldn't answer the question. He was asked to describe a superior performer on his team, the best salesperson. His retort: "That's the person who sells the most." In desperation, he was asked: "Well, how does she sell the most? What does she do to make all those sales?" His response: "I don't know; she just does it." This sales manager was focused, to a dramatic and an unfortunate degree, only on results. He didn't need a coaching program, at least not then. First, he needed to figure out how his best salespeople were getting those great results.

The coaching manager needs a sense of what good performance looks like in order to know what to look for and what kind of feedback is likely to be helpful. Tichy (1997) has described this as the requirement for the coach to develop a teachable point of view. Samantha understood what to look for when meeting with senior managers, for instance. She knew the value of keeping an eye on their body language to see when they were becoming annoyed or bored. She could see what caused them to perk up: presentations that integrated technical and commercial considerations. She knew that for George to demonstrate that he possessed the competence necessary for continued advancement, he'd have to be able to deliver such a presentation.

In Chapter 1, we asked you to consider your own coaching value proposition. Why did Samantha take the time necessary to coach? Her team was tasked with handling the installation of the company's products. These installations were complex and could have a significant impact on the customers' work flow. The installation period could be quite disruptive. The ability to deal with the political aspects of product installation was a key competency that she directly related to the business success of her group. She needed as many people in her organization as possible to have some abilities in that area. George wanted to learn to build his competency in an area that was very aligned with Samantha's needs.

George's interest in this area didn't appear out of nowhere. When Samantha took over the group, she began a series of discussions with the entire team, in staff meetings and in individual sessions, about this all-important competency even though this "competency" had not achieved any particular recognition corporate-wide. She was working on this skill set with several other members of the team who were engaged in activities similar to George's project.

It's important to note here that George didn't understand the term *executive presence* until Samantha and he had had a chance to talk over the actual meaning of the phrase. Defining success requires that both parties have a shared understanding of what the words in the definition actually mean. Only when such a concept as "presence" has been adequately discussed will team members understand its behavioral requirements. The organization (through its management) formally or informally defines the skills that are important to the organization's success. The coachee has to supply the all-important motivation to learn. If the hiring process has been effective, the employee will probably want to learn more about the skills (or attitudes or knowledge) that the organization considers important. Being effective in these areas helps an employee be successful in both the short term and the long term.

One final point: It's much easier to give feedback to someone who understands the rules of the game. If you know you have to be able to position your proposals to meet both technical and business needs, you'll be less surprised when your manager tells you that you need to revamp one or the other (or both). Sometimes negative reactions to feedback are driven by confusion over the behaviors and actions for which the organization is holding employees responsible.

A Coaching-Friendly Context

A significant component of that engine was an environment in which George and Samantha could hold frank discussions without fear of reprisal on George's part, in particular. This is perhaps the most important success factor in support of coaching. As we said in Chapter 1, you don't have to be perfect in holding a coaching dialogue, but you have to demonstrate that your intent to encourage development is meaningful and has equal prioritization with your job as performance evaluator.

We've been told on a fairly regular basis "that can't be done." We understand the challenge. Our evidence to the contrary: In every class and in every meeting in which we've talked about coaching we have found plenty of examples of managers who make it happen. And it's happened to us, on occasion, as both manager and employee. Can a manager eliminate every political or organizational concern that can impede the development of trust? No. Can a manager eliminate enough so that coaching can take place? Yes, in most cases, we believe that one can. (There are organizational environments so toxic that it is probably impossible for coaching to take place, we do concede. Most environments aren't that bad.)

How did Samantha make that possible? She did a number of things. Perhaps most important, she repeatedly signaled to those on her team that they should expect it. She expected team members to talk openly about key issues and about what they were trying to learn or having difficulty mastering. She made it clear that she wouldn't hold them responsible for being on the tough side of a learning curve when it was time for their performance appraisal. She liked to challenge people, so the occasional failure was, for her, to be expected, sometimes relished. Repeated failures, and team members' keeping problems to themselves, could be another matter, however. Finally, she made it clear that she didn't have all the answers. She expected those on the team to generate ideas and possible solutions that would lead to discussions and to feedback. Team members, including Samantha herself, would learn together. Her role was, in part, to ask questions that would aid in that process.

In a coaching-friendly context, employees develop a new set of assumptions about working with their manager. The employee who has learned coaching-friendly assumptions holds ideas such as the following:

- It is OK to talk with your manager about a problem, a personal performance goal, or a career goal. You won't be criticized for seeking out coaching. In fact, your manager believes it is part of his or her job to help you learn and improve your performance. You may ultimately receive more critical feedback if you don't seek out and make use of coaching and feedback.

- However, your manager isn't going to solve the problem for you. Coaching is profoundly different from a pat on the back (though sometimes it does include a pat on the back) or attending a lecture. Your manager is going to talk about what you're trying to accomplish, listen, ask questions, and challenge you to learn and to try new approaches to your work and your career. In a coaching-friendly context, employees expect a lot of questions, but not necessarily a lot of answers.

- Your manager will try, when possible, to put you into situations in which you'll learn, on the job, through challenge and feedback; the feedback will be constructed to help you deepen your ability to assess your own performance, not just to grade your performance. However, employees have to negotiate such opportunities. These opportunities aren't given as a gift; they are earned, and they must make some business sense. Employees have to keep in mind that development is a two-way street. Both parties, the organization and the employee, have to benefit at the end of the day, or developmental efforts will not be sustainable.

- Your manager *is* watching your performance, though without the intent to micromanage or usurp your responsibilities. Your manager is watching your performance to gain data that will help provide balanced feedback.

- Even if your manager is responsible for grading your performance through an appraisal system (a periodic event in most firms), coaching will be continuous. It won't take place only during periodic performance appraisal sessions. Coaching is, for most coaching managers, a higher priority than the performance appraisal. The performance appraisal, in a coaching-friendly context, is a review of the work that's been going on over time.

Though these assumptions all sound appealing, they must be in a sense "earned." Managerial and organizational actions are frequently responsible for developing beliefs in employees that are diametrically opposed to those outlined here. Further, some employees may not like to work for a manager who doesn't "tell them the right answer" or who is expecting them to engage in continuous learning. Others may not want to believe that they need coaching or that coaching has anything to offer. Many of us have gotten used to being quite independent over the years in our organizations. In a coaching-friendly context, employees don't experience their managers as trying to undermine their independence—far from it. In fact, a coaching manager is watching for the purpose of helping employees perform at an ever-higher level of effectiveness.

If you've never coached before, and if your employees are not used to your asking coaching questions (see below), signal them in advance that you are going to be trying something new. It may even be necessary to reassure them that coaching does not mean they will be constantly appraised about their performance. Then you'll have to "walk the talk": follow through on keeping it safe to honestly deal with important questions. Try asking others for coaching and feedback help and, in doing so, serve as a model coaching consumer as well as a provider.

The coaching-friendly context creates the market for coaching we discuss in Chapter 1 (Evered & Selman, 1989). If it won't hurt them materially or psychologically, people really want to know how they are doing and how they can improve. The desire to learn and grow is for all practical purposes innate. It is too often crushed in organizational life. Coaching occurs in part when the manager ceases to impede such naturally occurring conversations by creating unnecessary or self-protective political barriers. ("Don't talk to your boss about the job you'd like to apply for. That'll be seen as disloyal, and he'll get you for it.") The great athlete would not think of going to the Olympics without a passion for improving his or her performance and a coach to help in that process. We expect to see coaches, several of them usually, working with any team, even a team with the youngest athletes. If the coach left the sidelines, the team would, rightly, feel abandoned. There's no politics involved (for the most part). That is the model for a coaching-friendly context.

Creating a demand on the part of employees for coaching makes managing the conflict between development and evaluation easier. It also makes it much easier to be a coaching manager. Employees under such circumstances seek out opportunities to learn in discussions with their managers. The employee becomes a collaborator in the coaching process, not a subject of it. The implications of that change in mind-set could not be more important, as we'll see.

We should probably acknowledge that many of you may be thinking at this point that as soon as Samantha helped these people develop such a desirable leadership skill, they'd start to leave the team for other opportunities. You're right. Samantha was very aware of this dilemma. In fact, she relished it. She knew that if she could build her reputation as someone who was good at developing talent, she'd have no trouble replacing those who left with equally motivated people. As to those who might depart, they'd be her ambassadors, friends she could call upon for help in future projects. It was Samantha's business goal to create a developmental engine that would drive her business.

The "Coachable" Coachee

Samantha was a student of talent. She long ago was aware of George's interest in learning and developing himself. That's one of the reasons she requested that he join her group when she took over the management role last year. The term *"coachable" coachee* means exactly what you'd expect. Coaching managers encourage the development of "coachability" in a number of ways, including the following:

- Hiring the right people
- Spotting those individuals who are most open to coaching
- Assigning those people to work that will provide them an opportunity to pursue their goals when possible
- Creating a coaching-friendly context, as described above

We did not include selection in our model in the first edition, and we heard about that from readers and participants in our workshops. We went back and looked at the records of our interviews with coaching managers, and it was there all along. They are talent managers in the truest sense. The first job of a talent manager is to be able to spot talent and to know how to bring that talent into his or her organization.

What did our coaching managers say they hoped to see when they were looking at potential hires? In addition to the threshold capacities required to do their jobs, they looked for people who want to learn. In a turbulent environment, it's very unlikely that the job you're hired for is going to be the same job you'll be doing next year. The ability to learn, and to be motivated by the opportunity to learn, is key. We argue here that coaching experiences are cocreated by the coachee and manager. Our first piece of advice for future coaching managers is to look for people who can (a) do the job you need them to do and (b) help you cocreate the opportunities for learning, for everyone.

Of course, you may not always have the chance to select your team members, and people in fact can change, making them more or less, permanently or temporarily, unable to cocreate coaching conversations. George, at varying times in his life, may have had a different degree of openness to learning and the feedback that Samantha gave him. But he wanted to have an impact broader than he was able to have through the application of his technical expertise. He had a vision for his role that was powerful and that helped him deal with the highs and lows of development on the job. He was motivated and, as such, an able cocreator of the coaching enterprise.

In our experience, high-potential employees often possess this characteristic and are willing to take coaching if, and this is important, they see it as valuable. They like coaching best when it helps them stretch and develop a new skill that will increase their range.

Note then that Samantha couldn't change George. Only George could make the changes required to enhance his effectiveness and move his career forward. He had to want it. That's why mandatory coaching is so likely to fail. When the organization demands the individual change his or her behavior, regardless of the potential coachee's intent, the coaching isn't developmental; it's remedial or, worse, punitive. Adults don't like to be punished. Punishment, as opposed to feedback, does not facilitate change. The downward spiral often associated with remedial coaching is one of the reasons managers hate to "coach." If remedial coaching was the only kind of coaching we'd ever done, we'd agree wholeheartedly. It's no fun, you're the bad guy or gal, and it rarely works. Who needs that? Developmental coaching is something quite different.

There are other factors that can make developmental coaching difficult or impossible that we'll explore later. Some people can't tolerate feedback. Some have learned from previous experience never to trust their boss (this can sometimes be reversed, with effort). Some people are dealing with health or family problems that may make them temporarily or permanently resistant to coaching. Finally, some people are just in the wrong job. They don't have the foundational skills or sufficient motivation to make it work.

We have repeatedly seen good and even excellent coaching managers who were unable to get through to an employee. The results of a manager's and an employee's failure to establish a useful coaching relationship are unfortunate. Much time is lost in the process as well. The potential coachee hasn't learned much. Often, he or she will leave the organization and run into similar problems somewhere else. As we'll note later in the book, coaching managers are not reticent about moving people out of "the wrong job" if it's been determined that that's the source of a performance failure.

A Challenge That Can Provoke Learning

Most of us engage in a variety of activities at work. Some of them are challenging; some are not. If we already have mastery over the skills required to complete a specific task, coaching isn't likely to be all that helpful. George was a very skilled engineer. He didn't need nor did he want Samantha's help in that area. In fact, he was a bit bored with some of the technical demands of his job. He'd "been there, done that." What excited him was the challenge of having a broader impact, of dealing with big-picture problems and with his customers' senior managers. He and Samantha directed their coaching efforts there because the learning potential was so high.

A "Coaching Mind-Set" on the Part of the Manager

In order to be an effective coach, Samantha had had to expand her own repertoire of behaviors beyond the take-charge style that had brought her the success she had achieved prior to becoming more of a coaching manager. The reality for her is that she may not have had much of a choice. She needed leaders everywhere. She couldn't do it all herself.

To coach, in our experience, you have to assume a different frame of mind than when you are engaged in the day-to-day practice of making decisions as a manager. Experience suggests that there are two related components of a coaching mind-set: developing a coaching identity and learning to be helpful rather than or in addition to being evaluative.

As we discussed in Chapter 1, coaching represents a stretch task for many managers. They have typically achieved initial success by "doing." Coaching represents both a shift of one's attention toward the performance of others (probably not that big a stretch for many managers) and a shift of identity to "one who helps others do" (probably a big stretch). Some managers will not achieve this identity transition. They may have a very difficult time becoming comfortable with the role. Perhaps just as important, the motivational distance may be too great. Some managers are only happy if they are in the trenches, doing the work. You probably won't know how you feel about coaching until you have tried it.

The coaching mind-set also requires that managers ask themselves this question: "Do I really feel that what I am about to say will be helpful to the coachee receiving my feedback?" Interestingly, many managers who have learned to coach have told us that they experienced unanticipated personal growth from their efforts. They report a better understanding of the nature of leadership and teamwork, a positive feeling about themselves from helping others, and enhanced process skills that develop from the act of trying to teach those skills to others. They become better leaders.

Stopping the Action and Starting the Dialogue: Creating Coaching Opportunities

Coaching moments, moments with the potential for learning, occur all the time in most settings. This is particularly true when the employee has been given a challenging assignment as discussed above. What do potential coaching moments look like? An employee has a question, has a complaint, thinks out loud about a particular issue, or expresses concerns about a problem he or she is having. What happens next is important. Most busy managers confronted with a question will answer it. Confronted with a complaint, they will defend company actions. Overhearing employees chat about a new customer, they may throw in their own opinions. Coaching requires a different approach at such junctures. Coaching requires that the manager stop the action and instigate a dialogue using techniques of inquiry (Senge, Ross, Smith, Roberts, & Kleiner, 1994). This is where we start to run into trouble with some of those who may have found our argument thus far to be somewhat persuasive. Stop the action? You can't stop the action. There's no time. Yes, you can. However, we grant that sometimes this requires the manager to be somewhat clever.

Imagine that you're a nurse on an intensive care unit. You're rather new on the job. You've got to administer a difficult treatment to a very ill child. The child's parents are watching. How do you develop anything like mastery under such circumstances? You learned about the technical aspects of the treatment from a book or a class. You have practiced it on models or on your friends (up to a point). You have watched more seasoned nurses administer the treatment. There comes a time when you have to do it yourself. A more experienced nurse, a coaching nurse manager, is now watching you. You manage to get it done, but it takes much longer than it should have, and your patient is not so happy (and neither are his parents).

When's the best time for a coaching dialogue? It is probably not at that particular moment in the room, with the parents and patient. "Bedside coaching," as some of our hospital workshop participants have described it, can be very tricky. Do you wait till the end of the shift if you're the more experienced nurse? You'd better not, if you can help it. The end of the shift could be 6 hours, a lifetime, away. Eighteen things could happen to distract your attention. If you want to make sure your younger colleague has a chance to improve her performance, you had better talk about it soon, but down the hall, in a private place. It won't take long. You grab an office and don't even sit down. (We've heard, but we promise we did not make up, the term *drive-by coaching* for such interactions. And we heard it at a hospital!)

Then, do you start by telling her the things she did wrong and right? You might. That would be better than no feedback at all. Think about it, though. Would she really feel more or less overwhelmed or attacked by such an approach? She's already stressed out, in all likelihood. What about if you first asked her, "So what did you think? How did that go?" Immediately the playing field gets leveled a bit. She can talk about her experience. She may be right on target about what went wrong. As the coaching nurse manager, you may just have to listen, and nothing more. She begins to tell you where she had some troubles, and she says she was nervous. You concur with that. Who wouldn't be nervous? But she got it done, and she thinks she knows what she could do differently next time. Again, you concur. She's getting there, and in this case, she diagnosed the challenge (it's not a problem; she's on a learning curve) herself. She's beginning to breathe again.

The new nurse has to learn to think for herself. Telling her the answer doesn't achieve that goal. Helping her learn to critique her own performance is key here. You won't always be there. She's got to learn to handle situations like this independently. A dialogue, rather than a "telling" session, makes people feel like, as one of our nurse participants once told us, "I'm a participant in my own learning," not a victim. She's learning to be a reflective practitioner, and she's just learned that it's OK to talk with a senior colleague about her struggles. Interactions like this occur every day, many times each day, in your average well-run hospital. If those folks can do it, so can you. (Granted, your situation may be very different from theirs, and as such, you'll need to modify your approach.)

Should the manager try to engage employees in a coaching opportunity every time an apparent coaching moment appears? Early in their efforts to become more effective as coaches, we often find that some managers can be a bit aggressive in grasping for such moments, overcorrecting in a sense. It is also our experience that employees tend to understand and appreciate the effort. Once it is clear that coaching is a routine part of life in the work group, managers can take their cues from the employees. They, the employees, start to clearly signal when they need or want coaching. Again, if you've just given them a stretch assignment, you should assume that more coaching will be required.

Note that Samantha and George actually used a more formal process for their coaching. They held regularly scheduled meetings. Given how often both were out of the plant, that's really the only way they could make it work. Even so, they focused on coaching moments. Samantha liked to look at very specific situations that confronted George. She found it not terribly useful to speak in generalities. By being specific in her focus, she was able to stop the action even though several days had passed.

Stopping the action sets the stage for a dialogue between coach and coachee. The question that the coaching manager should keep in mind is this: "What do you, the coachee, want to learn and/or need to learn?" The coachee and coach need to be engaged early in the process in an effort to mutually define the scope of the coaching effort. Simple questions such as the following are useful ways to get started:

- "What was that experience [the focus of the coaching effort] like for you?"
- "How do you think you did?"
- "What is your own critique?"
- "What could you have done differently?"

The coach asks questions that will help the prospective coachee self-assess his or her performance and, on the basis of that self-assessment, define a learning goal or need. (Of course, the coachee isn't likely to describe the outcome of this process as a learning goal per se in most cases. Typically, the coachee will say something like "I think that approach didn't work. Maybe I should try . . .") Self-assessment represents a foundation for learning. But self-assessment, reflection if you will, is not just a listing of good and bad grades. The process of reflection, as we've already stated, is a necessary part of learning. Reflection works even better, as we'll discuss, when others are involved in the process.

Finally, the coaching dialogue also helps address the all-important issue of ownership. By asking the coachee what he thinks, where he's running into trouble, and what he thinks he should do, the coaching manager is clarifying the fact that it is the coachee who has to deal with the issue at hand. Obviously the coaching manager will ultimately be responsible for what takes place on her team. The dialogue, however, makes the coachee responsible for actively participating in the work and the growth.

Again, a dialogue may not always be possible. What can a coach do if an employee sees no problem or no need to learn more about his or her performance? Such a response suggests that the individual is not ready for coaching. Feedback that the individual respects will likely be the only force helping him or her see that there is actually a need for developmental work. We'll address this when we talk about the management of performance problems in a later chapter.

Observing Effectively and Providing Balanced and Helpful Feedback

Obviously coachees' perceptions, or self-assessment based on personal reflection alone, may not be enough to help them clearly see how they are doing and what they need to learn to improve their performance. Feedback is a component of coaching that may be necessary to clarify key issues, suggest specific actions, reveal blind spots, or help coachees prioritize action steps. Giving feedback may be one of the most difficult aspects of coaching. On the other hand, some managers confuse feedback and coaching. Feedback isn't coaching because feedback by itself does not encourage critical thinking, independence, self-monitoring, and the other outcomes that can be supported through a coaching dialogue.

Feedback should be used to support an individual's learning. Too often, though, feedback is in fact used as a punishment. If you have to punish someone, so be it. You may find it useful or necessary to explain to the individual being punished the nature of his or her transgressions. Rationales for punishment should not be confused with feedback, however. Think of feedback as providing data to fill in missing elements in the coachee's and the coaching manager's understanding of what is taking place. George didn't realize the degree to which he had lost credibility with senior management. He didn't understand the importance with which they viewed his ability to consider the commercial aspects of his work.

Samantha confronted him with this information not to punish him but rather to help him fully comprehend his situation. She held up a mirror in a tactful but direct fashion. George then had the courage and commitment necessary to look squarely in the mirror and draw his own conclusions. There are two components to the coaching mirror: defining what is important to observe and observing effectively (which can be surprisingly difficult to do).

We stress here, though, one often overlooked aspect of providing effective feedback. The coaching manager ideally needs to be able to spot, to observe, examples of good and poor performance so that she'll be in a position to provide feedback when appropriate. This requires that the coaching manager keep her eyes open and be sensitive to potential opportunities to observe the coachee's actions. It also requires that the coaching manager try to maintain a position of objectivity. We saw how Samantha struggled with this particular issue. She liked George, but she had to think clearly about his abilities. Feelings about the coachee, positive or negative, can make it harder to really evaluate the coachee's actions.

Of course the virtual world we inhabit now doesn't make this any easier. In many companies, George and Samantha might have actually been working in separate countries. They might see each other once or twice each year, if that. How can Samantha be effective at helping George if she doesn't see him in action? This is a challenge that does not succumb to easy remedies, we must admit. We'll talk more about this thorny issue later in the book. Needless to say, we do believe that it's not an all-or-none situation for the coaching manager, though it may require some clever thought.

In addition, however, the psychological processes of perception and cognition tend to degrade the data we do obtain. We can see a single behavioral act, for instance, and easily misjudge its meaning. We live harried lives. It saves time to (often unconsciously) draw an inference or, as we more commonly state it, jump to conclusions. Samantha could have easily misjudged the difficulties that George was having in relating to senior management. She could have assumed that he just didn't care about their concerns. After all, it looked that way. But in fact he was concerned. He just didn't think that it was his role to speak up. Coaching managers can be a bit like scientists. They observe and then form tentative conclusions about the object of their observations. But they are tentative. What those observations actually mean can usually be determined only through the coaching dialogue. Samantha observed George's failure to bring up key business issues when meeting with senior management. She could correct him. Or she could share her observation and then ask him, "Why?" In doing so, she would learn the real issue.

To preview one of our basic tools, we've found it useful to think about observing for and providing feedback that is directed at one or more of the following three aspects of action:

Intent—What the coachee was trying to do. George was trying to deliver a helpful presentation. He was also intending to avoid discussing commercial factors that he felt were probably more the territory of others. He was not intending to ignore implied but not stated concerns of senior management.

Action—George actually delivered good technically competent but commercially superficial presentations.

Impact—This was the area that George was missing. He had a blind spot here, and Samantha was able to spot it and communicate it effectively to George. The category of impact is increasingly important in a diverse, virtual, and global business context. It is easy for well-intentioned people to try to do the right thing, do the wrong thing, and have a significantly adverse impact.

Of course, when coaching managers personally deliver feedback, a caring attitude is essential. If coachees define learning goals, they are allowing themselves to be vulnerable to the process of receiving feedback. They have let their defenses down, at least with regard to particular learning needs. It is the coach's job to help maintain individuals' sense of comfort, to the highest degree possible, so their collaborative efforts can continue.

However, this does not mean that such feedback can't be critical. Indeed, it often has to be critical. According to our interviews, coaching managers find that to withhold critical feedback as a means of supporting an employee is often seen as gratuitous. In a coaching-friendly environment, critical feedback is taken less personally, particularly if it is directed at the learner's actual goals. Balanced feedback helps the employee see him- or herself as clearly as possible.

Collaboratively Interpreting the Meaning of Performance Gaps

Through their dialogue and Samantha's tactful but direct use of feedback to supplement George's own self-awareness, they were able to understand what needed to change and why. George needed to step up more in his ability to demonstrate command of the business context of their work. His intent was fine up to a point. His actions needed to change. He needed to be much more sensitive to the impact he was having, particularly on his own management. So George was going to have to do some skill building. But there was more to the challenge he faced.

This was going to require real growth on George's part. It was critical that the two of them understand that George, technically trained and acculturated over the years, was going to be working outside his comfort zone. He could be his own worst enemy in this endeavor. They needed to have more than just a superficial understanding of his need to "be more commercial." He would more likely have some blind spots in his self-awareness. He might "relapse" more easily from time to time. He might need more rehearsal during which he could receive feedback. He also might need encouragement. There is an emotional aspect to learning on the job. The support of a coach can be enormously helpful in maintaining the coachee's morale in tough times.

Such a more comprehensive approach is not always going to be required. Let's assume that George actually had decided to pursue a purely technical path. He might be very comfortable in doing so, and he'd be building on some considerable strengths. He might need far less support from Samantha. We'll talk about the change process in a later chapter, but for our purposes here, we'd encourage the coaching manager to consider, as did Samantha, the goals George was trying to achieve and the various ways that progress could falter. The two need to create an action plan. A good plan leverages support but also addresses possible barriers to goal achievement.

Creating a Plan for Change and Following Up

George and Samantha then gradually put together a specific plan. Notice that there were really several plans at work here. There was a business plan, which required work. George was to lead the effort to implement the robotic inspection product at Building Co. There was, however, a development plan in play as well. George was going to build his ability to influence key players at Building Co. from both a technical and a commercial perspective. The business plan, and the work that it required, was used to drive development.

Samantha and George were both realistic about what could be accomplished in a one-week executive development program. They were right to be skeptical. Change usually doesn't occur through a short classroom intervention. The classroom experience provided some useful ideas and tools, but those needed to be put into practice in the field. Coaching managers never expect the classroom by itself to result in sustained behavior change. Developmental coaching is about on-the-job learning.

The actual development plan, which in this case was understood but not written down, involved regular meetings between Samantha and George during which they could engage in a coaching dialogue and Samantha might be able to provide George feedback on his ideas and business plans. The regular coaching sessions helped Samantha stay on top of both the business issues and development progress. She was not abdicating her responsibility. She was really delegating that responsibility. She held both of them accountable for staying with the plan, at least to the degree possible. (It's a given that sometimes the greatest learning occurs when the plan falls apart. Again, in those instances, the manager and the coachee are positioned to work together to repair the damage and learn from the experience.)

As You Experiment With Coaching

We have tried in this chapter to provide you with an overview of a model of developmental coaching that can work in fast-paced, new-economy companies. As we stated at the outset of this chapter, the model is simple conceptually and doesn't take a great deal of time to execute once you have established a coaching-friendly context. However, we work with people on a regular basis just as you, our readers, do. The devil, as they say, is in the details, the multitude of issues and problems and opportunities that emerge as two or more people are trying to work together. To learn to coach, you must try it, self-assess how it goes for you, obtain some feedback, and think about what you need to do to close the gap between current and desired performance.

In the chapters that follow, we hope to give you a clearer picture of competency as a coach on the part of a practicing manager. Chapters 3 through 6 describe what we call the setup for coaching. You can consider these enabling factors that you can influence: your reason for coaching, the coaching context, your own behavior, and making sure you're coaching the right people. If you get these right, to an extent you can rest assured that some good coaching will take place, naturally. In the remaining chapters, though, we will dig into coaching conversations in much greater depth so that you can get a clear sense of what they look like in practice.

Defining Success as a Coaching Manager

3

In this chapter, you will learn the following:

- The business orientation of managers who coach
- How you can define competencies that will help you coach, and help your business
- Ideas for spreading the word about what is important
- The connections between selection and coaching

We've argued that there isn't enough coaching going on in most business organizations. Managers who do coach, though, are acutely aware of the connection between their coaching efforts and business results. As mentioned in Chapter 2, they spell that connection out clearly. In this chapter, we'll look at some ideas for making that connection clear. These ideas should help you not only in talent development but also just as importantly in talent selection. Though the latter is somewhat beyond the scope of this book, we'll spend some time linking the two at the close of this chapter.

Coaching Managers Focus on Running a Business

We have found that coaching managers may not define themselves as coaches, and they may not define what they do as coaching. The word *coaching* has obviously become a part of the popular culture, given the attention it has received in the media. However, effective leaders have been engaging in behaviors that have what we would now define as coaching as their intent throughout the history of civilization. Why? The coaching managers we met are businesspeople first. In other words, effective coaching managers don't appear to be more "touchy-feely" than anyone else in the business world. They work hard and tend to be very task and results oriented.

Although some have strong beliefs about the humanistic or even spiritual importance of helping others learn and grow, most enjoy the business life and wouldn't give it up to become social workers (with all due respect to that noble profession). It should come as no surprise that most effective coaches very much like their work. One of the reasons they like to coach is that they are enthusiastic about what they do, and they genuinely want to help others succeed in their fields. It also turns out that being grounded in the running of the business or organization is a highly effective aid to the coaching process.

The coach who is a business leader (not necessarily the CEO, but a formal or informal leader in any size business unit) is likely to have a great deal of what psychologists call *source credibility* (London, 1997). Feedback from someone who is seen as having skills or as having been successful in an area linked with the aspirations of the coachee is likely to be difficult to ignore, even when the feedback is critical in nature. Even more important, if conditions are right, feedback from a credible source is likely to be sought out. Perhaps a simple story from one of the founders of the field of management will illustrate the point.

Erich Dombrowski was the editor of Germany's largest afternoon paper in post–World War II Frankfurt. That newspaper, *General-Anzeiger,* served as the place of employment of management writer Peter Drucker. Drucker has described how he learned the newspaper business from Dombrowski. In the years following the Second World War, Dombrowski had very few resources with which to work. In particular, he had no experienced journalists. He was forced to hire an inexperienced staff. Drucker tells the rest of his coaching story as follows:

> None of us had ever worked on a newspaper. And he [Dombrowski] did two things, one, there was no limit to the responsibility that he heaped on us, and he took the whole editorial staff, 15 people, 16 people, sat down from Saturday evening, when the paper went to press, until Sunday afternoon. And each of us reported [to Dombrowski] and all the others asked questions and criticized. . . . At the end he [Dombrowski] summed up and gave each of us a specific goal. This is what you will have to learn. . . . This is where you have to change the way you do things. . . . This is the additional dimension. And I learned to sit down with myself once a year at least and look over the work

I did over the preceding 6 or 12 months, what did I do well, what could I or should I have done better, what could I or should I have done that I didn't do, and what do I get rid of because it is just surplus baggage, how do I reshape priorities? That is what I learned from him. (Peter F. Drucker Foundation for Nonprofit Management, 1998)

Drucker has written extensively of his observation that good leaders subordinate themselves to the mission of their organizations. In this case, Dombrowski didn't coach for the sake of coaching or even for the sake of developing his staff. These were not his primary goals. Drucker explains, adding something of a punch line to the story:

After I went back to Germany in '53 or '54, I cornered him, and I said, "You don't remember, but I want to tell you how much I owe to you, how much I learned from you, how much you made me face up to things, and you have been my mentor and teacher," and he took a long look at me, and said, "This never occurred to me. All I was ever interested in was next month's newspaper." (Peter F. Drucker Foundation for Nonprofit Management, 1998)

Dombrowski was a leader. He did many things to get his newspaper out. Coaching was one of those activities. His ability to coach not only made him a more complete leader, but it also helped support his business. Coaching represents, at perhaps its best, one aspect of what might be described as a "bundle" of leadership behaviors or roles (Nannus, 1992). Dombrowski coached, but he also delegated, gave his employees challenging assignments, let them do their best and sometimes fail, and kept his eye on the mission of getting out the newspaper. He also helped his organization adapt to a very difficult and resource-poor environment.

In the process of engaging in these activities, as we would expect of a successful business leader, Dombrowski spent a great deal of time with his people. The young journalists probably did make many mistakes. The tone of Drucker's comments, however, suggests that the editor carefully listened to what they were doing, encouraged them to reflect on their work, encouraged them to help each other, and then gave his own thoughtful feedback. His feedback was heard not as critical but as informative and challenging. And it was given in the service of helping his employees work toward a goal to which they were presumably committed, that of being effective journalists and newspapermen and -women.

In Chapter 1, we discussed what we have come to term the "coaching value proposition." It is very important that you understand how your business goals are linked with your talent management goals. Again we ask, how can talent development help your team or organization? Dombrowski had no choice about becoming a coaching manager, at least in his own mind. He saw that it was necessary. What's your reason?

Not Just Results, but Process: How the Work Gets Done

In order to assist you in answering that question, we need to ask you to indulge in a bit of strategic thinking about the nature of the work that takes place in your unit. In an effort to understand the work you do, it can be useful to distinguish between process and results. *Process* refers to "how the work gets done." Unfortunately, some managers dislike focusing on the processes by which employees get their work done, as long as whatever path the employee takes is within some reasonable limit. They also may want to avoid undermining the autonomy of their reports. They don't want bright, well-educated employees feeling as though they are being watched under a microscope. Other managers may fear that a focus on process is too "soft" or analytical and will reflect a lack of emphasis on results. Nothing could be further from the truth. Results represent the goal. Process is how you get there. An effective manager is interested in both. Processes can be captured in elaborate models or informal ones. You can think of them as the best effort to accumulate wisdom about how to achieve success.

Results, on the other hand, are really what it's all about. It is the desire to achieve those results and the meaning of those results to each individual that serves to drive learning and efforts to improve. (We say this knowing also that many people enjoy the journey as well as the destination. That's fine, but some awareness of the destination is extremely helpful from a motivational perspective.) Results then drive an interest in learning and are absolutely essential to effective coaching. Employees are typically focused on results, too. This is fortunate because results are what you, the coaching manager, and your employees are paid to "deliver."

What Should the Coaching Manager Pay Attention To? Competency

The best way to think about processes for our purposes here is to consider them as being built from a series of activities. It is the ability to perform those activities well that represents talent in action. The coaching manager pays attention to the behavior, values, or skills that are causally related to the organization's desired outcomes. If your employees develop the behaviors or skills linked to organizationally necessary outcomes, they will have learned something valuable while helping the firm. Firms offer their managers and their employees varying levels of help in directing their attention to what their people should be doing well. Many firms now have what are called *competency models,* or descriptions of the behavior, values, and skills related to success, for at least the firm's most critical roles. From an individual, process-oriented perspective, competency models capture what is important. We say this knowing that some readers will already be skeptical about the value of competency modeling. We'll deal with those concerns shortly.

Competency models have been growing in popularity for the past 80 years, building on work from two sources. They were initially developed by the federal government to help define needed skills in the armed forces during the world wars of the past century. In the 1950s, AT&T became one of the first industrial organizations to develop a competency model (though it did not use the term) for the firm's various management levels. The job of the first line supervisor is of course very different from that of the senior vice president. AT&T and its human resource management and industrial/organizational psychology staff studied jobs at each of the firm's management levels and were able to specify behaviors that would be likely to predict success at each one (Bray, Campbell, & Grant, 1977).

This line of analysis was greatly extended by psychologist David McClelland (Spencer, McClelland, & Spencer, 1994). His research indicated that the techniques then in use for selecting employees, such as unstructured interviews or IQ tests, were not particularly helpful as they failed to predict success in work or in life. His suggested solution was deceptively simple.

McClelland and his colleagues began to interview and observe individuals in particular job roles who demonstrated exceptional performance in the eyes of their peers, customers, or leaders. They also interviewed and observed individuals in the same roles whose performance was average or adequate, and individuals whose performance was poor. They were able to isolate specific behaviors or skills for various job roles that could differentiate the three levels of performance. Importantly, when they went to confirm their findings by testing their competency models in new settings, they found that the particular behaviors associated with superior individual performance were consistently related to better business performance. In some studies, superior performance has been demonstrated to yield a 1,000% dividend over average performers! The best salespeople surveyed in a study of *Fortune 500* firms produced $6.7 million in sales per person compared with $3 million in sales per person for the average salesperson (Goleman, 1998). The comparison with poor performers was even more staggering.

McClelland and his colleagues defined the behaviors associated with a particular effective performance as *competencies.* A competency, then, can be thought of as an underlying characteristic of an individual that is causally related to effective or superior performance in a job (Boyatzis, 1982). Competency can result from individual characteristics, such as motives (what one wants), traits (personality characteristics), or self-concepts (the way one sees oneself). Competency can also be built from content knowledge and cognitive or behavioral skills. The ability to function effectively as a leader, for instance, is usually associated with certain motives, such as having an interest in power (McClelland & Burnham, 1995). Competency in leadership is also often associated with emotional intelligence and a highly developed set of interpersonal skills (Goleman, 1998). Competency in C++ programming, however, is associated with a talent in analysis (a personal trait) as well as specific learned skills in the language itself that build on that analytical talent. It is likely also associated with an ability to concentrate independently for an extended period of time. They began to find that competency was more complicated than just the ability to perform the technical aspects of a job.

Not surprisingly, the kinds of jobs that we ask people to do today are increasingly complex and involve the application of technical knowledge in relationship with others in the organization (the team) and with customers.

Threshold competencies (typically the technical skills necessary to even be considered for a job) and what might be called "price of admission" (Lombardo & Eichinger, 2001) competencies (basic skills such as oral communications that are widely distributed in the workforce) are places to begin when thinking about competencies. Most experienced talent managers would recommend selecting for these skills if you can. (We leave aside here the question of fit with a culture, however. Many would argue that you need to select for a good cultural fit as well. Personality can't be developed.) More sophisticated skills such as strategic thinking, project planning, the ability to negotiate and influence, and organizational savvy may not be as widely distributed in the population from which you can select candidates for a role. As such, you may have to help develop such high-level skills.

Our point here is to encourage you to think about competency and its relations to success broadly. This is *not* like writing a job description. Don't just stop at the technical competencies. An effective description of the talents required for success in a role should include the following:

- Technical skills—technical abilities required for the job
- Interpersonal skills—leadership, teamwork, influencing skills, and other abilities associated with working effectively with others inside and outside the organization as required
- Cognitive skills—the ability to problem solve and deal with ambiguity and other intellectual challenges

If you haven't had the opportunity to engage in this kind of thinking, try Exercise 3.1.

Exercise 3.1   The Great Performer

Find someone who does a great job at whatever role he or she has been given. You can find such people everywhere (perhaps except when you most need them). You can try this anywhere. One of the more interesting locales is a fast-food outlet.

Observe them, interview them, or interview those who work with them. Ask them what they do that promotes success. Be careful though. One person's great performer may be another person's poor performer. Take the individual who is great at customer service. He's friendly. Always tries to help. And whenever there's a problem, he takes care of it. But note, does the problem get taken care of in a fashion that always costs his company extra money? Someone who is great at customer service from an organizational perspective must find ways to help the customer *and* do so within budget. Managing those trade-offs is the tricky part. It can be helpful to ask yourself whether or not a variety of individuals who might be considered stakeholders in the individual's performance would be equally pleased with that person's competency.

Based on your observations and interviews, build a simple "competency" model. (It can't be a formal one using this methodology. To do an actual competency model you'd ideally study a number of superior performers and compare them with individuals who were average and even below average to test the hypotheses you're about to develop.)

Take note of the competencies you think are important. Consider the technical, cognitive, and interpersonal skill sets required of this performer. This kind of exercise can help improve your ability to observe talent as well as your ability to coach.

Now take it one step further. Put on your business mind-set. Try to prioritize from your list. What one or two items seem to be the most important from a competitive standpoint? What does this person do that makes his team more competitive? Does this individual's performance enhance the ability of his or her outfit to achieve business success? Then consider your own team. What kinds of competencies are truly mission critical to your team's ability to succeed? This is where the demonstration of competency has its greatest value.

The potential of describing a pattern of behavior or skills for any particular role that is highly predictive of success has led a number of organizations to spend the time, energy, and resources to build customized formal competency models for their individual firms. They then use these models as guides in selection, development, and, in some cases, even compensation.

Naturally, a number of consulting firms have emerged to service this market, particularly for those organizations that don't have resources to develop a competency model internally. The list of organizations that have established competency models for their executives, for instance, includes some of the best companies in the world: American Express, Eli Lilly, Hewlett-Packard, PepsiCo, and others (Briscoe & Hall, 1999).

Competency models have also been developed for a variety of middle management, individual contributor, and professional roles (Rosier, 1994). The service account engineer competency model for Landis & Gyr Powers, Inc., for example, includes competencies related to leadership, total quality management, interpersonal skills, and technical knowledge (Rosier, 1994). This competency model was built by data gained from focus groups made up of people in the role and those who interfaced with people in the role; they were asked to define effective performance in the role.

A competency model provides focus. In our coach training programs in which students are the ultimate coachees, we work with six simple but powerful competencies: leadership, teamwork, decision making, oral communications, ethical awareness, and listening. Each competency is defined by behavioral attributes or examples of what effective, average, and weak performance for each of the competencies look like to a trained observer. The participants in the program who serve as "coaches" know that these are the competencies for which they will give feedback. We've included a description of the competencies in more detail in the Appendix to give those of you who have not had experience in working with a competency model an idea of the kinds of descriptions that can be useful when trying to describe talent in action.

Not everyone will agree on the definitions of each particular competency. Even within companies, lively debate can take place, for instance, about the behaviors that characterize effective leaders in a specific organization. It is critically important, we believe, for these debates to play themselves out so that a shared understanding of *customer service, project management, software development,* or any other role can emerge. It's easy to imagine the potential for chaos if everyone interfacing with the customer had a different understanding of the meaning of those terms! One of the key roles played by the coaching manager, then, is to make sure, when any kind of competency model is in use, that everyone involved comes to consensus on what effective performance looks like. An important implication, then, of the idea that one of the most important functions of a competency model is to aid all parties in focusing on how particular tasks are accomplished is that such models must be public, particularly to employees with aspirations to learn and improve their performance. Descriptions of competencies represent descriptions of effectiveness that offer employees guidance on how to make developmental choices.

We are motivated to learn what we think will help us achieve our goals. But we have to know what to learn. A useful competency model helps in that regard by pointing toward a vision of superior performance in a particular role.

A competency model can help an employee aspiring to a management job understand the expectations and requirements for entry and success. Employees considering such major career transitions are often at a loss. How do you convince someone that you're worthy of being given a chance to manage when you've never held a formal managerial role? If, however, the employee knows that managers at her firm are expected to prioritize and plan work, to select team members and lead team meetings, to provide feedback on her performance, and so on, then she is better positioned to (a) consider how her current and previous experience might in fact be helpful in demonstrating *competency* for a role, even if she hasn't been *in* the role, and (b) identify areas for further development that can help prepare her for future roles. Keeping the competencies required for advancement secret doesn't help anyone.

This discussion of competency models is offered with the intent of trying to persuade you toward a point of view that, until recently, most managers did not accept: There can be a "right way" to approach even the most sophisticated tasks. This is true even when the job is brand-new or the terrain is deeply ambiguous. When selecting or developing candidates for a job that will require confrontation with extreme ambiguity, the competency "able to work under ambiguous conditions" becomes extremely relevant. Without some sense of what might work from a process point of view, coaching can be very difficult, if not impossible.

We would take this several steps further. With some idea of what to pay attention to, far more people can coach effectively than we might have guessed when we started this work. We had the chance to see this in action at the Whirlpool Corporation. Whirlpool is of course the largest appliance manufacturer in the world. The appliance business is tough, very tough. Until recently, the only way to be successful in that business was to pursue a strategy of operational excellence and shave every possible penny off the cost of the product. Now, of course, things have changed a bit, in no small measure because of the creative thinking of a large number of individuals at Whirlpool.

Whirlpool makes extensive use of a variety of forms of coaching (Hunt & Weintraub, 2007). The firm strongly encourages its managers to coach. This is a significant change for the company and is somewhat countercultural. Yes, Whirlpool is a company that has placed a great value on relationships. However, it has been a company that focused on management more than leadership. Coaching, until the past two decades, was not the kind of activity that was prioritized there. The CEO at the time, David Whitwam, became acutely aware that the company needed to redress that imbalance, to focus more on leadership, change, and creativity. He and his own team developed a very simple competency model (they did not use that term) that helped them communicate effectively to their people about the kinds of changes they were trying to make and how to get there (not just results, but the personal road map for change). They had had positive experiences with coaching themselves and also upped the priority they wanted Whirlpool managers to place on coaching and talent development.

Many of those managers, with strong backgrounds and successful careers in engineering and operations, for instance, had to make significant changes in their own behavior, such as learning to coach. In our interviews with those managers we found consistently that the competency model, known as the Whirlpool Leadership Model, was an invaluable tool. "I don't think I could do much in the way of coaching without some guidance" was a sentiment we heard time and again. Think of your competency model, formal or informal, as a playbook, to use the athletic terminology. It doesn't guarantee success, but at least it gives you some ideas as to what to do to achieve success.

An understanding of what is important is thus the foundation for coaching. Most professionals and managers should come to the job with a basic technical knowledge base in their chosen fields, be it programming, marketing, or human resources, but they also need to understand the processes in their organization that lead to success. Next, we'll talk about how to put this idea into practice. We consider first what to do if your company has a competency model in place and then what to do if your company does not.

If Your Company Has a Competency Model

If your company does have a competency model, you should first try to get a sense of how the model was developed. Competency models are developed by companies in three ways (Briscoe & Hall, 1999). Some firms use a research-based approach similar to that of McClelland and AT&T. This approach involves interviewing individuals who hold particular roles and who are perceived by others in the organization to be superior, not just adequate, performers. These interviews, typically conducted by human resource consultants, ask the interviewee to tell specific stories about his or her performance. These stories are then analyzed and grouped together by themes. For example, highly effective executives in a start-up division may offer a number of stories suggesting that they and their teams are capable of making very rapid decisions. These stories indicate that an important competency might be "the ability to make decisions in a timely fashion."

Whereas the research-based approach describes past superior performance, the strategic approach to building a competency model forecasts the competency requirements for the future. In a highly dynamic work environment, what worked in the past might not work in the future. The strategic competency model describes those skills, attitudes, or behaviors that it is thought will help the business unit move in a new direction. A company entering a new market, for instance, will likely be able to predict that certain kinds of marketing skills and the ability to manage change will be important to its future success. When a work group takes on a new task, such as that of consulting with a new type of client, it can likewise predict that the skills sought by the new client are likely to be helpful.

Finally, the managers in charge of a group may believe that certain competencies are necessary as a reflection of their values. Integrity, the pursuit of quality, or a team orientation, for instance, may be critical to success in certain firms; to behave otherwise would be counter to the cultural values prevailing in that particular organization, as promoted by the organization's leaders. The Ritz-Carlton hotel chain is one example of an organization that has created such a model of what it describes as "service values" such as "I am always responsive to the expressed and unexpressed wishes of our guests" (Ritz-Carlton Hotel Company, 2009). You'll note that the hotel chain doesn't use the term *competency,* but it does offer enough detail about the process by which it hopes employees will achieve business results (presumably customer satisfaction) so that employees and managers can hold reasonable useful conversations to that end.

Once you have clarified the purpose of the competency model, as a reflection of how it was developed, you will then need to ask what turns out to be a surprisingly tough question: Is the model actually used? This is where for some of you the skepticism comes into play. Some companies have well-developed competency models that are poorly understood and/or sit on the shelf. This represents a substantial waste of management or consultant time and company money. However, if the competency model was developed at the behest of managers who are no longer at the firm or was developed a number of years ago, times may have changed and the competencies once thought to be important may no longer be so important. If that is your current situation, see the section below on what to do if your company doesn't have a competency model.

More commonly, we've seen companies that have what ought to be useful competency models but weren't well understood by managers or employees because of the reluctance of senior managers to engage in teaching. Again, unless the model is understood by all those affected by it, it will not serve as a developmental or coaching guide. Beyond that, it is poor management practice to appraise people against particular competencies without their having a good understanding of what those competencies mean. The Whirlpool Corporation did not use an external consulting firm to develop the Whirlpool Leadership Model. It was developed by the top eight line managers in the corporation. They used words that made sense to them. The fact that they took a personal interest in its development means of course that it had a lot of credibility with line managers further down in the organization. It was a useful tool because it was developed by those who had to use the tool (Hunt & Weintraub, 2007).

What can the coaching manager do? Take the competency model off the shelf and talk about it. We've seen coaching managers do an excellent job of drawing everyone's attention to what is important by reviewing the competencies in meetings with employees; they encourage everyone to fully participate in discussing what the competencies actually mean for them, in their particular settings. "Timely decision making" as a competency may seem rather straightforward at first glance. Each word, however, is open to interpretation. To an emergency medical technician or an ambulance crew, "timeliness" means something quite different than it does to a biomedical scientist or marketing director.

The exercise of talking about what the competencies actually mean is not a trivial one. If one believes that superior performance of a particular competency is linked to business results, then it is likely to be worth the coaching manager's time. If the coaching manager can define what the "super person" does to achieve such results and help an average but well-motivated performer move in that direction, the potential payoff can be enormous. Unfortunately, coaching won't be effective if all performers don't know what they are striving for and what competency looks like.

How do you talk about it? We recommend that you start with the orientation of new hires. The coaching managers in our studies often talk with new employees about what it takes to get ahead, as part of their orientation to the business unit. Communication involves more than just giving someone a copy of the model or presenting it on overhead displays in a staff meeting. It means using examples, telling stories, and then making sure people understand when they are doing something right. Recognition lets them know that they are executing around a competency in a way that truly creates value. It may also be useful to talk about the origin of the particular competency. Many people want to know why certain attitudes are thought to be important to success. Does the model say something about the way things have always been done, does it say something about where the business is going, or does it say something about the values of the firm's leadership?

Some firms also use competency profiles as vehicles for career development. Career progression in some consulting firms, for instance, involves movement from consultant to manager to partner. Progress from one level to the next usually involves a number of factors, including (a) time in a particular level, (b) results (of course), and, increasingly, (c) the development of a progressive level of competency in skills deemed to be of importance to the firm. The competency of leadership may be defined for consultants as the ability to influence clients and others in the firm to work toward a particular goal without incurring hostility. Competency in leadership for the manager may involve the ability to lead a team. Leadership competency for a partner may involve the ability to set and communicate a vision to outside constituents, such as investors.

As stated above, linking a discussion of what is important to career development obviously has the potential to serve as a powerful motivator for ambitious employees. It also helps them understand what they should be learning over time. In the worst-case scenario, the link between competencies and career development can help employees understand why their progress is not as rapid as they may have hoped.

All these effects can be gained from simply talking about what people need to do to be successful and to grow with the firm. If your company has developed such a model, these discussions shouldn't require a great deal of time. The real learning will take place while the competencies are actually in play, and that is where coaching comes in.

If Your Company Does Not Have a Useful Competency Model

If your company does not have a useful competency model, then your task is to develop one. Relax. You can do this. You could go out and hire an industrial psychologist, but you probably have neither the time nor the money to do so. Likewise, the important competencies for your organization may be more future-oriented and strategic, or they may reflect the values of the organization. Rather than thinking that you as manager have to build an elaborate model, we encourage you to think of the challenge as being more along the lines of articulating what you, and probably most of the more experienced employees on your team or your fellow managers, already know.

We have used an approach toward articulating competencies that can be replicated in a short period of time by business units, both large and small. We call this exercise "Building the Success Manual" (Weintraub, 1996). The steps of the exercise are listed in Box 3.1. The results of the "Success Manual

Exercise" can help you identify what is important that is specific in your company or business unit's culture.

BOX 3.1   The Success Manual Exercise

This exercise can take place in a staff meeting, or any context in which small groups can address the following questions. If you have a large organization and want everyone to participate, you can break the larger group into smaller groups of four to six. Ask each group to record its answers to the following questions on flip chart paper and be prepared to report to the larger group.

1. What does someone have to do to be successful here? (If your group performs many different tasks, you may have to be more specific, rephrasing the question to "What does someone have to do to be successful at selling to larger customers here?")

2. What results must we achieve to be successful?

3. What are the most important processes for the members of the group to follow that lead to success?

4. What does someone have to do to fail or get in trouble here?

SOURCE: From *The Success Manual*, by J. Weintraub, 1996, Wellesley, MA: Organizational Dimensions. © 1999 by Joseph Weintraub, Organizational Dimensions. Used by permission.

In one of our recent executive development programs, there was near unanimity among the 20 or so participants that "you have to know the details, the raw numbers, to be effective at presenting (at their company)." Similarly, there was near unanimity that one had to be "good at working under pressure" to be successful at the firm. The coaching managers at this firm knew that if they were to help their employees develop, they would need to address these competencies. The articulation of these competencies took no more than 2 hours.

This particular method is what might be termed a "bottoms-up" approach to competency articulation. It is particularly useful with experienced individual contributors and other managers. Everyone is knowledgeable and can make meaningful contributions to the discussion. However, if you are hiring large numbers of new employees into a particular kind of position, those new employees may need more guidance. Under those circumstances, we suggest that you partner with managers or individual contributors who have some experience to articulate, through a similar process, the competencies you believe you should be teaching to the new hires.

Tom Gillett is a manager in a large customer service unit of a financial services firm whose mission is to provide value-added services to a wealthier clientele. He and his colleagues (other managers in the same organization engaged in similar work) collaborated to develop a simple list of competencies to which they could train and coach newer employees, particularly those coming from outside the firm. Importantly, each manager had intimate and expert knowledge of the customer service processes in question. Over the course of several meetings, they talked about superior performers and ultimately articulated three simple competencies having to do with sales, product knowledge, and customer relationship management. For each competency, they described a set of "anchors," or examples, that illustrate the successful execution of a particular aspect of the competency. Under relationship management, for instance, "listening to the customer" is an important behavior that can help strengthen the relationship.

These competencies are taught to new employees. Tom also makes extensive use of developmental coaching and can use observational data from call monitoring to aid in the learning process. He and individual sales associates review the content of recent telephone calls, each reflecting on the associate's execution around the three competencies. Given the nature of their business, which is to provide a high level of customer service, the most frequently used coaching dialogue question is this: "What else could we have done to please that customer?"

More rigorous researchers may question the validity and reliability of competency models developed by such a method. The reality is that Tom and thousands of managers like him are constrained by time and other resources that make the development of a research-based competency model prohibitive. Perhaps more important, the prevailing attitude in most organizations today is "Let's move ahead." Static competency models that require a great deal of time and money to develop and that look backward rather than forward may in fact lack credibility. What is important is that coaching managers and those who work for them have a practical sense of what effective performance looks like, to the highest degree possible.

Coaching and Selection

As we indicated earlier, developmental coaching needs to be thought of as but one of the activities that coaching managers execute to build talent in their organizations. There are of course other activities that are required as well. Appropriate reward systems as well as performance measurement systems can have a tremendous impact on employee behavior, values, and motivation. In Chapter 2, we mentioned particularly the role that selection plays in the talent management process. We can't stress this enough; it's key. It's not sufficient, but it couldn't be more important. Again, an in-depth exploration of the selection process is beyond the scope of this work, but we do want to make a few important points.

From our research, it appears that coaching managers tend to approach selection in a way that is very consistent with how they coach. They tend to think first about the work that needs to be done to help the business. You have options then about how that work gets done. Depending on a variety of factors you may reassign work from others, seek outside consultants, or decide to add staff to your team. The latter action of course should reflect a greater commitment on your part. While organizations seem to be able to "right size" at will, we know the toll that letting people go, for cause or economic reasons, takes on all those involved. You want to avoid that if you can. Likewise, we know the incredibly significant economic impact of poor hires on an organization.

So our first question is, given the importance of selection, do you spend enough time to ensure a strong selection process? We know it's tough, but are you doing as good a job as you should be doing? Do you spend as much time on selection of a new regular employee as you spend on assessing a new software package for your unit? Are your best people involved in the selection process in an appropriate fashion? Are you directly involved? If it's your business unit, do you lead the selection effort (or delegate to one of your best), or do you "let HR do it" and then get it done as quickly as possible? The latter approach of course yields predictable results. As with coaching, the time you spend has to be seen as an investment in order to attain the best possible business results. Having the right people in the right jobs makes coaching possible.

Furthermore, an unsystematic, unstructured approach to selection is not much better than playing the lottery (at least in Massachusetts, in the United States). If you don't have a systematic approach to defining the talent you think you need and assessing that talent, then as with any other out-of-control process you'll get what the quality control people refer to as "sample variance" big time. (And since you get lots of that anyway, given that we're talking about human beings, you might want to try to minimize it if you can!) So enough with the sales job. You get the point. If you're feeling guilty about not spending enough time on selection after this brief rant, good.

What does an effective process look like in action, one that is aligned with the work of talent development (you can think of selection as talent acquisition)? There are a number of good references available today, but one quick and widely available read is "Hiring Without Firing" by Claudio Fernandez-Araoz (1999). If you want a more in-depth exploration of the topic, we recommend his book *Great People Decisions* (2007). Among his other suggestions are the following.

- *Invest in the problem definition:* Look carefully at the work that you need to have done here. Don't just take the old job description or competency list and assume it's still valid. Think about the tasks your team will face going forward. Think about why the last person failed, if in fact that was the case.

- *Work as a team:* Seek the input of others. You may in fact choose to involve others directly in the selection process up to and including the point at which the decision will be made by a team consensus. There is a continuum here, but in most cases, the advice suggests that you not do the analysis by yourself. Get data from other stakeholders. If in fact the new hire is going to have to work closely with team members and no significant team changes are desired, you may bring others into the decision-making process (beyond involving others in the analysis, or as interviewers who may advise you). If you are hiring a change agent, involving others in the process may be trickier.

- *Do your homework and define the competencies:* Think through carefully the competencies that will be needed. Try to spell them out clearly and get agreement among those involved that "this is the kind of person we'll be looking for." You will likely need to prioritize here. Which competencies are "must have" versus "nice to have"?

- *Use a structured approach to interviewing, involving others if possible:* An open-ended, unstructured interview adds very little to your ability to predict whether or not a candidate will be successful in his new role. In general, past performances are predictive of future performances. Even if the person is moving into a stretch assignment, how he handled previous stretch assignments will likely be a good indicator of how he will handle his next. The best way to assess past performance is to see the candidate in action. Give him some work to do, be it teaching a class, writing software, or handling a mock sales situation. It's not a perfect way to assess a candidate, but there are no perfect assessment tools. The question is whether you can use several tools to enhance the odds of your being correct. Usually, though, the interview is a prime tool for selection. We strongly suggest that you consider utilizing behaviorally based interview techniques in the selection interview process. Fernandez-Araoz describes the use of such tools in his paper. In general, behavioral questions explore, in some detail, past performances. The interviewer doesn't ask only about aspirations

(How would you handle a particular problem?) but also about actions (What did you do to handle a particular problem?). Behavioral interviewing for selection should sound familiar. It's a little bit like creating a coaching dialogue through the use of effective questions.

The art and science of selection continue to evolve. Coaching managers and those who aspire to be coaching managers should stay abreast of what we're learning about selection and hold it as a cornerstone to their talent management efforts. If you have been given a team and don't have a chance to hire, you will still be required to assign work. Every delegation, every assignment, is a mini selection process. You're trying to match talent, opportunity, and demands. This provides you with an opportunity to think through whether or not you make such assignments on "autopilot" or based on a talent management vision.

Summary

Defining success represents defining what people need to do in order to achieve desired results. Thinking through the kind of talent that it takes to be successful, and then communicating that with others, gives everyone a sense of "how we hope things will be done here." Yes, you may say, "We need to change how we do things here." The problem is the same. OK, you want to change the process by which results are achieved. What would that look like? Yes, there is room for some individual variation, but if the level of variation rises to that of anarchy, you probably have some issues to consider. Defining success helps you coach, and helps your people learn. We're now going to look at how you set up the organizational culture and expectations that make coaching possible, by creating a coaching-friendly context.

Creating a Coaching-Friendly Context

4

In this chapter, we describe the following:

- The values and norms that characterize a coaching-friendly context

- How individual managers can create a coaching-friendly context in their organizations and teams

Learning requires a level of openness that some managers and employees find challenging and even threatening. In our experience, though, once they are used to the value of holding such candid conversations as we've described here, employees and managers will find it helpful and even stimulating. In this chapter, we describe what both can do to make this possible.

Let us stress from the beginning that all parties involved have to work together to create a context that makes learning possible. The manager sets the tone but can't do it alone. In a coaching-friendly context, those involved feel that talking openly about problems and challenges with a goal toward learning from them is the norm. (Norms represent a shared but often implicit sense of the way to behave in a particular group. One can feel their power. In the United States, for instance, it is the norm to walk on the right-hand side of the sidewalk. If you walk on the left-hand side, you can feel yourself pushing a bit against the prevailing behavior of the group. But of course, sometimes people do walk on the left-hand side. Norms aren't laws; they are more like probabilities.) This is what we mean by a *coaching-friendly context*. The coaching-friendly context, when fully developed, helps create and support the emergence of a market for coaching and learning. At that point, the coaching manager may even spend less time formally coaching because coaching is going on almost everywhere, on a fairly routine basis. The coaching manager coaches team members. Team members coach each other, and they also probably coach the manager.

Most employees do not experience their context, the workplace, in that way. For most of us, when we use the term *context*, it is easier to think about contexts that interfere with learning, rather than promote it. Does the situation we describe in the following case sound familiar?

Case 4.1: Financial Co.—A Learning Context?

Times are tough at Financial Co. (the name and industry have been disguised). Born of a set of companies that were strung together through difficult-to-fathom merger and acquisition activities, Financial Co. was grasping, unsuccessfully it seemed, for some sense of purpose or vision. Many of its product lines were in very bad shape. Mismanagement over the years had turned cash cows into obsolete bureaucracies. Competition had successfully encroached from all sides.

Employee turnover was high, in part driven by the (accurate) perception that senior management was ruthless in its focus on the bottom line. The stock price had dropped so low that with any further decline, delisting of the stock from the exchange would become a very real possibility. Managers were expected to hit their financial targets by any means necessary. "If you can't get it done immediately, we'll find someone else who can, and you're out!" was the explicit message from the CEO. Fear and mistrust were rampant. Mistakes were not to be tolerated.

New hires were told that they needed to be able to "hit the ground running." You had to be really good at what you were hired to do. There was no time to develop new talent. (Of course, this begs the question of why anyone who was "really good" would want to work for such a company.) Many managers expressed open disdain for the corporation, when they had the time to think.

Is coaching, the development of others, possible in such an organization? Isn't it true that this type of short-term focus is anathema to thinking about employee development? If managers receive no reward—indeed, run the risk of being punished for spending time coaching employees—won't all such activities cease?

What do you think? Could you imagine trying to help the people who work for you develop while you are working under the weight of such intense pressure? Taking this from an action-planning point of view, if you wanted to try and help your employees develop, what would you need to do?

We suggest that you start by making sure that you and the members of your group take a bit of time to reflect on your work and what is going on around you. When surrounded by a sense of panic, people rarely feel as though they have the time to reflect. They feel the urge to *act*. Of course, as we discussed in Chapter 1, the tendency to act without reflection probably leads to doing more of the same, which ultimately won't help Financial Co.

After creating some pockets of time for people to reflect on their work, you would then have to make them feel that it was safe to do so. Would they trust you enough to talk openly about their work, rather than feeling as though they needed to stay out of the way and "keep their heads down"? Even if they did trust you, would they trust that you could protect them? After all, to learn from their performance and their mistakes, they would have to talk about them with you. Perhaps you would be forced to talk about these kinds of problems with your own boss. Perhaps one of the peers on the team would let it be known that this was a group with problems. Word would get out, and some careers at Financial Co. would be over. Nevertheless, we have repeatedly seen that even under such harsh conditions, coaching can and will take place. Coaching is not completely dependent on the larger organizational context in most cases. In our experience, managers who want to take active roles in shaping positive developmental opportunities for their employees will find a way to make it happen. They protect their employees from a toxic environment to the extent possible and in the process create something approaching a coaching-friendly context. A coaching-friendly context can then be very local. A team within the even more toxic environment found in a place like Financial Co. can support coaching, particularly if the manager and some of the team members try.

We were fortunate to have a manager from Financial Co. attend one of our coaching manager training programs. He was there because of his capacity as a team leader. His team was involved in an innovative project at Financial Co. that even the CEO hoped would help improve the firm's business situation. The task of the team leader and his group in bringing this project to completion was extraordinarily risky, however. If they failed, they would quite likely all lose their jobs.

The team leader reasoned that the only way he could get some of the best minds in the company to work on the project was to make sure that they would learn a lot from their experience, learning that would be valuable for them in the future, no matter what the fate of their current project. He also felt that he had to play an active role in helping them integrate the experience with their own career plans. He was given no support from corporate but was simply determined to make it possible for his people to develop, even under such difficult circumstances. He managed to create a coaching-friendly context under bitterly harsh conditions. He was coaching, and his employees responded very positively to his efforts.

Evidence from other researchers supports this rather provocative contention: In most cases, the manager may be able to promote a coaching-friendly context even if the larger environment is hostile. Amy Edmondson (1996) studied team learning in hospital-based nursing units. Nurses, of course, work under very difficult circumstances. Their work can entail very high risks and is technically demanding, tedious at times, and heavily regulated. When a nurse makes an error, people can be hurt. Doctors, hospitals, and nurses can be sued. Such incidents can make the front pages of the newspapers. Politicians get involved, and so it goes. Is this a coaching-friendly context? Wouldn't such conditions create an absolute intolerance of mistakes that would make it practically impossible for people to talk about their performance? Not necessarily.

Studying a number of distinct nursing units within the same hospital, Edmondson (1996) found statistically significant differences from group to group in nurses' willingness to talk about medication errors. In some groups, to talk about a medication error was a tacit admission of guilt and responsibility, and one's career could be threatened. In other groups, medication errors were considered too important not to talk about. In those teams, nurses expressed the view that they needed to learn more about what went wrong and what could be done to improve their accuracy.

The more open groups did report more medication errors than the more closed groups. (When you make it possible to really talk about the work your team is doing, you may not always like what you hear. Be prepared for that.) Digging deeper into the problem, Edmondson (1996) found independent evidence that strongly suggested that the rate of errors was actually not higher in the open groups. Rather, individuals in the more closed groups were actively suppressing discussion of errors. They were covering up to protect themselves from punishment. The nurse manager's actions and behavior played a significant role in determining whether or not those who worked in such units believed that it was acceptable to learn from their performance and their errors. (If you were sick, in which kind of unit would you like to be hospitalized?)

This is the challenge our coaching managers put before you. If you are lucky enough to be working for a supportive and open company, such as Southwest Airlines, or you are part of an enlightened entrepreneurial start-up or a family business that places a high value on employee development, go ahead and coach. You are probably in a coaching-friendly context already. (Again, though, you will likely find pockets of a "coaching-unfriendly context" in even the most progressive companies. Managers and employees work together to create a coaching-friendly context. A frightened or incompetent manager can create a coaching-unfriendly context all by him- or herself.) Your employees may even be expecting you to coach, so you'd better do it. Look around you and watch how other managers in your firm coach and create learning opportunities. Borrow what you see that is consistent with your own leadership style (assuming that you want to incorporate coaching into your leadership style).

If the larger organization in which you do your work is not quite so supportive, or even downright resistant to the idea of talent development, we believe that you will need to *intentionally* shape the immediate context around and within your work group to make your efforts at coaching and learning productive. You will also need to consider carefully how you introduce new members into your group if you want to engage them in any kind of a learning process. To do so, you will have to manage yourself and your relationships with the other members of your group. In certain circumstances, you may also need to manage the relationship between your group and the surrounding organization (by protecting them, for instance). However, before describing actions that can help you create a coaching-friendly context, we'll describe the look and feel of one in more detail. (Please note that this description of a coaching-friendly context is also relevant to CEOs or entrepreneurs who are seeking to build or shape a company culture.)

The Values and Practices of the Coaching-Friendly Context

In the coaching-friendly context, learning is taken for granted to be an important, if not always directly discussed, ingredient of both personal development and business performance. People in a coaching-friendly context naturally and informally reflect on their actions, discuss their problems and goals, and ask for feedback and advice. The values and beliefs that serve as a foundation for such a coaching-friendly context, along with those that don't support a coaching-friendly context, are listed in Table 4.1. Where appropriate, we use examples from one of the more coaching-friendly contexts we've run across, the after-action review (AAR) program of the U.S. Army, to illustrate what one organization has done to promote learning and reflection (Garvin, 2000).

Table 4.1   Organizational Values and a Coaching-Friendly Context

Supporting Values	Inhibiting Values
Trust and openness	Mistrust and fear
Tolerance of mistakes, learning from them	Intolerance of mistakes, blaming of the perpetrator
Careful attention to hiring the right people	Lack of careful attention to hiring that supports competence
Learning for the long term is important	We should focus single-mindedly on evaluating today's performance
Reward systems shouldn't punish time spent developing people	Reward systems focus only on short-term results
People should feel valued as individuals	People are a "means to an end"

Trust and a Large Measure of Openness

As is the case with much of leadership, trust in the relationship between manager and employee is probably the most important element of a coaching-friendly context. The employee must believe that he or she can be open with the manager without fear of punishment. The manager must consistently behave in a fashion that reinforces such trust. The manager must act with integrity in this regard. Trust of this kind between manager and employee makes it possible for employees to support their managers even when times are tough. Such trust is based on (a) an explicit awareness of what is important to each individual in the relationship and (b) the knowledge that they will make sincere efforts to help each other meet their goals. We can't emphasize this latter point enough: Trust is built between individuals. The coaching leader must have a relationship with each individual on his or her team to successfully help them learn through coaching.

Tolerating Mistakes Because They Are Useful for Learning

Mistakes are not usually viewed from an evaluative perspective in a coaching-friendly context. Yes, mistakes do create problems for any business. Certainly, some mistakes are intolerable. On balance, however, in a coaching-friendly context, mistakes are viewed as opportunities for learning.

A famous coaching story from the early days of IBM illustrates the point. An executive responsible for a particularly important and expensive project came to Thomas Watson Sr., the founder, to report that he had failed. The executive then offered his resignation to Watson. At this point, Watson supposedly responded, "Why would I want to lose you? I've just invested a lot of money in you." The considerable financial costs of a failed project were important, but Watson felt that in the process, the executive had learned something even more valuable.

The after-action review (AAR), described briefly in Chapter 1, offers an example of how trust and an officer's tolerance for mistakes are intertwined as a vehicle for learning. The official policy of the AAR program holds that whatever is said in the AAR will not come back to injure a soldier's career. Inclusion of a soldier's input from an AAR into his or her personnel record is explicitly forbidden. However, policy by itself is not enough to ensure trust. Policies are carried out by individual managers. Our interviews with servicemen and -women who have been through AARs indicate to us that the perceived value of the exercise was very much dependent on the integrity with which the officers involved stuck to a focus on learning. If information about mistakes made were to somehow "leak" out, and the careers of individuals who participated in an AAR were injured because those individuals had been candid, even the army's AAR policies wouldn't be enough to ensure a coaching-friendly context. The policy can help because it backs up the manager, but the integrity of the manager is the factor that determines the real value of the AAR.

Hiring the Right People—Redux

We've talked about the importance of hiring at some length. What we want to emphasize here is how effective hiring builds trust. Obviously, no organization has an infinite capacity for error, and we would never suggest that managers tolerate any and all mistakes. The answer to this seeming paradox can be found in research on "psychological safety" and learning in high-performance teams. Edmondson (1999) found that psychological safety on a work team represented a shared sense of trust, a caring for one another as people, and respect for each other's *competence*. Those three factors created a context for team learning that resulted in improved group performance. We draw your attention to the last of the three factors, respect for each other's competence.

It is easier to trust people, even to allow them to make mistakes, if you see them as fundamentally in the right job and being able to perform that job to at least a minimal degree. This means that they can make a credible claim to being up to the basic tasks of the job, though they may still need to learn more. If that underlying sense of competence isn't present, a mistake understandably becomes much more threatening. One condition for a coaching-friendly context, then, is that the team or the organization has been relatively successful at getting competent people in the right jobs. This requires paying attention to competence and not just gut reaction in the selection process, as well as hiring people who are open to learning. It is much easier to coach good or adequate performers than performers who are failing. It is simply easier to trust that they will, on balance, do an acceptable job and responsibly try to learn from their mistakes. In our view, effective hiring is an essential foundation for effective coaching. Mutual respect as an outcome of an effective hiring process provides the foundation for trust.

An Interest in Learning for the Long Term, Not Just in Today's Performance

Financial Co. runs the risk of consuming its own feedstock. Although today's business performance is important, a company's long-term competitiveness is rooted in the ability of its people to learn and adapt. Even during the worst of times, attention to learning is visible, for instance, when the firm doesn't eliminate its training budget, uses downtime for strategic or important projects that will help the business, creates opportunities for personal learning on the part of employees, and demonstrates a recognition of the priority placed on learning. Attention to learning, which ultimately validates a manager's efforts to coach, signals to everyone that the group exists for both today and tomorrow.

One might expect that the U.S. Army would have a rather short-term, performance-oriented focus. After all, when the battle is over, army personnel are undoubtedly glad to be finished. Yet the senior commanders have explicitly and forcefully committed themselves to the idea that personal and organizational learning are essential for *tomorrow's* effective performance. This commitment is communicated through the army's insistence on the regular use of AARs. They are not considered optional. The learning that emerges from the AAR is, then, used as part of the army's knowledge management system.

Of course, one could also argue that it's easier to imagine the armed forces of the world thinking long term than many of our businesses today. In communications with one of the authors, David Whitwam, former CEO of Whirlpool, acknowledged that it isn't easy to focus on the long term, given the relentless pressures associated with being a publicly traded global company (Hunt & Weintraub, 2007). He also puts forth the notion, though, that the ability to manage the tension between today and tomorrow, to get work done today while not losing track of tomorrow, is part of the work of leadership. The reality is you have to do both. The great companies are able to do this well enough that they can perform over longer-term time horizons. So while we acknowledge the challenge of advocating for the long term, we hold firm to the need to do so.

Reward Systems That Encourage Managers to Spend Time Coaching

Closely related to a value on learning are reward systems that create tangible positive outcomes for managers who are effective at employee development. If managers are paid solely for today's results, that is what many managers may focus on. Our point here is to watch out for pay systems that actively discourage coaching. However, we issue a cautionary note about the use of pay for performance as a vehicle for changing managerial behavior when it comes to encouraging coaching (and almost anything else). There is a growing body of evidence suggesting that external rewards (pay) undermine intrinsic motivation (performing because it fits with your personal need or motivation). Jeffrey Pfeffer (1998) is one of a number of management researchers who have shown that more extreme pay for performance serves to make people feel controlled and make them do what the controllers (those with the money) want, rather than exercise personal judgment.

Managers who coach "for the money" are not necessarily operating with the motive of trying to be helpful (see Chapter 5). For instance, a small number of lawyers, consultants, and psychotherapists who have appeared to be profoundly greedy in the conduct of their business affairs have made the practice of their professions suspect to the rest of us. Employees need to trust that they will get their manager's attention for reasons that go beyond the paycheck. Certainly, compensation systems should reward a manager's work in the development of employees. The reality is that coaching managers are often not compensated directly for such efforts but keep coaching anyway. (They would argue that even though they are not directly compensated for coaching in most cases, coaching helps them reach their business goals, so the reward is indirect.)

This is not a book about the latest debates over compensation practices. However, we encourage organizational designers and human resource executives to consider whether the reward systems in play in their firms support coaching or inhibit it. Reward systems that place an enormous amount of a manager's pay at risk on the basis of the quarter's business results can get the attention of even the most dedicated and gifted coaching manager. You may be willing to coach your employees for strategic or personal reasons even if the payoff is not fully tangible in the short term. However, you probably won't want to coach if it will cost you and your family a substantial amount of money.

The U.S. Army doesn't use a compensation system to encourage unit commanders to hold an AAR. It is an expected part of their jobs. A failure to do so would be considered a performance problem of the highest order.

People Are Valued for Themselves, Not Just as a Means to an End

The last value that promotes the emergence of a coaching-friendly context is perhaps the least tangible, yet it serves as a foundation for much of what has already been discussed. A coaching manager says to himself, "George (an employee) is under way too much stress at home to deal with all this. I may need to lighten his load for a little while." Such a manager has put himself in the position of the employee and thought about the needs of the whole person. Employees are people first, who learn and perform. The process is not mechanical. Significant status differences between managers and employees can undermine organizational performance (Pfeffer, 1998). Status differences can make individuals feel undervalued. People who feel valued are much more likely to want to learn. They feel that there is a more genuine overlap between the organization's goals and their own personal goals. Likewise, people who are overwhelmed and burdened by stress may be in no condition to learn. We'll talk about the timing issues that arise while trying to create a coaching moment; suffice it to say that being sensitive to the needs of others is critical to the coaching and learning process.

Although soldiers are ultimately a "means to an end" in the sense that they serve a purpose that is higher than their own self-interests, officers have for centuries known that the personal relationship between commander and soldier is an essential part of the bonding that holds a unit together. When the commander listens to a soldier in an AAR, respects his or her opinion, and takes his or her feedback seriously, the soldier feels valued.

The Coaching-Friendly Context and the High-Performance Organization

Note that the values and practices that we believe support a coaching-friendly context also characterize many high-performing work organizations (Pfeffer, 1998, 2000). High-performance work organizations significantly outperform their competitors and view the workforce as a crucial competitive weapon. These six sets of values and practices are also consistent with recent research that demonstrates the linkage between managerial practices and profitability, customer service, and employee retention (Buckingham & Coffman, 1999; we'll discuss this research in more detail in Chapter 6 as it also offers us insight into the all-important question of "what employees want"). These are the values cited by our sample of coaching managers. For this reason, we have become absolutely convinced that there is no contradiction between developmental coaching and business success. What, then, should managers try to do to create coaching-friendly subcultures in their own business units?

Creating a Coaching-Friendly Context in Your Business Unit

The suggestions listed in Box 4.1 and described in detail below should help you create a coaching-friendly context in your business unit. Our list here was compiled from the suggestions of our coaches and what we've seen while we've had a chance to watch them in action. Of course, these will not all be appropriate to every context, but in our experience, they are based on some fairly generalizable observations. Implementing some or all of these suggestions should help signal to your employees, implicitly and explicitly in some cases, that it's OK to talk about the challenges they face, what they are learning or need to learn, and their aspirations.

BOX 4.1   Checklist for a Coaching-Friendly Context

Here is a checklist of actions you can take to build a coaching-friendly context in your own unit:

1. Have you explained your management philosophy, including your approach toward mistakes:
   - To your group?
   - To new members of the team?

2. Are you able to "walk the talk" and be true to your management philosophy?

3. Are you accessible? Do you make it clear that you do want to know:
   - When people have questions?
   - When people think they need help?
   - When things are not going well?

(Continued)

(Continued)

4. Do you convey in words and actions an interest in your employees when they ask to speak with you?

5. Are you clear in your own mind about the distinction between coaching and evaluation?

   - Have you communicated this distinction to others?
   - Do your coaching efforts support or conflict with your performance appraisal program?

6. Do you demonstrate through your actions that you want others to coach you?

   - Do you listen to feedback without retaliating?

7. Do you help the members of your group deal with threats of punishment from outside the group?

Explaining Your Intent to Coach

We advocate that coaching managers consider explicitly informing the members of their group that they will use coaching as part of their day-to-day approach to leading the group. In addition, we suggest that coaching managers clarify how they will react to questions from their employees, performance problems, and mistakes that employees make. This is particularly important when the manager is taking over a new group or orienting new employees in an existing group. We say this with some trepidation because we have also been told by some very assertive businesspeople that managers shouldn't make a "big deal" out of the fact that they coach. We do acknowledge that for some managers, or on some teams, all this can happen naturally. Our recommendation here is taken from most of the managers we've interviewed as part of our research who tell us that it pays to be explicit about what you are doing as a coaching manager if for no other reason than that most employees are simply not used to it. (If you're not comfortable with the word *coach*, then by all means use another title, such as *debrief*.)

One of our coaching managers has a series of in-depth meetings with each new group member. She gets to know her employees as individuals but also tries to help them get to know her. As part of this process, she explains how she hopes new employees will make use of their twice-monthly individual meetings and weekly staff meetings. She explains that new hires can bring up anything they want to discuss: career issues, work problems, good ideas, and bad ones. She tells the new hires that she'll probably listen and ask questions because that is her style. She also tells them that it is OK to come into her office and ventilate their feelings: "Better they do it with me than with a client."

We aren't suggesting that managers exaggerate their emphasis on coaching. Indeed, they should consider communicating their expectations to employees as well, as a way of aligning their work with that of their team members (Bradford & Cohen, 1998). However, we are concerned that unless managers are explicit about their intent to coach and what they expect of people who work for them, some, perhaps many, of their employees won't know how to effectively participate in the learning process. We've asked our coaching managers whether or not new employees are surprised that coaching is a normal part of business activity. They answer, "Yes, many are," unless they've had a mentor or coaching manager before (which most haven't). Consider the assumptions that many employees hold on the basis of previous experience:

- How many of us have heard, "Don't come to me with problems; come to me with solutions"? Although we can understand the harried executive making such a statement, this advice has reached the status of folklore in the American business culture. This statement, probably the most anticoaching statement we've heard, is, ironically, derived from a command-and-control model of leadership. The leader is too busy to talk things over with others because he or she is making all the really important decisions. In a coaching-friendly context, the leader delegates work to others. The leader then helps people doing the work by providing consultation and other resources. The leader has to be available for meaningful consultation under such circumstances.

Consider the alternative statement used by one of our coaches: "Don't come to me with a problem until you have spent a little bit of time thinking about it and have thought of at least one possible solution. It doesn't have to be the right one; it can even be a crazy one. I just want you to do some thinking before I jump in." The meaning of this message is very different. This statement doesn't convey "Don't bother me." It conveys "You need to take some responsibility for this, but I'll help."

- Most employees expect to be evaluated, not coached. Remember that this is the experience of almost everyone in every kind of organization today. They may have never been coached. If you start trying to coach them before you've set the stage by explaining your actions, they may think you are laying a trap.
- Many employees are told what to learn. "Get *your* job right before you go thinking about mine" is the control-oriented manager's dictum on learning. When employees are told not to think "outside the box," some may give up on learning in resignation.

It is worthy of note that the army does make a "big deal" out of coaching, though that's not the term it uses. We suspect that such an effort has been necessary because the previous environment was so toxic to the kinds of interactions required for learning. We suggest that if you find yourself taking over such a group, you may need to work very hard to communicate your own focus on learning to others and how you expect them to participate in that effort. The "big deal" may be quite warranted.

Making Yourself Accessible

Having explained your management philosophy and your approach to coaching to your employees, follow-through on your part is critical to sustaining your credibility. Your interest in following through is communicated by your attention in words and with body language when a coaching opportunity occurs. Consider the following example.

Case 4.2: Fred, the Coach

(The following is a true story. The names are disguised.) Have you ever "been there"?

Jane was a group manager in a well-respected consulting firm, one known for its interest in the development of its employees. She had just returned from an unsettling client engagement. One of the senior managers in the client firm accused her of not being committed to the project and felt she was not sufficiently available to the client team. This information was in direct contradiction to the verbal and written feedback she had received in the client review meeting 2 days earlier. Sitting in her office with the door closed, she felt deeply discouraged about her performance and her career. She wasn't even sure what she had done wrong.

Feeling an overwhelming need to talk, she was relieved when she heard the familiar sound of keys in the door to the office next to hers. Her director, Fred, was coming in from the field as well. Though she didn't normally talk about her own doubts or her failures with others in the firm, let alone her boss, she felt as though she had no choice. She needed to talk and to figure out what had gone wrong. Also, Fred spent a lot of time "preaching" about the merits of coaching and prided himself on being an avid practitioner of the latest management development techniques. Jane felt it might be safe to talk with Fred.

When she knocked on Fred's door, she heard, "Come in," in his usual, somewhat stuffy manner. After an exchange of small talk while Fred was unpacking his briefcase, Jane began to explain what had happened with the client earlier in the day. Fred kept unpacking, never looking at Jane. Jane continued to describe the problem, obviously in distress. Fred began to read his e-mails while offering a perfunctory "Too bad." Jane knew he wasn't listening. And why should he? This problem won't affect his bonus, let alone his career, she thought to herself. But she continued to feel a powerful need to talk. She kept trying, to no avail.

All at once, Fred began to complain to her about the e-mail he had just received from the company's CFO. Jane could tell that everything she had said about herself, her worries, and the client had never been heard. Fred had gone on to *his* next issue. As he continued to rant about the CFO and the finance department, Jane eased herself out of the room, saying, "Excuse me, I think I heard my phone." She left feeling very much like a nonperson and wondered why she had even bothered going to her boss in the first place.

Obviously, Fred communicated in words and body language that, at this particular time at least, he wasn't interested in coaching Jane. This is one example in time and may not represent Fred's typical behavior. However, it will not take many such instances for Fred to undermine his efforts at creating a coaching-friendly context.

Fred preaches coaching but isn't accessible. He doesn't listen to Jane. He doesn't ask helpful questions. He turns away from her and starts reading his e-mail. Finally, he changes the subject from her concerns to his own. The message to Jane is twofold. First, Fred doesn't help Jane figure out what went wrong, which is one of the most basic responsibilities of the coaching manager. Second, Fred apparently doesn't care about Jane. In Fred's defense, he may have been busy or tired himself. He may have been in no mood to coach Jane. If that were the case, and he wanted to maintain a coaching-friendly context for the long term, he might have said to Jane, "This sounds very bad. I'm afraid that I'm just exhausted. Let me catch my breath and then let's talk, say at 4 p.m. today." In that case, Fred would have delayed the coaching dialogue but stayed true to the ideal that coaching is important. He also would have communicated to Jane that he does care about her and wants to help.

Contrast Fred's behavior with the report from another coaching manager. Jack coaches a global marketing team. He coaches by telephone. He prefers to talk with his team members from a conference room rather than from his own office. "I know myself. I'll look at the e-mails or start glancing at whatever is on my desk. People can tell when you aren't really focused on what they are saying, you know. I have to put myself somewhere I can really focus. I want to encourage them to pick up the phone and call me when something's going on."

Accessibility involves open-door management. One coaching manager rearranged his office rather than have people see his back as they entered the room. Another coaching manager gives group members his home telephone number and encourages them to use it. Most coaching managers practice management by walking around. They'll stop in at an employee's cubicle or office and chat, sending out a clear message: "I'm here; let's talk."

But it takes more than open-door management. It takes an awareness of the fact that as a leader, you're always sending signals. Your behavior has an impact. Does your behavior signal that you're interested in the employee, or not? Underlying all this is your attitude, your interest in being helpful to someone else. We'll talk about this more in Chapter 5.

Clarifying and Communicating the Distinction Between Coaching and Evaluation

Ultimately, as a manager in most organizations, you will also have to evaluate your employees. You will have to make decisions that will influence your employees' pay. You may have to terminate an employee for nonperformance. Don't these responsibilities make it more difficult to create a coaching-friendly context? We say that they can, but they don't have to. Coaching can actually support the process of evaluation when the two are kept distinct.

To coach effectively, you must first of all be clear in your own mind as to when you are evaluating and when you are coaching. Organizations that both coach and evaluate tend to use a variety of rituals that help them punctuate the transitions from coaching to evaluation. Many now explicitly separate performance management and coaching feedback.

Regardless of the timing, the conflict between performance appraisal and developmental coaching is most likely to occur when the manager has not done enough developmental coaching. One of our coaching managers resisted the notion that there was a conflict between the two. "I coach all the time, so when performance appraisals are given, no one is ever surprised. The data are already clear. They know I have tried to help. The performance appraisal is when we tally the score."

While coaching, you may not formally tally the score—the coaching manager focuses on learning from a particular situation. Ultimately, though, the manager has to tally the score if the learning in question is critical to the success of the employee and the business unit. If the manager has done a great deal of coaching around an important developmental goal, the process of evaluation has actually already taken place, implicitly and informally. Employees know that their manager will ultimately formally evaluate them. The question is: Will it be done in a just fashion? If the employee has not been coached, when the appraisal or evaluation does occur, it will have a much greater sting.

In our view, the problem with evaluation has as much to do with day-to-day behavior as it does with formal performance appraisals. Looks of disapproval, undue or humiliating criticisms, a withdrawal of friendliness, and other behaviors following a problem, though implicit, are powerful signals to the employee that say, "You screwed up!" As one of our coaching managers put it, "If I say, 'Don't worry about it' and don't back that up, walk the talk, then I'm going to blow it with that employee. I can't say, 'Don't worry about it' and then keep bringing it up in a critical way. I have to grit my teeth and let it go."

We all want to feel that we're OK in the eyes of others who are important to us. This is a particularly powerful dynamic between leaders and followers. The leader's verbal and nonverbal cues to group members are probably more powerful messages than losing 1% of a raise. Another coaching manager told us, in that regard, "You have to hold your temper. If you get angry, sometimes just once, you may make it impossible for that employee to really come back and tell you the truth." This statement sets a high standard. After all, we're only human. Nevertheless, we draw your attention to the importance of managing your own emotions as a key success factor while trying to create a coaching-friendly context.

Encouraging Employees to Coach You

We have been told, repeatedly, that one of the best ways to encourage a coaching-friendly context is to encourage people in your unit to coach you. The reasons are probably obvious. The manager models openness, how to take feedback, an interest in improving his or her performance, and an interest in learning. The manager shows others in the group how to receive coaching in the process. This is important because, as we've stated repeatedly, most employees haven't been coached and as a result don't know how to use it.

Many coaching managers have also told us that they discuss their interest in being coached with new hires. They explicitly encourage upward feedback. An important payoff to encouraging employees to coach is that they can learn coaching skills as well. Most of the coaching managers we have talked to report that they do rely on peer-to-peer coaching within their work groups.

Helping the Members of Your Work Group
Deal With Threats From Outside Your Group

The following quotation from a division vice president in one of our training programs says it all: "If someone is trying to do 10 things, does 7 right and does 3 wrong, that's OK with me. We'll talk about it and try to figure out what went wrong with the other 3. I just have to make sure that corporate doesn't find out. They somehow don't believe that a batting average of .700 is adequate." (For those who don't know the game of baseball, a batting average of .700 means that a batter has gotten a hit in 7 out of 10 trials. No one in history has ever come even close to such a batting average. Averages of .290 to .350 are considered exceptional.)

This challenge represents, we believe, one of the most difficult tasks facing the coaching manager whose larger organizational context is not coaching-friendly. In addition to the politics of trying to protect your team, this issue has an ethical dimension as well. In some industries, there may be a legal problem in withholding information about an employee's difficulties from your own manager. Auditing firms, energy companies, and health care institutions, just to name a few, must follow very strict guidelines or risk running afoul of a variety of governmental regulations.

Having stated that this is a tough challenge with an ethical component, however, we don't mean to say that the dilemma is without creative resolution. Trust in most businesses isn't total and doesn't have to be. Trust does have to be adequate, however. Follow-up interviews with an executive who had been the recipient of some very helpful and effective coaching put the matter into some relief. "I don't talk with her (the coach) about my love life, my health, things like that. I don't know that I'd trust her with all that personal information. I talk with her about work. I do trust that she's trying to do a good job when it comes to work, and that's good enough for me. This coaching stuff doesn't have to be too personal to be helpful." Employees, at least mature ones, understand that they have to manage communications with even the best bosses from time to time. Ironically, this can help create sufficient trust between both parties so that useful work can be accomplished. Employees working for a coaching manager must trust that, on balance, he or she will support them. This doesn't mean that managers will cover up for serious mistakes, but they will help employees deal with these issues when they come to light. Managers lose a significant level of credibility when they don't represent their employees to the outside world. Sometimes, that representation must be personal and assertive.

Protecting a Coaching-Friendly Context Over Time

As you look at the list of questions back in Box 4.1, you might consider how well you've done in creating a coaching-friendly context in your business unit. You may feel good that you can answer most of the questions in the affirmative. Unfortunately, we have bad news: You should not rest on your accomplishments to date. A coaching-friendly context as a set of norms and expectations exists within a larger dynamic environment. It is subject to change. It needs to be constantly nurtured if it is to survive, particularly in difficult times. One of our favorite companies, an extremely innovative family-owned manufacturing firm, created enormous excitement in its highly unionized workforce by engaging its employees heavily in collaboration and learning. After 5 years, the firm and its employees had made enormous gains.

After 10 years, even though there was no change in leadership, the firm had slipped back a bit. Coaching had taken a backseat to other more pressing activities. There was a renewed sense of suspicion between labor and management. Quality (the business rationale for coaching in the first place) began to decline. The CEO told us, "I think we became overconfident, didn't pay attention to what was really important to us all. We just got caught up in the day-to-day." With this renewed awareness, the firm was able to recapture some of its energy for learning. Coaching activities and other learning-oriented initiatives resumed.

This small but dynamic firm had started to look more and more like Financial Co. We suggest that if a leader strongly embraces the ideas of coaching for learning, he or she should do so because of the belief that coaching and learning are essential for business success. If that is the case, then safeguarding that effort for the long term is critically necessary. Note that the CEO of the firm didn't say, "We didn't have time for coaching." In fact, he readily admits that that wasn't the problem. Coaching doesn't take a lot of time. The firm had simply stopped paying attention.

The Future of the Coaching-Friendly Context

We would be remiss in not engaging in some informed speculation regarding changing societal norms and new technology when it comes to assessing the possibilities for the coaching-friendly context of the future (or the present in some organizations). It is a given that this book focuses on the traditional hierarchy, the manager and the employee. That hierarchy still holds enormous mental and actual power. It is still the prevailing structure of our lives, probably as it evolved from familial relationships.

But that's not the only game in town, as they say. We've hinted that in a coaching-friendly context, there might be more going on than just top-down coaching. Peer coaching, for instance, might be more observable in a coaching-friendly context.

In fact, we now know that personal and career development is fostered as much by what Higgins and Kram (2001) describe as a "developmental network" as it is by service under a great coaching manager. The concept of the developmental network suggests that there are a variety of relationships upon which we might depend for learning. Hierarchical, peer-to-peer, and what might be called diagonal relationships can and frequently do play a part.

Fast-forward to current times and the growing use of Web 2.0 technologies by members of the so-called "Net Gen" generation (Tapscott, 2008). These folks, at least many of them, utilize Web 2.0 technologies as well as instant messaging to stay in touch on an ongoing basis. The impact of this social phenomenon is yet uncertain, but it looks to be quite important. The question then becomes to what extent these social networks that are facilitated by technology can become vehicles for what has been called "informal learning," another term we feel references developmental coaching (Bingham, 2009).

In the coaching-friendly context of the future, the manager may increasingly be called upon to manage the environment, particularly the social environment, within which such informal learning can take place. Our assumption is that many of the concepts described here will be relevant, but will likely need to evolve. The question of accessibility, for instance, changes when people view accessibility via texting to be more symbolic, or a stronger signal, of the value of coaching and learning than an open door, which was traditional in previous generations. Some managers may be more comfortable in the new social and technological environment, and some will likely be less. Thus, the competencies and attitudes of the coaching manager may need to evolve as well. This does suggest the value of a closer look at the development of the coaching manager and his or her competencies and attitudes, which we'll address in the next chapter.

The Development of a Coaching Manager and the "Coaching Mind-Set"

5

In this chapter we'll describe the following:

- How managers become coaching managers
- The attitudes and beliefs and behaviors that characterize the "coaching mind-set"
- How you can assess your capabilities as a coaching manager

In Chapter 4, we talked about the challenges of creating a coaching-friendly context and ended by commenting briefly on how the competencies required of the coaching manager may need to evolve to meet future demands. This can be a bit anxiety provoking, we realize. We share that anxiety to the extent that we steadfastly adhere to the notion that being a coaching manager doesn't require you to be superhuman. Some of you are probably thinking that maybe you could handle coaching baby boomers, but now the rules are going to change? Again, it's not a matter of rules. It's as much a matter of attitude. Yes, you have to stay in touch with your people, and the way you do that will have to change. Yes, you have to signal your intent, and the way you do that may change. But you don't have to be perfect at all this. You have to be good enough to make coaching possible. In this chapter, we want to focus on the attitudes that make coaching behavior possible and how those attitudes develop.

We discussed in some detail in Chapter 3 the fact that one attitude characterizing most coaching managers is that coaching has a business, or organizational, value. They believe that it's a rational thing to do, to help develop talent. They believe that it has a business payoff. But we've also referred to their attitude of helpfulness. We'd like to explore the development of that attitude in greater detail. Some managers seem to be "natural" coaches, and their struggle is one of finding a credible outlet for their talents. Others learn to coach as they might pick up any other skill, though it appears that even they need to have the proper foundation on which to build coaching skills. Regardless of the pathway, however, managers who do become coaching managers have much in common, particularly with regard to a set of attitudes and beliefs that we describe as the *coaching mind-set*.

The Naturals

In Chapter 3, we referred to the story of Peter Drucker and his boss, Erich Dombrowski. How Mr. Dombrowski actually learned to be such an effective coach is something of a mystery. We speculate that he might share certain characteristics with the kind of coaching managers we call "naturals." It is certainly doubtful that he received any formal training in coaching. Drucker and all his colleagues at the paper were extremely fortunate that Dombrowski was such a good coach. The coaching done at that time was probably limited to that which was provided by the naturals. (The same is probably true today for the most part, though the number of individuals who have learned coaching as a skill is increasing.) Naturals are those people who like to help others, are very good at *doing it,* and have been that way most of their lives with little or no training.

Judy Giger, marketing manager at a technology company, remembers people coming up to her throughout her life, wanting to talk. While working her way up the ladder from small businesses through large ones, she found that people routinely sought her out. For a long time, she didn't know why. Those around her report that she is a good listener. She doesn't remember ever having to learn to listen, however. She likes people. She conveys that outlook with natural warmth and a routine expression of respect for others. She is also good at keeping confidences. Interestingly, she has had more than a few people come up to her over the years and say, "You were my mentor." Much like Erich Dombrowski's reaction, this surprises her. She uses her natural coaching style routinely yet does not necessarily think of herself as coaching.

Judy has been asked by her boss to provide support to people in their marketing group who are in the early stages of their careers or are new to the group. It is her responsibility to "bring along the talent." If someone is having trouble with a presentation, dealing with organizational politics, or considering another career move, her role is to do what she has always done: listen, try not to judge or criticize, ask useful questions, observe her "clients" (really her colleagues) doing their work when she can, provide feedback, and on occasion provide advice. The underlying concept that guides her work is that of helping people figure out what they want to do and what they do well. She then helps them leverage their personal motivation and skills to achieve their personal goals, inside her group or out. If she ends up advising someone in the wrong role to find another job, she considers that a win for everyone. She does not believe in trying to change people.

Judy enjoys this aspect of her work a great deal. However, she has never seriously considered going into human resources or other roles with which one might intuitively associate a natural helper. She likes business, and she likes marketing. She is an example of a natural coach.

Although Judy's story as told so far sounds straightforward, she has had her own struggles. Many naturals find barriers to the expression of their given talents. They may work for managers who are suspicious of people who seem to be confidants of others within the organization. They may be stymied by managers who fear a loss of control. They may be discredited by managers who think that coaching is not work at all, but rather a waste of time. Judy's current manager offers two important sources of support. First, she validates the importance of Judy's coaching activities. Judy doesn't have to worry that the time she spends coaching will appear to be time wasted from a business perspective. Second, Judy's manager has actually found a semiformal outlet for the expression of Judy's talents.

The last point can't be emphasized enough. Those who have a strong interest in helping others and yet want to pursue a business career must look for managers and roles that allow them to express that strength. Unfortunately, unless naturals have done a bit of homework, they may not even know that coaching is a valid business activity. They may be concerned about sharing their interests with others for fear of appearing too, yes, "touchy-feely." Naturals, once they have identified their interest in coaching, need to intentionally pursue opportunities for the expression of that interest as part of their own career planning.

The Manager Who Learns to Coach

The low frequency with which we find naturals suggests that we are much more likely to find managers who, if they are coaching, have intentionally learned the skills necessary to coach. We anticipate that their numbers will swell with the growing awareness on the part of business leaders and human resource professionals that the ability to coach represents an essential competency for an effective manager. We emphasize here that these people are probably not without some of the talents one finds in naturals. However, these talents may be less fully refined, and their expression may have been given a lower priority over the course of time.

Our work has shown that those who learn to coach go through a two-step process. They first identify the need to learn about coaching, and then they must internalize a model of coaching that helps guide their actions. The coaching model they ultimately work with can be an academic one or one they have learned "on the job."

The first step is necessary to point out because the future coaching manager may not even know that coaching is a legitimate business activity. The personal identification of the value of coaching may take place in a number of ways. Some managers may feel that they just don't have any choice. Like Erich Dombrowski, they may have to work with undeveloped talent. They can't do it all themselves, and they come to realize that becoming a teacher is their only hope. Some may hear about coaching; intuitively think that it is a good idea, perhaps because it fits with their values; and start the learning process. Finally, some identify a need to learn more about coaching through very personal and often difficult experiences.

Stan is an information technology director with a major U.S. consulting firm. He is on the career track to becoming the chief technology officer of the firm if he so chooses. His coaching efforts play a significant role in how he runs his group. He takes the development of the members of his team seriously. He was not always aware of coaching or the role that it could play in his leadership style. He had no idea that there was a technique or a model one could use to guide efforts to help others develop. His eyes were opened to the importance of understanding how to help his employees in one very traumatic experience.

Several jobs and companies ago, his manager suddenly and without warning confronted him on the perceived shortcomings of his leadership style. Basing her criticisms on feedback from the management of another group in her organization, she attacked his interpersonal effectiveness in particular (though her attacks were very nonspecific). Stan was left in the dark as to the specific sources of the feedback. She made it clear to him that she felt he had no talent for leadership.

Without concrete details or clear knowledge of "who said what," he was left feeling devastated and helpless. His overriding sense was that his manager, even if she had a point, had not been in the least helpful. He went back to his own group and sought out their feedback, which was largely positive. He then took it on himself to go to a leadership training program that, though he left with some good ideas, also validated the fact that he was actually doing pretty well for a young manager.

There was a problem, however, but it was a cross-functional one. Stan had run into a serious political problem that had nothing to do with his top-down leadership. His manager had been of no help in that regard, either. Her surprising feedback merely generated mistrust in an already highly charged atmosphere. Stan eventually moved on to greener pastures. His insight, however, stayed with him. He did have a problem, but his manager's actions had only exacerbated it. One should expect more from one's manager.

Stan resolved to help his own people in a very different way. He began an effort to create the kind of environment in which his employees could help him (as they had done during his crisis) as well as each other. We'll hear more of his ideas later. Suffice it to say they include being open to giving and receiving timely, useful, and specific feedback delivered with the dignity of both parties in mind at all times. His motivation to learn was actually quite simple: "I don't ever want to do to anyone else what she [the former manager] did to me." When asked what he worries about, as a manager who coaches, he says, "The thing that keeps me up at night when I'm trying to coach somebody is whether or not I'm having a positive or a negative impact. I still worry about that."

Role modeling is one of the major sources of learning in the career of a leader (McCall, Lombardo, & Morrison, 1988). Managers can learn to coach from managers who coach, such as Dombrowski. Many of our coaching managers have told us that they learned a great deal from their first managers, people gifted at helping them develop. The experience of receiving no coaching or, worse yet, destructive coaching early in one's career can also shape an awareness of the importance of humanely helping others to develop.

Whether from the impact of a good or bad manager, the realization of the value of helping has to occur for people to move to the second step: actually internalizing some kind of coaching model. Our experience suggests that many people would like to do more coaching at work but don't because they are anxious. The idea of intentionally trying to influence the path of another human being scares them. "I'm not a therapist" is a common refrain. We were quite surprised by this early in our work in this area. It's very ironic, after all, that managers would express the fear of "playing God" and at the same be prepared to terminate someone's employment. (Not that most managers would do so happily; they wouldn't. Our point here is that firing someone seems to be a more comprehensible part of some managers' construction of the management role than helping someone.) If they don't believe it is important, they won't work to get beyond that anxiety. The comments of one participant in a coach training program, an engineer, are illustrative in that regard:

> Coaching appears to be more difficult than it really is. First, I was nervous, but as the session started, I realized I had to and I could do my best to advise [the coachee], drawing from what I learned in the training, at work, and in life. The coachees [learners] made this easy, as they were open to feedback and eager to see how they did. My confidence has built up, and I am ready to go through the coaching process more effectively next time, whenever I need to coach.

We have had new coaching managers tell us that they lost sleep the night before their first coaching efforts. However, as this quote illustrates, the anxiety is largely anticipatory, probably based on the fear of doing the wrong thing and hurting the coachee. As managers come to understand that effective coaching involves sharing responsibility for learning, this anxiety abates considerably. The mental models that such individuals hold of coaching begin to change, and to become much more realistic.

Another coach participant, a research and development manager, stated,

> In the past, I have been afraid to do the wrong thing or give the wrong input, so I kept quiet. I now feel that I know how to have a discussion on nontechnical topics that will be constructive and helpful, rather than upsetting and inflammatory.

This individual has to build a team out of a group of scientists. He knows that if he is going to be successful, he is going to have to help them. In his eyes, a coaching model and a little experience completely reframe the problem. Being well beyond the anxiety, he can anticipate coaching more in the future. Step 1 on the road to becoming a coaching manager intersects with Step 2.

Through feedback we have received from the coaches who have attended our training programs over the years, we have found that a useful model of coaching needs to be simple and realistic. The language of coaching needs to be clear and businesslike. Perhaps most important, managers need to have a realistic understanding of what coaching is supposed to accomplish, for whom, and how. In our training programs and work in organizations, we find that managers usually become noticeably less anxious about coaching once they understand the following:

- The learner is responsible for much of what takes place in coaching. The coach doesn't have to take responsibility for all aspects of the process or the outcome.

- Developmental coaching focuses largely on learning from the work at hand. Yes, it can involve career discussions as well, but the coaching manager may be much less able to help in that regard. The coaching manager helps contribute to an individual's career development by helping him or her take on new challenges and build competence by learning from those challenges.
- Coaching does not mean changing someone's personality. Learning takes place incrementally. Small learning gains are usually enough to help people improve their performance toward even stretch goals. Developmental coaching should not be confused with remedial coaching, as we've discussed.
- Coaching doesn't have to take a great deal of time once one has become comfortable with the process and has created a coaching-friendly context.
- A manager's ability to coach will usually improve with practice, reflection, and a bit of feedback. Coaching is learned the way one learns any other skill.

Most managers find that they are very effective at executing some aspects of a simple coaching model, but not so effective at others. Stacy McMullen, an information technology manager, ran the Help Desk function at a large multinational retail company. Throughout her career, Stacy worked to develop her leadership skills in a variety of ways. She decided to learn more about coaching through a course-based training program and to apply what she had learned in working with her employees.

In our coach training program, her coaching session was recorded as she worked with a coachee (this was known to the coachee who understood that Stacy was trying to improve her coaching skills). Listening to the tape, she realized that she had not done a good job of using questions to help create a coaching dialogue. Out of her own anxiety and lack of practice, she began to "tell and sell" her point of view to the coachee, rather than asking questions to get the coachee's point of view. She ended up talking far more than the coachee and taking complete responsibility for the conclusions that emerged from the coaching interview. The next day, Stacy was scheduled to hold a meeting with one of her employees to discuss that employee's development goals for the year. She was determined that this meeting would not go the same route.

Stacy decided to literally bite her lip after asking a question, consciously and quietly waiting to see what might happen. This is quite uncomfortable for most people unless they have really worked on their ability to tolerate silence. Nevertheless, it is a great way to keep from dominating a conversation and encourage the other person to think. After a few awkward silences, the employee began to open up with Stacy. In the space she had created between her questions, the employee began to share his ideas about the strengths and weaknesses of his performance and what he felt he needed to work on. Stacy found herself learning things about her employee that she hadn't known and was quite pleasantly surprised in the process. The result was a development plan that made sense to both of them.

Stacy is a bright, well-motivated manager with good interpersonal skills and an openness to learning. By gaining a conceptual model of coaching, trying out some new behaviors, getting some feedback, and practicing, she was able to learn to coach in a rather short period of time. As with any skill, she'll need to continue practicing, however, for that learning to stick.

Can Anyone Learn to Coach?

So some managers—we believe many—can learn to coach. Can anyone? Probably not. Several basic premises of adult learning are relevant to this question. First, development often involves building on strengths. For Stacy, the ability to coach builds on a set of previously existing strengths. She is a good leader, an effective communicator, and usually patient and mature. Not everyone has such a foundation. As the CEO of a firm that values coaching told us, "I might hire an engineering manager because he is a great engineer. That is his strength. That doesn't mean he'll be a great coach." Does this mean that if there isn't clear evidence of a foundation of interpersonal strengths, you shouldn't give it a try? We think not. A second premise of development is that the learner has to set the goal. If you think it is important for you to learn to coach, there is a much greater likelihood that your efforts will lead to success. Studying biographies tells us that many gifted teachers, counselors, and business and political leaders came from psychologically disadvantaged backgrounds. They made their way through difficult circumstances and were able to have a very positive impact on those around them.

Several of the coaching managers with whom we've worked have suggested to us, though, that the distinction between the natural coach and the coach who has to learn how to coach can represent a false dichotomy. In reality, they have said, the two represent extremes along a continuum. Some people are very gifted and need little additional help to become effective coaching managers. For others, much practice is required.

We have had managers tell us that they really didn't know how to hold a conversation with their employees until they learned how to ask questions and to coach. Not good at small talk, they avoided talking about almost anything at all. They wanted to enhance their ability to just talk with their employees, and coaching represented a vehicle for doing so.

To help you better assess whether or not you are working from a foundation on which effective coaching skills can be built, we describe in some detail what the naturals and those who have learned to coach by more traditional means have in common. As is the case throughout this book, in compiling this list, we draw on our experience in training managers to coach, interviews with coaching managers, and the writings of those who have coached or studied coaching.

The Coaching Mind-Set: An Attitude of Helpfulness

Managers who become coaching managers, by whatever route, appear to show most if not all the attitudes or behaviors we will be describing (see Box 5.1). Before listing them specifically, we will simply summarize them by the word *helpfulness*. Managers who coach want to *help*, as opposed to fixing or changing others. They like seeing others succeed. They seem to get a kick out of having a chance to admire the good work of others. As one coaching manager told us, "I keep track of them in their careers. I hear about their accomplishments. I like to think that in a way, I have contributed to their success."

BOX 5.1 **What Coaching Managers Have in Common**

- They have an overriding attitude of helpfulness when trying to coach others.
- They don't believe in the "sink or swim" theory of employee development.
- They believe that by helping their employees develop, everybody comes out ahead.
- They show less need for control.
- They believe that most people really do want to learn.
- They show empathy in their dealings with others.
- They are open to personal learning, to receiving feedback, and to being coached, even by their employees.
- They set high standards.
- They don't try to "fix" people.
- They don't believe that people are a means to an end.

The reader will recognize several of these values from our discussion of the coaching-friendly context. This is appropriate. The context set by the manager reflects his or her value system. We would like to look more closely at several areas we have not discussed at length that have more to do with the coach's attitude and competence when working individually with direct reports. These factors go into creating that overriding sense of helpfulness we describe here. Indeed, as we will discuss further in other chapters, one of the most important things that the coaching manager has to consider before creating a coaching dialogue is this: "Do I feel I am ready to be helpful?"

Coaching managers don't believe in the "sink or swim" theory of employee development. Morgan McCall (1998) has studied the leadership development practices of a number of companies and has concluded that the "sink or swim" approach to development is probably the most common, even in some very progressive firms. In this approach to development, individuals are given challenging assignments. If they are successful, their careers advance. If not, their careers stall. The individual is given no coaching, mentoring, or other learning supports.

The coaches we have worked with find this a wasteful and invalid practice. As McCall (1998) points out, who knows how many more would be successful with a little help? Consider the political mistakes that would not be made, the time that would not be lost as an individual makes the same mistakes over and over, and the bad habits that even some of the successful "sink or swim" candidates probably learn along the way, in the absence of feedback.

Interestingly, many of our coaches, when asked why they think coaching is a good idea, say, "Because no one ever coached me!" They struggled to learn and advance in their careers, often without help. They are the victims of a "sink or swim" mentality and see what has been lost in their own careers. They do believe in giving people challenging assignments, but they also believe in helping out with support, advice, and feedback—in other words, coaching. The "big pit" theory, digging a hole and throwing people in to see who crawls out, is a waste of resources and a poor way of demonstrating that you care!

We would add that there is increasing research support for dismissing the "big pit" theory of leadership development. It is becoming increasingly clear that challenge, in the absence of support, offers diminishing returns from a learning standpoint. Think about it realistically. Significant challenges involve quite a battle. What if you were facing significant challenges, of any sort, but didn't feel like your performance was improving? Let us look at one simple example that may be painfully close to home for some readers.

Golf, as an industry, has a problem. It seems that too many individuals give up golf after around 3 years of participation in the sport. Some of you can guess the reason (Hurst, 2002). After 3 years of steady improvement, their game begins to level off. The process of golfing does not readily supply the kind of feedback that would lead to continued improvements beyond the basics for those who are self-taught. That sand trap on the 17th fairway turns out to be the "big pit" theory of golfer development. The answer to this problem is, you can guess, to hire a coach. Closer to our concerns here, researchers are now coming to understand that what one can learn by one-self by facing continued leadership challenges begins to level off at some point. We are no longer learning from experience and seeing improved per-formance as a result. Again, the answers are feedback and coaching (DeRue & Wellman, 2009).

Coaching managers believe that by helping their employees develop, every-body comes out ahead. In our consulting practices, we have repeatedly run across one of the most insidious barriers to coaching by managers. That bar-rier is represented by the belief that managers shouldn't try to help their employees develop because in doing so, they will lose the best ones. Employees naturally despise this assumption because it means that they are ultimately just being used by the manager as tools for the manager's self-serving agenda. This assumption and the practices associated with it are par-ticularly dangerous to a business in a tight labor market. Given that employees have options, they will go elsewhere if an opportunity to develop is closed to them.

The coaching managers we have worked with assume that by coaching their employees and aiding their development, they will build the overall capability of their businesses. They also are quite aware that, although they will lose some good people along the way, in the end, they are likely to be even more successful. By taking a developmental approach, their employees are challenged and satisfied. Problems are dealt with more quickly. Morale and commitment are high.

We've asked managers whether or not all this work on development isn't just a bit inconvenient at times. After all, you are always in the business of bringing people along when you operate this way. One coaching manager answered us in jest, "Only when they say they want my job!" For the most part, coaching managers believe that they *should* be preparing people to take their jobs and view it as an essential means of succession planning. They feel it is their obligation to their people and to the business.

Coaching managers show less need for control. At the 1978 Gator Bowl, storied Ohio State Coach Woody Hayes ran onto the football field and hit an opposing player who had previously intercepted a pass. Hayes was sub-sequently fired (Schwab, 1999). This now rather pathetic picture (with apologies to Ohio State) speaks to just how difficult it is to be a coach rather than a player. The coaching manager sometimes has to subordinate his or her own wish to be in control and to be on the field, taking care of business, in order to let the team play the game and keep learning. This can be gut-wrenching. Note that the characteristic in question here is called *"Show* Less Need for Control." It does not say "Have Less Need for Control." Self-control is the key.

The tasks of the manager have traditionally been described as those of planning, organizing, directing, and controlling. Managers are held accountable for results. They are rewarded for success and punished for failure. The rewards and punishments with which they must contend are powerful. This emphasis on "results no matter what" can make it hard for managers to coach rather than do.

Given that development requires, among other things, a challenging assignment (Van Velsor, McCauly, & Moxley, 1998), those who are offered such assignments might just fail. Although failure should probably have some consequences, if the consequences are too dire, development will stop, as discussed in the previous chapter. The coaches that we have witnessed doing the best jobs are those who are able to tolerate the potential for at least some failure. They can delegate, turn over a task to another individual, and then stay in the coaching role even when the situation becomes difficult and failure is a very real possibility. That doesn't mean that coaching managers set their employees up for failure or don't step in to help when needed. Rather, they don't rush in at the first sign of trouble.

Perhaps most important, an effective coaching manager has to be able to ask questions rather than provide answers, enough to make it possible for the coachee to struggle with the challenge. Mr. Hayes evidently was not convinced that his players could take back the game. He crossed the white line that distinguished coaches from players. In organizational life, we have no such white line. Sometimes we have to cross the line, and sometimes we don't. How good are you at holding back and not offering advice? This is a key aspect of the coaching dialogue, but if you're honest with yourself, you know that it isn't easy. After all, you may have the right answer. Why not just give it up and get this over with? When you wait and see what your coachee has to say, you are giving up a bit of that sense of control that you fought to grasp.

Coaching managers believe that most people really do want to learn. The effective coaches we've known have tended to be very good "systems" thinkers. By that we mean that they understand that many people don't *appear* to want to learn because they have been trained not to. They don't believe, however, that most people really don't want to learn. (We'll talk more about this topic in the next chapter, from the coachee's point of view.) They believe that it is their obligation to create a context in which learning is possible. More than one coaching manager has told us about a "salvage job" he or she was working on. This kind of salvage job refers not to the employee who has a severe performance problem, but rather to the employee who is afraid to learn. Some managers are so hostile toward employee development that they can literally leave a talented employee demoralized, cynical, and greatly inhibited when it comes to learning. A coaching manager involved in a salvage operation might speak of an employee as one might describe a child who was raised in an abusive home: talking about the need to take a lot of time, build some trust, and convince the employee that it is OK to talk about work, his or her career goals, or what he or she is having trouble with.

Coaching managers are really much like gardeners. They plant the flowers (hire the right employees), create a context, provide some support, and are there to help out. However, having done that, they don't always expect every effort to bear fruit. Most coaches report that, as they mature, they come to accept that some people don't want to be coached and that they may not be able to make a difference in their development.

Coaching managers show empathy in their dealings with others. As the previous example indicates, effective coaches tend to be able to put themselves in another person's shoes, rather than judging an individual solely on the basis of surface behaviors. They are interested in what makes people work and in the role that work plays in people's lives. One coaching manager, in describing his work, was adamant about the importance of understanding the family or personal lives of his employees. "How can you expect them to take on a tough assignment, one that might really be stressful, when somebody is sick at home or when they are going through a divorce?"

Effective coaches use empathy to help them understand the coachee in his or her totality. This stands in sharp distinction to managers who are so focused on results that they delegate tasks to an already overburdened individual, creating the conditions for failure as well as a lack of learning in the process. Interestingly, however, most of the coaches we've talked with insist that they maintain very high standards with regard to performance. In fact, they use high standards as a tool to keep themselves and their people motivated and focused. They also use the high standards they have set as a framework within which to coach.

Coaching managers are open to personal learning, to receiving feedback, and to being coached, even by their employees. Effective coaches like to learn about themselves, about others, and about their work. They often enjoy being surprised by what they don't know. Coaching is, for them, a tool that helps them foster their own learning. It also helps them know what is going on in their business units, always a desirable outcome.

They also seem to enjoy learning about themselves from others. Frequently, managers who create what we call "coaching-friendly contexts" are very likely to encourage employees to coach them. This is a way of modeling the giving and receiving of feedback. However, it is done for more than just the purpose of modeling desired behavior. They genuinely want the feedback. They have come to believe that they really don't know it all and that the perceptions of others, even critical perceptions, are essential to hear and understand.

In this sense, they are comfortable admitting what they don't know and how they might be wrong. This is particularly noticeable when they are gathering performance information about coachees, positive or negative. Rather than taking the attitude, while gathering information, that they have to prove their own positions correct, they're more likely to seek information that will add to or change their perceptions, in an effort to find out what is really going on.

Coaching managers set high standards. We mentioned above that the coaching managers we have interviewed are very rigorous businesspeople. Their rigor is seen in the high standards they set. They expect their employees to be able to meet those standards. The difference is they are willing to help. They offer help through coaching as well as through other interventions. One of our coaching managers told us, "People are surprised at the fact that I can be tough. The toughness comes out when I make it clear to everyone that I expect this group to be successful, to be the best group in our division. They think that because I'm interested in people, I am inevitably going to be soft. Not true. I set high standards, though I do think they are achievable. I stick to them; I don't back off."

This particular characteristic is extremely important. In the absence of this, coaching might in fact be too "soft." Workshop participants have told us repeatedly that their best managers expected something from them that they didn't feel they could deliver. "She saw something in me that I didn't see in myself." "He expected me to perform even when I didn't think I could." We have said that challenge by itself may not foster continued development, but it is a very necessary condition for development. People have to stretch themselves to grow. High standards for a team promote stretch opportunities for everyone. The manager who has high standards serves as a personal role model for performance. This is where the power of the developmental coaching model can become apparent. High standards are coupled with support for reaching those standards.

Coaching managers don't try to "fix" people. We have repeatedly noticed that managers who seem to take coaching most to heart also seem to be most accepting of others' strengths and weaknesses. They pay attention to strengths and weaknesses in the hiring process (see Chapter 3) and work hard to create opportunities for people to use their strengths and, where appropriate, work on weaknesses. On the other hand, they can also accept that an employee may not have the right talent for his or her role or the right fit for the business unit. They are able to accept that someone may need to move along to another role or business unit or company and are quite willing to make that happen, even though they may feel bad about the need to do so. To put it simply, they aren't afraid to fire someone if that person is in the wrong job. Most coaching managers, then, don't assume that coaching can fix everything. They are willing to give coaching a try when serious performance problems arise, but such remedial coaching isn't the primary focus of their developmental efforts.

We have seen this problem from very close range in our coach training programs. Some managers, including some who are clearly well-meaning and interested in other people, show tremendous frustration when their coachees seem unmotivated or abrasive. Despite our best efforts, such coaches will confront coachees on admittedly unappealing behavior without first building relationships with them. You can envision this as the psychological equivalent of "giving them a swift kick for their own good." The "fix 'em" obsessed managers don't stop to understand people, their contexts, and, most important, their goals. The results usually range from unproductive to disastrous. The coachee feels abused and highly defensive. Sadly, we suspect (though we can't prove) that coachees who have been the object of a coach's efforts to fix rather than coach are less likely to seek coaching in the future.

The frustration of the coaches does not abate as they realize that they cannot simply change people. This isn't coaching! The true coach, as stated above, has to be able to tolerate giving over control of the process to learners and be accepting of the fact that things may not always work out for him or her.

Coaching managers don't believe that people are a means to an end. We can summarize our description of coaching managers by describing their approach to the age-old business paradox: Is the business run for the sake of shareholders, and perhaps customers, or for the employees? Coaching managers dismiss the view of wealth creation or need fulfillment as being dichotomous in relation to the needs of the employees. Their assumption is that the business should meet the needs of both groups: Employees do the work of the organization, but one does not build organizational capability (or "human capital," as it might now be called) simply for the sake of putting out a better product, though that is important. In this view, the development of employees is an inherent part of what makes a business unit worthwhile. Espousing this ideology can create some tension, however (see the earlier comments about human resources).

The Coaching Manager

Would you like to work for the kind of coaching manager we've just described? Unless you are a very exceptional person, the answer is probably an unqualified yes. Why wouldn't you? These attitudes combine an interest in success with an interest in helping others be successful. Is this just too good to be true? Think about it.

Is there a manager in your organization whom everyone seems to talk about? If it takes place among other managers, is such discussion occasionally tinged with more than a hint of jealousy or envy? Do you ever fear losing some of your good employees to that person? Chances are, he or she is a manager who runs a successful group and is also interested in helping people develop through coaching.

Great organizations tend to be well-known both for being successful and for being interested in their employees. As a result, they don't suffer any shortage of talent. Southwest Airlines, for instance, in one recent year, had over 100,000 job applications for fewer than 5,000 openings. The recruiters and hiring managers got to choose the best individuals from a very large pool.

Managers who coach will likely experience something very similar, on a smaller scale, of course. People want to work for them because those managers help them succeed in both the short term and the long term. The work is challenging and interesting. Growth and career movement are likely outcomes. Coaching managers are able to think about moving people up or across the organization because they know that someone else is waiting in the wings to join their group. They can choose from among the best. In the eyes of potential employees and other company managers, the coaching manager has a sustainable competitive advantage.

SELF-ASSESSMENT 5.1: Your Foundation for Learning to Coach

We've spent considerable time in this chapter and previous chapters discussing how the coaching manager provides a personal and organizational context for coaching, using her own behavior and attitudes as primary tools. Setting the context and reinforcing that context with your own personal actions of helpfulness make coaching possible, make it possible for you to help others without being perfect at doing so, make responsibility for learning shared, and just might make your work life a bit more fun.

In the next chapter, we will take a closer look at the other partner in the learning process, the coachee. Before leaving our exploration of the coaching manager's perspective, we want to provide you with a more concise and systematic opportunity to assess your own strengths and needs. This "Coaching Manager Self-Assessment" was originally developed by our colleague Suzanne Levin Glazier (Hunt & Weintraub, 2007). These competencies represent an effort to capture the wisdom of the coaches with whom we've had a chance to work, in response to our question to them: "What does it take to be an effective coaching manager?"

We encourage you to look carefully at each of the competencies described below and the questions related to each competency. How would you assess your performance? Ideally, you should also ask members of your team for their feedback. It may be easier in that regard to use a rating system. Rate yourself as a "5" if you see your performance as very strong and, using a graduated scale, as a "1" if you see yourself as needing significant developmental work in this area.

1. Demonstrates Self-Awareness

   - I encourage others to give me honest feedback.
   - I take time to reflect upon the best course of action rather than jumping to conclusions.
   - I encourage others I work with to reflect on their work.
   - I handle myself in a calm manner when things become hectic.

2. Promotes Learning Among His or Her Team Members

   - I encourage the ongoing learning and development of others.
   - I take time to develop my own skills and abilities through continuous learning.
   - I give timely feedback that helps others understand their own work performance.
   - I view mistakes as learning opportunities when appropriate.
   - I use questions to help others think through an issue or a problem rather than immediately telling others what I think is the right solution.
   - I encourage others to share new ideas regarding work, even if they are contrary to my own.

3. Is an Effective Communicator

- I share information with others in a timely fashion.
- I communicate my management philosophy and expectations with those around me.
- I impart a clear vision of what successful work performance should look like.
- I communicate clearly to others regarding their roles and responsibilities.

4. Is Accessible

- I have an open-door policy—when others need assistance they know I will set aside time to address their concerns.
- I respect the confidential nature of my discussions with others when appropriate.
- I schedule a future time to meet with others when I am not immediately available to meet their needs.

5. Demonstrates Effective Listening

- I do not interrupt others when they are speaking.
- I pay attention to the manner in which others are speaking as well as their words (using cues such as body language, tone of voice, etc.).
- I stop what I am doing and pay attention when someone is speaking.
- I restate others' words to ensure that I have a proper understanding of what they are trying to say.

6. Creates a Trusting Environment

- I help people feel comfortable discussing issues with me by acting in a non-judgmental manner.
- I recognize the people I interact with as unique individuals who have different needs and goals.
- I create an environment in which people want to make decisions related to their own development.
- I support people when they have dealings with others outside our team, when needed.
- I look for competent, self-motivated candidates for open positions, particularly those who have a desire to grow with the organization.
- I follow through on my commitments.

The "Coachable" Learner $\qquad$ 6

In this chapter, you will learn about the following:

- The evidence suggesting that most people want to learn on the job
- The indicators that point to an individual's ability to engage in a coaching relationship
- The barriers to "coachability" created by potential learners
- Tactics for engaging the coachee

The Question of "Coachability"

In Chapter 5, we described the characteristics of an effective coaching manager. Talk of "characteristics" can be a bit misleading, however. The coaching manager–coachee relationship actually functions as a system. Effective coaching is largely dependent on the nature of the relationships between managers and the people who work for them. One manager might be very effective at coaching someone whom another manager would find difficult to reach. Nevertheless, we do believe that it is possible to draw some useful conclusions regarding who can benefit from coaching and who might not benefit from coaching, on the basis of the experience of the managers with whom we have worked. The bottom line is that most, but not all, people are in fact coachable if conditions are favorable. As we move forward, however, it is important to keep in mind that we are to an extent the architects of what we see in others.

In this chapter, we will share some of what has been learned regarding the question of coachability. The following case example illustrates the two basic questions we must confront. Is coachability a reflection of an individual's personality? Alternatively, is coachability a reflection of the environment within which an individual works and of the way that environment shapes a worker's response to coaching efforts?

Case 6.1: The Reluctant Coachee?

Part I: Aren't You Glad You Got This New Job!

Congratulations. You have just been promoted to director of all credit functions at your company. As part of the package, you find that you are Roger's new manager. (Roger manages the International Credit Group.) You've known Roger for only 3 weeks, but you've already had more than a few complaints. The company has been coming down hard on managers who are seen as abrasive. (You note to yourself the irony with which your company's actions can be viewed. After all, didn't its emphasis on short-term results create problems like Roger to begin with?) Retention seems to be "in"; beating people over the head is "out." You review the results of your most recent survey of Roger's employees and peers. Here is what they tell you:

Roger is (in no particular order)

- ruthless;
- aggressive;
- demeaning to subordinates (intolerant of mistakes and likely to become very angry publicly when mistakes are made); and
- someone who intends to get his way, regardless of the cost.

Even more intriguing, his former boss told you, "Don't try to give him any advice. He already knows it all." (You again register a mild sense of irony. You had always thought that Roger's former manager knew it all or at least thought he did.)

Consider a few questions to get started with the task of assessing Roger's coachability:

1. On the basis of what you already know, do you think Roger is coachable?

2. What role does the company's culture play in your thinking as you try to make this determination?

After asking yourself why this had to happen to you, you buckle down to the task of trying to do something with Roger. At this point, you might make some of the following inferences:

- You've known the Rogers of the world, and of this company, for a long time. There are plenty of them out there. They are usually so arrogant that they end up running into serious political problems as they move up the corporate ladder. Yes, they do get results, but through the use of brute force. They aren't necessarily bad people. They just don't take others' needs into consideration. They often offend people. Ultimately, they offend the wrong customer, senior manager, or product engineer, and suddenly, their careers go into a nosedive.

- You might blame the Rogers of the world for not being smarter and more skillful in their drive for results. After all, Roger has an MBA from a good school. Shouldn't he have known that you have to work effectively with people?

- You might blame his previous manager. You've attributed part of the problem to the fact that Roger's last manager was notorious for encouraging exactly the kind of behavior that Roger is now demonstrating. Certainly, his previous manager was not someone who would confront Roger about his interpersonal behavior.

- You might ultimately question the culture of your company. It hired and promoted Roger and his previous manager. Now it is suddenly saying that it wants both results and a team-oriented environment and process for getting those results. It wants people to feel valued and to learn. How can those who run the place expect Roger to change his behavior overnight? Roger has been with the company for 5 years. He's learned a lot of bad habits. One of the habits he learned was to reject the coaching and advice of others. After all, those who couldn't solve their own problems were labeled by the previous management as "wimps."

After going through all the diagnostic possibilities in your mind, you're still confronted with the problem of figuring out how to deal with Roger. Should you try to coach him or not?

Part II: A Day in the Life of Roger

Perhaps out of the kindness of your heart, and your own efforts to embrace the new corporate philosophy, you decide to give coaching Roger a try. You see him sitting alone in the lunchroom. You grab a cup of coffee, walk over to him, and ask if he'd like some company. He is more than ready to tell you about himself and his problems.

Roger reports that he has had a rough day. Three of his direct reports "hinted" that they might be looking for work elsewhere. They also "hinted" that it was because of Roger. He knows this won't look good to the higher-ups. But hey, he's gotten the results. He deserves a shot at that next promotion. Sure, there are some whiners in his group, but they wouldn't be where they are today without Roger. Roger is pretty sure that his career has advanced because

(Continued)

(Continued)

he's known who the right people are upstairs and made certain that they were happy, regardless. No one ever doubts whether or not he's going to make his numbers. That, after all, is the point of business. Having completed his monologue, he promptly gets up from the table, informs you that he has a very important meeting, and leaves the cafeteria.

If the story were to end here, you might again reflect on your own current challenges and come up with a few more inferences:

- This guy is even more arrogant than I thought! Perhaps he is beyond help. He didn't even ask me about how things were going in my new role.
- He doesn't want coaching. He just wants to complain about other people without really exploring anything of substance with me.

You might then ask yourself the following questions:

1. Is there any way to get through to him, to get him to open up about his own problems and be open to some input from others?

2. If I try to coach him, how much of a drain is the effort going to be on my own time?

3. If I can't coach him, what am I going to do with him?

Part III: A Happier Ending?

Perhaps through a combination of techniques (some drawn from this book, we hope) and good luck, you actually get Roger to tell you a bit more about his management style and its origins. Would the following story, if Roger decided to share it with you, change your impression?

The next day, you and Roger again find yourselves talking over a cup of coffee in the cafeteria. Roger remembers that when he first came to work, he was a real idealist. He wanted to make sure that everyone was happy. He thought worker satisfaction was the key to productivity. He started bending over backward to help out his employees, but boy, did he get burned. Some took advantage of him. His own boss at the time threatened to fire him unless he got his people in line. The company didn't want to hear anything about his dreams of high performance and happy workers. Roger had a family to support, and he decided he'd better do it "their way."

What inferences might you make now? Here are some possibilities:

- Roger has at least some ability to reflect on his behavior and its history.
- He has in fact learned some very bad habits. Those habits have unfortunately been rewarded financially and in other ways.

- Roger may have some ability to alter his style a bit. We actually don't yet know because no one has ever tried to help Roger improve his ability to work with others. There was a time, when he first started working here, that he might have gladly accepted coaching about his leadership style.
- It probably won't be easy for him to change. This set of habits has, unfortunately, been in place for some time.

Roger will likely represent a coaching challenge regardless. You may wonder whether or not this is developmental or in fact remedial in the sense that he is now in serious performance trouble. We've learned that that can be a difficult distinction to make, even though it's a distinction we find necessary. Consider, for example, the brilliant analyst who is also a "table pounder" (has very little ability to restrain himself when angry). If he continues pounding the table, his progress in his career may be blocked. However, his company really wants him to succeed and is deeply committed to him. His company sees coaching for him as developmental, even though his problem is serious. The developmental versus remedial distinction refers not only to the severity of the problem but also to the individual's level of support in his organization. As Roger's manager noted, Roger had support, up to a point. Then, things changed. So the judgment as to an individual's coachability goes beyond that of his immediate manager in many cases.

But back to Roger's manager; notice that the question of whether or not someone is coachable is likely to involve the making of an inference or a whole series of inferences. (We talk about making inferences, "jumping to conclusions," in detail when we talk about gathering performance data in a later chapter.) The reality is that the question of whether or not someone is coachable is one you will probably have to resolve with incomplete data. Almost no one will tell you that he or she is not coachable or that he or she doesn't want coaching. That stance is probably no longer politically tolerable in most organizations, even organizations that don't particularly care about the development of their people.

Most coaching managers we have interviewed tell us that arrogance, as they see it, is likely to be the number-one block to coaching. Yet as can be seen in the case of Roger, the *appearance* of arrogance can reflect a personality problem, but it can also reflect previous learning in an organizational culture that actually teaches and rewards arrogance. It may be easier then to begin thinking about what a lack of coachability looks like, by looking at the baseline, the average coachable employee.

What Do Employees Want From Their Managers?

The Gallup Organization, using more than 20 years of survey and interview data, identified 12 "core elements" or needs of employees that are statistically linked to increases in employee productivity, profitability, customer service, and employee retention (Buckingham & Coffman, 1999). These core elements give us a clear picture of what workers want and what motivates them to make efforts that result in these organizationally desirable outcomes. The 12 core elements are listed in Box 6.1.

BOX 6.1   The 12 Gallup "Core Elements"

1. I know what is expected of me at work.

2. I have the materials and equipment I need to do my work properly.

3. At work, I have the opportunity to do what I do best every day.

4. In the last 7 days, I have received recognition or praise for doing good work.

5. My supervisor, or someone at work, seems to care about me as a person.

6. There is someone at work who encourages my development.

7. At work, my opinions seem to count.

8. The mission/purpose of my company makes me feel my job is important.

9. My coworkers are committed to doing quality work.

10. I have a best friend at work.

11. In the last 6 months, someone at work has talked to me about my progress.

12. This last year, I have had opportunities to learn and grow.

SOURCE: Adapted from *First Break All the Rules*, p. 28, by M. Buckingham & C. Coffman, 1999, New York: Simon & Schuster.

These are findings drawn from a wide range of industries and organizational cultures, and as such, not every factor is likely to be relevant to every organization. Many people comment on "I have a best friend at work," asking, "What does that have to do with work?" Initially it seemed like a spurious finding to us, but continued dialogue with participants in our own program suggests not. "I have a best friend at work" suggests that relationships are important to people. Interestingly, compensation is not one of the core elements. That finding suggests that compensation systems themselves do not differentiate superior performance. (It does not suggest that compensation isn't important for other reasons.)

Managers and management educators everywhere should be humbled by these findings, which drew on data from literally millions of workers. Some core elements are intuitively obvious. The first two reflect an employee's need for clear direction and logistical support, though we would suggest that the first element is related to "defining success." A review of the Gallup elements in general, however, gives the distinct impression that the relationship between the manager and the employee has the greatest impact.

What about coaching? The word isn't used in the study, but as we review these results, we suggest that almost every question relates to coaching, even if indirectly. Certainly, active coaching managers can be well aware of whether their employees' needs are being met. However, we can be more specific than that.

The following elements are directly related to coaching: having the opportunity to do what one does best, receiving recognition or praise, feeling cared about, knowing that someone is interested in one's development, discussing one's progress, and having the opportunity to learn and grow. Our interpretation of the results of the Gallup study is that there is powerful and quite specific evidence from business organizations showing the strength of employee interest in coaching that will lead to learning and personal or career development. This suggests that managers should assume, until proven otherwise, that people at least want to be coached, even if they don't show that behavior explicitly or if they don't know how to be effective coachees. We suspect that even Roger would like to learn. The question is whether or not he can allow himself to learn with his manager and other members of his team: That is the real meaning of coachability. A review of the characteristics of coachable learners sheds light on what it takes to learn with someone else.

Hallmarks of the Coachable Learner

What behaviors does the individual demonstrate who is capable of effectively engaging with a coaching manager? Despite the diversity of styles, personalities, and cultural backgrounds found in today's workforce, it is possible to make some useful generalizations. The hallmarks of coachability are listed in Box 6.2. Consider the degree to which Roger, the star of our case at the opening of this chapter, demonstrates such behaviors. The coaching manager should also consider the degree to which his or her behaviors demonstrate his or her own coachability. As we saw in Chapter 4, the manager's coachability can be an important step in creating a coaching-friendly context that encourages employees to express their interest in being coached.

BOX 6.2   Hallmarks of Coachability

The most effective coachees show the following characteristics:

- They can reflect on their actions with at least some desire for objectivity, without undermining their own self-esteem, and are able to accept their humanity (that they aren't perfect but are a work in process).
- They are curious about their actions and the actions of others.
- They are able to accept that someone else may be more knowledgeable than they are.
- They are not bound by shame that inhibits their ability to share their self-observations with a coach. (Some people are all too aware of their humanity but feel they must hide it.)
- They are able to listen, particularly to balanced feedback, without deflecting all feedback back to the coach.
- They are motivated by coaching and are anxious to keep trying to improve and to learn.

First of all, a coachee must be able to reflect on his or her behavior—to step back and examine it from a somewhat objective frame of reference. If you had a particularly troubling meeting with your team and you want to learn something from the event, you need to be able to describe to yourself and to someone else what happened. Furthermore, you need to be able to think about what you did differently this time in contrast to your previous efforts. You need to be able to see and accept that you did some things effectively and other things not so effectively.

This rather dispassionate stance is not always easy for an individual to take, particularly if his or her self-esteem is closely bound to his or her work effectiveness. If whether or not you see yourself as a good or worthwhile person depends on your success, it may be threatening to objectively observe yourself while you are in the process of learning something new. Things will likely not go as well as you might have hoped. The ability to reflect requires an acceptance of your mistakes and your humanity without a great sense of distress. Ideally, effective coachees are curious about their performance and the challenges of continuous improvement. The coachee is like a scientist, trying to understand the laws that govern his or her actions and the actions of others and to exercise some control through that understanding.

As already implied, you, as the effective coachee, also need to be able to acknowledge that others may be able to help you. This means that you will need to accept that someone else may have more knowledge or be more effective than you are. You may be good, but you can become even better. You need to be able to see that you're on a learning curve. The alternative is to believe that your lack of perfection indicates that you are defective. The emotion of shame, which accompanies a sense of being defective, makes us want to hide our concerns or problems. Feelings of shame make an individual want to keep awareness of his or her mistakes from others, which can make coaching nearly impossible. Effective coachees are able to honestly raise their concerns with their coaching managers, rather than succumb to such inhibition. Ideally, effective coachees are sufficiently free from a sense of shame, which makes them able to proactively seek out coaching.

The effective coachee needs to be able to listen. He or she needs to be able to tolerate balanced feedback and consider the meaning of what the coach is trying to say. It is interesting to talk this issue over with those in the arts. If they have had formal training, they are used to being "critiqued." Eventually, they start to crave it. They come to believe that feedback can be worked with, or played with, and that ultimately it's a key component of lifelong learning. One of us has witnessed (and been a participant in) many photographic critique sessions. We have all had the experience of giving someone else feedback only to be met with a defensive attack in which each and every point of the feedback is rebutted ("Yes, but . . ."). Although the feedback is heard, it is not understood. It's normal to want to deflect the criticism back on the coach. But ultimately, the best coachees come to realize that that does very little good. Listen, think about and see what you can learn from it, and represent the attitudes and actions of someone who wants to learn.

Finally, coachable coachees are motivated by coaching. Having talked things over, perhaps received feedback, considered its meaning, and considered what they might do differently next time, they are anxious to practice. They take full responsibility for change and want to exercise their responsibility so that the learning can continue and they can assess their progress.

Not every coachee will display these behaviors in the same way and to the same degree. The coaches we have interviewed report that in their experience, no one is coachable all the time, as we'll discuss in detail below. *Timing* is important. Everyone has bad days, and on those occasions, the coachee might be particularly prone to defensiveness. The best coaching managers are good at spotting windows of time when coachees seem more available and ready to learn, the stress level isn't too high, and the coaches themselves have the time and energy to focus on the coachee.

We can see now that our subject, Roger, has trouble on several counts. He doesn't seem to be an effective observer of his own behavior. More important, even though he is facing some difficulties in his work, he appears reluctant to discuss them with his manager. At this point, he doesn't seem to want to be coached. We can't know that for sure, however, because he hasn't known his new manager very long. He may have important concerns about how he looks to his new boss. This concern with "looking good" goes beyond any sense of personal embarrassment or shame that Roger may experience. The need to "look good" has a political dimension as well.

The Problem of Impression Management

If we can accept the assumption that people want to learn, then why aren't more of them even loudly insisting that they get the kind of coaching they feel they deserve? Unfortunately, there is a cost to seeking out feedback. Susan Ashford (1986) and her colleagues have drawn our attention to the idea that feedback is actually a resource and, as such, has a certain value. In particular, it can help us be more successful in our efforts to adapt to or master the world—or, more specifically, our jobs. The effort to master our environment requires that we get to know and understand it. This requires exploration, interpretation, mapping, and organizing what we come to know about our context. Feedback, specifically coaching, can greatly aid in this process.

What has a value may also have a cost. If appearing to be self-assured is required for success in your job, there may seem to be a substantial cost associated with asking for helpful feedback. And the reality is that asking for explicit feedback is not essential in order to survive at work; there are other ways of learning. After all, opening yourself up for help is to admit your vulnerability. Viewed by one, albeit unrealistic, set of standards, admitting that you need help can represent a blow to your self-esteem: "You are not self-sufficient."

To avoid the problems associated with exposing one's vulnerabilities, we can watch others, read, overhear the conversations of others doing similar work, and engage in trial-and-error learning, among other strategies. These "implicit" strategies of learning have a much lower cost, at least in some environments. It must be noted, however, that trial-and-error learning by itself is very inefficient. Implicit learning strategies in general are likely to be less effective in the absence of some opportunity to reflect, with someone else, on what one believes he or she is seeing and interpreting. Of course, implicit learning strategies may also be feedback-poor.

Nevertheless, implicit strategies of learning allow us to have greater control over the impression we believe we are creating in the minds of others: "If I look like I know what I am doing, then I'll probably be able to make it here." This concept is accurately captured in the notion of heroic leadership (Bradford & Cohen, 1998) and the idea that success comes to those who have all the right answers.

The ultimate point of this perspective is as follows: People probably won't appear to want coaching unless the cost of seeking it is less than its perceived value. Creating a coaching-friendly context in part requires the manager to make sure that there are few, if any, costs to an employee who seeks out coaching. However, we encourage you to make the assumption that many, if not most, of your employees are consciously managing the impression they want to project to you. You need to ask yourself, "Am I signaling to them in any way that I don't want them to ask for coaching?" Roger has been in his firm for 5 years. There is at least some evidence that he learned the importance of impression management early in his career with the firm. He somehow got the impression that only "wimps" asked for coaching. If that is the only real barrier to his coachability, his stance may change over time.

Barriers to Coaching: What Does an *Apparent* Lack of Coachability Look Like?

Once again, we issue the cautionary note that most people are coachable. Here, we'll look at the exceptions. On the basis of our interviews and a review of the management literature, five potential barriers stand out as being very likely to be confronted by the coaching manager. The first three reflect characteristics of the individual employee. The final two reflect a *mismatch* between employee and manager:

- A disconnect between self-concept and observed performance
- A lack of interest in the job and in learning what the manager has to offer
- The employee who is burdened with too much stress, particularly personal or family stress
- A significant cultural barrier between the coaching manager and his or her employee
- A mismatch between the career stage and needs of the employee and between the career stage and needs of the manager

Arrogance: The Overestimator

As one of our coaches put it, "Arrogance—you know, they've got all the answers. Doesn't seem to matter whether or not they actually do have all the answers; they just think they do. They don't really want to talk with you at that point." This particular coaching manager doesn't give up on people who display such arrogance. Rather, he waits and chooses the right time to address this most difficult of coachability issues. He admits that coaching the arrogant employee can be more than a bit of a challenge.

The word *arrogance* summons up a great deal of emotion. Just the thought of dealing with an arrogant individual can be annoying and even intimidating. It brings up memories of meetings dominated by a team member who was sure of his or her perspective, regardless of the input of others; memories of discussions that went nowhere; memories of a tyrannical pursuit of results, no matter who got hurt; or memories of the sense of intimidation one experienced while trying to address a problem with an arrogant person. Arrogant people have a destructive impact on those around them. (In the interest of fairness, we should add that not everyone feels this way. Some people admire the extremely confident, even cocky, individual who "says it like it is, even if you don't want to know." In fact, one could argue that there is a place for such behavior under certain circumstances.)

However, personal style or method of presentation isn't at issue here. The issue here is whether or not the arrogant individual can engage in a learning relationship and benefit from coaching. The research to date is not promising. First, we should define more specifically what we mean by arrogant in this regard.

Rather than use an emotionally loaded approach, it is more useful to think about the cognitive framework that underlies what appears as arrogance on the surface. The problem is one of self-assessment versus the assessment of others. Researchers now have many years of experience in the use of multirater feedback instruments. *Multirater feedback*, or 360-degree assessment, as it is also known, allows an individual to receive feedback from not only the boss but also peers, subordinates, and other key stakeholders in relation to his or her effectiveness. Raters are usually chosen by the individual who is the subject of the assessment but are sometimes chosen by his or her manager; they rate the individual in relation to both outcome and process measures, such as interpersonal savvy or the ability to build an effective team.

The subject of the assessment is also asked to rate his or her own effectiveness. Self- and other-ratings can then be compared. Researchers can also compare the relationship between these two sets of ratings with other data in an effort to understand the meaning of gaps between self-assessment and other assessment.

Yammarino and Atwater (1997) describe four different relationships between self- and other-ratings that are useful for any manager to consider while coaching. These relationships are presented in Table 6.1. When an individual sees himself or herself as effective, and others agree, that individual is very likely to be successful and help the organization. Individuals who have negative self-assessments with which others agree will probably be neither successful nor helpful. However, they may have insight into the problem and can work on changing their roles.

Table 6.1   Self- and Other-Ratings

Type	Ratings	Likely Outcomes
Overestimator	Self-ratings higher than other-ratings	Very negative; the employee is unaware of weaknesses
In agreement/Good	High self-ratings similar to high other-ratings	Very positive
In agreement/Bad	Low self-ratings similar to low other-ratings	Negative
Underestimator	Self-ratings less than other-ratings, which are high	Mixed, because the employee may not recognize skills and talents that could help him or her take on greater challenges

SOURCE: Adapted from "Do Managers See Themselves as Others See Them? Implications of Self-Other Rating Agreement for Human Resources Management," by F. Yammarino and L. Atwater, 1997, *Organizational Dynamics, 25*(4), p. 40.

The individual who has a negative self-assessment with which others don't agree, the underestimator, presents an interesting problem that we will discuss further. The most negative outcomes for both the individual and the organization, however, are observed when an individual's self-assessment is consistently higher than the assessment of that individual by others.

Most of us overestimate our effectiveness in a few areas of activity. That is simply human nature. However, individuals who broadly overestimate their performance are likely to be unconsciously engaged in denial. Their self-concepts do not allow them to take in or effectively work with information, probably readily available from the environment, which suggests that their performance is poor. The manager will almost certainly have to address the problem but will find the employee uncooperative, or worse.

Truly arrogant individuals are people, in the eyes of our coaching managers, who don't realize they are arrogant. They are intimidating to others but have no insight into the magnitude of their intimidation. The combination of problematic behavior, a rigid self-perception, and a lack of insight create a very difficult circumstance for the coaching manager in such a situation. By way of contrast, we all know people who are perhaps generally overconfident but who, under the right circumstances, will own up to a fault or two. Gentle confrontation of their arrogance can lead to a self-deprecating confession and sometimes even a genuine effort to respond. The coaching-friendly context, as described in Chapter 4, can aid in such self-acknowledgment.

What can a coaching manager do with an overestimator? The managers we've interviewed typically don't give up on such an individual, particularly if he or she still has some overlapping goals with the business. In addition, it is often the case that the origin of the individual's inflated self-assessment stems from the presence of an ability that the individual has actually been able to demonstrate to a successful end (Kaplan, Drath, & Kofodimos, 1991). In fact, it is difficult to be arrogant in the complete absence of talent. If the overestimator does have some special gift, he or she is very likely to feel like a victim when confronted. Ultimately, the decision as to whether or not to keep trying belongs to the coaching manager.

Our coaches have confirmed the research in this area suggesting that in working with the overestimator, timing and the ability to use solid performance data to build a case are key (Ludeman & Erlandson, 2004). They have to look for a moment to deliver powerful and credible (data-based) feedback to the individual. Arguing with an overestimator is not a powerful intervention—just the opposite. The overestimator would then have reason to discount whatever content and data are in the message and feel even more misunderstood.

Every coaching manager should view his or her efforts to coach as an experiment. While conducting an experiment, one looks for results. If the desired results are not forthcoming in a reasonable period of time, another intervention may be called for. We encourage the coaching manager not to spend all his or her time trying to get through to every employee. Arrogant, chronic overestimators are actually fairly rare and often come to the attention of coaching managers when they find themselves spending an inordinate amount of time putting out the fires started by such individuals.

What of the other three varieties of self–other agreement or the lack thereof? The best performers who are seen as being very strong, as we have discussed, are often ignored. Our suggestions to the coaching manager who's lucky enough to have such strong performers on his or her team are, first of all, to try to keep these people challenged. They got to be such strong performers through their willingness to take on challenges and learn from them. Secondly, don't ignore them. Make yourself available by mutual agreement to "chat" with them about how things are going. You'll likely be relying less on feedback and more on your ability to ask useful questions. You'll probably also learn a great deal. Unless you're too intrusive, these folks won't feel that you're stepping on their autonomy. If you are concerned about micromanaging, then ask them for their feedback. The simplest question in the world is "How can I help?"

Those who aren't doing a good job and know it deserve very serious consideration, and assistance. They may simply be in the wrong job. We'll talk about this in our discussion of career issues at the close of this book. There are many reasons that people pursue careers for which they are not suited. Again, your ability to create a coaching-friendly context is key here. If you can appear helpful, you may be able to engage in some mutually very beneficial problem solving. We will have more to say about this topic in the next section of this chapter.

Finally, there are those folks—and their numbers are not small—who underrate themselves. The danger here is that they may not deploy their talents fully because they don't see themselves as being effective, even though they are. This can at its most severe represent a mental health issue, and we'll discuss that question a bit further below. More commonly, however, this is a self-confidence issue. Managers can't build self-confidence in their reports directly. Efforts to do so through offering excessive verbal support can in fact be counterproductive, as they may appear overly sympathetic or gratuitous. Here, your ability to carefully assess your employees' talent and challenge them appropriately is key. In the best-case scenario, the employees will learn from success that they have to adjust their self-concept a bit. We might refer to this as simply "learning to cut yourself a bit of slack." The developmental coaching model, objectively applied, offers your best opportunity to provide that extra bit of support that may help someone lacking in confidence rise to the occasion. Of course, seeing someone who is talented but unsure of her- or himself blossom into a top performer can be one of the most gratifying experiences in a coaching manager's career.

An Apparent Lack of Interest in the Job

A number of the managers we've talked to believe that some of their biggest coaching successes occurred when they accepted that an individual was in a job for which he or she was not suited—and, worse, did not like. The successful outcome involved helping the employee remove him- or herself from the job or the organization in a positive way.

In an era in which a focus on retention of employees seems all-important, such "successful" outcomes may seem counterintuitive. However, once the amount of time, energy, and stress required in order to try to help someone change his or her mind about a job is totaled up, the logic becomes clear. Many managers would be better off with no one in the job than with someone who is unhappy and is not going to get any happier, regardless of what anyone does.

We have stressed several times so far the importance of being careful about whom you hire. Unfortunately, the reality is that most managers are likely to take over a group built by someone else, perhaps even for another task (the "inheritance tax"). Given the rate of change in most businesses today, the work that was once of interest to a particular employee may permanently disappear.

When the task of a group changes radically, all employees will react with anxiety and some with a sense of loss. It will take time and managerial support to help employees adapt to such change. Many will. Those who find new work today that is consistent with their pattern of interests will probably make such an adjustment while working under a reasonably effective manager. However, some may not.

Once the manager has been able to determine that most employees have adapted and are moving ahead with new work tasks and processes but that some individuals have not, interventions in addition to developmental coaching per se may be called for. Interest patterns are rather stable and tend not to change over the course of our lives, even though the work we do to satisfy those interest patterns may change dramatically (Holland, 1992). Contrary to what many managers believe, we cannot make ourselves like something we don't like. For example, a manager who, as a supervisor, loves hands-on contact with her employees may find the political demands brought on by the growth of her unit and her de facto rise to upper-middle management to be both boring and stressful. The computer scientist who loves interfacing with customers may find the work of sitting at a terminal writing code to be abjectly uninspiring. As the old saying goes, promote your best salesperson to sales manager, and you may lose a good salesperson and gain a lousy sales manager.

Failure to confront and accept an individual employee's lack of interest in a particular job can lead to hard feelings, declining morale, and poor performance. Managers can become increasingly frustrated by the failure of their attempts to help individuals change. Employees may display a variety of reactions, including anger at their managers, as well as anger at themselves about their inability to "get on board." Both would be better off considering the possibility of helping an employee find stimulating work inside or outside the immediate coaching manager's business unit, as appropriate.

Managers should also be aware that many employees don't know how to manage their own careers. Even the brightest people in your organization may not understand the importance of thinking about what they really want out of life. Secondary and higher educational institutions in the western world don't always help, either. Take it as a given that some of your people will be in the wrong place at the wrong time and not really know it. This may represent the most common barrier to coachability.

The Impact of Personal Stress

When an individual, even a great employee, is caught up in a significant personal or family dilemma, he or she may be far less able to engage in learning activities at work. One of our coaching managers described the importance of "paying attention to the whole person." It may be important to understand the basic problems associated with having too many stressors in one's life. We discuss this problem in much greater detail in a later chapter. Here, we offer a few important points.

People actually need a certain level of stress in order to function effectively. Stress is the natural outgrowth of our efforts to adapt and master the challenges in life. You can think of each of us as having a kind of "set point" at which we are at our best. We may feel anxious, but we feel challenged as well. We're in a good fight, but we think we have a chance of winning.

Confrontation with additional stressors when we are already at the set point can take us to a state of distress that impairs our ability to function. The more threatening the stressor, the more distress is added to the individual's burden. Illness, child care issues, divorce, problems with an elderly parent, alcoholism or drug use, and emotional crises are just a few of the problems that can bring with them an acute level of distress. Coaching managers should be aware that the percentage of individuals in the workforce who are experiencing such levels of personal stress could be higher than they might expect. Some researchers estimate that as many as 25% of workers suffer from stress-related disorders (Sperry, 1993).

The coaching manager's approach to the individual who is experiencing a stress-related problem might be somewhat different from that of trying to engage the individual with low self-esteem, the underestimator. The matter may be one of timing. The stress-related problems may be transient. An employee with family problems may respond well to a solution, such as moving to a part-time status, which has been negotiated between the employee and his or her coaching manager. Such a solution may involve providing support or time off to the employee while the impact of the stress is being felt.

In both instances, we recommend that coaching managers be prepared to call their company's employee assistance program, human resource staff, or company medical consultants for support. Trying to work with an employee who is engrossed in a serious stress-related or self-esteem-based problem can be very stressful in and of itself. The manager needs focused support from someone knowledgeable about the role that personal stress can play on learning and performance.

When Diversity Becomes a Barrier

Given the diversity of the workplace, it is likely that coaching managers will find themselves coaching people from a different gender, age-group, race, ethnic group, cultural group, sexual orientation, or country of origin. The question we now confront is "To what degree is diversity between coach and employee a potential barrier to their ability to build an effective coaching relationship?" In discussing this challenge with our coaches, we hear near unanimity in the belief that diversity represents a challenge but should not be seen as representing an insurmountable barrier to effective developmental coaching. It is essential that the coach, and if possible, the coachee, be vigilant regarding the potential impact of diversity of experience, background, outlook, and even personal style. Diversity represents a potential challenge to the coaching relationship in several ways.

First, diversity can make effective communication more difficult. Coach and coachee may not understand what the other means. The word *leadership,* for example, can have very different meanings when viewed through a cultural lens. Some think of the leader as facilitator, whereas others think of the leader as director. Making sure there is agreement on the meaning of important words is essential in defining and interpreting performance processes, goals, and outcomes.

Diversity also represents a challenge to empathy, the ability to put oneself in the position of others and see the world through their eyes. Most of our coaches have told us that empathy is possible once the impact of diversity is understood and mutually explored. While talking about leadership, sales, or other interpersonal activities, coaching managers will often ask questions such as "How might you address this back home?" Hearing how the coachee sees the situation, which may be quite different from the perspective of the coaching manager, helps the coaching manager step into the coachee's point of view. The coach needs to ask for the help of the coachee to make this leap of understanding. If the coach ignores the notion, for instance, that it might be difficult to be the only person of color on a new team, he or she may be missing a very important influence on that individual's development.

For this reason, some scholars have suggested that the greater the level of similarity between coach/mentor and coachee/protégé, the more likely the coaching or mentoring relationship is to be successful (Kram & Bragar, 1992). Similarity of race, age, gender, or culture of origin between manager and employee, however, is no longer possible in every case, nor is it always desirable, for a variety of reasons. It is typically important for both coach and coachee to learn how to work cross-culturally in order to do their jobs. The coaching relationship then offers a vehicle for growth for both parties. At the same time, there may be a limit to how far even the best coaching manager and coachee can go toward closing the diversity gap. The coaching manager can't be all things to all people, and neither can the coachee. The reality is that we all probably need a bit of support from someone who has personally experienced and understands our culture, as well as support from people who are quite different from ourselves.

Gail McGuire (1999), in her study of a large financial services firm in the United States, found that Caucasian women and women and men of color were able to access coaching or mentoring help with a frequency approximately equal to that of Caucasian men; this suggests that the barriers of diversity do not inhibit the building of coaching connections. However, she did find that what was discussed in the coaching relationship was influenced by the gender and race of both coach and coachee.

McGuire (1999) also found that similarity seemed to have an impact on the degree to which emotional closeness developed between coach and coachee. Role modeling and friendships were less likely to develop in the absence of similarity of background. However, it was not clear whether similarity of gender or race had an impact on the degree to which coach and coachee addressed more career-related concerns, such as performance coaching, feedback, and assignment of challenging work.

As we have stressed, coaching and mentoring are not the same. Coaching is more focused on the work and is less likely to involve the kind of emotional closeness found in mentor relationships. As such, coaching might be particularly well suited to a diverse workforce and a diverse world. Expectations of coaches are different from those of mentors. Although much research remains to be done on this critically important area, we can only conclude at this time that dissimilarity of backgrounds can be a barrier to coachability, but it doesn't have to be. The challenge is for the coach and coachee to move beyond dissimilarity and create an effective enough coaching relationship so that learning can continue.

A Mismatch Between the Career Stage of the Employee and the Career Stage of the Manager

Many of our coaching managers have told us that they may vary their approaches to coaching in response to, among other things, the career stage of the employee. Some coaching managers report that they tend to coach newer employees more frequently. Some report that they coach senior-level employees less. Some coach highly experienced employees only when directly asked. In working with senior-level employees, they focus on making sure that they get very challenging assignments and have the right resources to address them.

This finding is consistent with the findings of management researchers Lloyd Baird and Kathy Kram (1984). They came to the intuitively appealing conclusion that at different career stages, people have different needs. They described five distinct career stages, all of which are relevant to coaching. Those stages and the associated needs that are paramount at each stage are listed in Table 6.2. The five stages are establishment (just getting started), early career, advancement, maintenance, and exit.

Table 6.2   Career Stages and Coaching

Career Stage	Personal Need
Establishment	The new employee probably has the greatest need for coaching.
Early career	Continued need for coaching and support, though the employee is increasingly able to work autonomously. May need more career guidance as part of coaching.
Advancement	Exposure to senior management and challenging work. Sponsorship and support for taking on new challenges.
Maintenance	Autonomy in his or her work. Opportunities to help others develop.
Exit	Consultative roles that still have an impact.

SOURCE: From "Career Dynamics: Managing the Superior/Subordinate Relationship," by L. Baird and K. Kram, 1984, *Organizational Dynamics, 12*(4), 54.

Early in an employee's career, during the establishment stage and just beyond, there is an acute need for coaching and feedback because the employee may know very little about how to survive and be productive in the new career and organization. Employees in the establishment and early career stages have the most to learn in the shortest possible time.

In the advancement phase, individuals need to take on more work independently and show what they can do. In essence, they become progressively more capable of thinking through and solving problems on their own or with their teams, and they need less basic guidance. The individual in the advancement stage may be strongly focused on his or her own career and have less interest in or energy for helping others. We remind the reader again that given the apparent desire for autonomy on the part of individuals in the advancement stage, it's easy to ignore them. In many cases, this is unwise. They may still want the help of at least a "sounding board."

In the maintenance phase, particularly if the individual has been successful, he or she is expected to coach. The employee, now often a manager, has significant responsibilities for taking autonomous action and feels less of a need to "prove" something to others. He or she may have more interest in building an organization and in the development of others. Again, such an individual may be ignored. The same cautionary note is sounded. The fact that someone has "made it" doesn't mean that he or she doesn't want and need developmental coaching and certainly feedback.

Finally, in the exit stage, the employee's upward mobility is limited. He or she has already contributed to the firm and/or the profession but still wants to have an impact. Many employees at this stage find the opportunity to help others develop to represent a very meaningful contribution, a dignified and helpful way to close out a career.

The potential barrier for coach and coachee emerges when each has expectations of the other that are "out of sync" with their career stages. If the coaching manager tries to coach a senior-level employee in the same way that he or she coaches a junior-level employee, the senior employee may feel infantilized and rebel. Coaching and feedback become destructive rather than constructive.

A more senior employee will probably not wish to have his or her technical judgment questioned but may be open to coaching on strategic and political issues. Unfortunately, a younger coaching manager may have much less to offer in this regard. Likewise, the very new employee may have a great need for coaching. However, a manager caught up in the advancement stage may perceive that he or she has less time and energy for coaching than the new employee would like.

We caution against the view that lack of synchrony between the career stage of managers and employees has to be an overriding barrier. We have known many good coaching managers who are still early in their careers. As long as they are skilled at the use of coaching tactics and don't claim to be expert in areas or ways they are not, their effectiveness will not be undermined by their age or career stage. Likewise, we argue to managers in the advancement stage of their careers that coaching could help them advance even more rapidly. We have also seen many senior-level employees make good use of rich coaching relationships that address their real needs. This makes sense given the nature of today's work.

The concept of the career stages we have just outlined may in fact be changing in the new economy; organizations have shorter life spans, and those that do survive have to adapt to very rapid change. (Some readers who look at our list of career stages may wonder whether anyone makes it to the maintenance stage at this point!) Yet senior-level employees who accept that they may have to start their careers over from time to time, to keep up with such rapid change, may find the opportunity to engage in the give-and-take of coaching to be very useful.

An experienced manager, Jack Welch, former CEO of General Electric (GE), took advantage of (and insisted that his peers at GE do so as well) a "reverse" mentoring program. Executives needed a hands-on knowledge of the World Wide Web to guide the firm into the era of e-commerce. The best way to learn was to tap the younger, Web-savvy generation of GE workers for help. Junior employees, chosen to serve as technology coaches to senior executives, met regularly with their "coachees" to help them learn how to "surf the Web" (Schlender, 2000). Such a coaching model can work, even though the career stages of both coach and coachee may clearly seem "upside down."

Coaching managers who tell us that they coach more experienced workers just as much as newer workers say that coaching focuses on more sophisticated issues. Strategy, leadership, and client relationships are examples. This group of coaching managers believes that coaching needs to continue as part of succession planning within their business units.

Finally, we should stress again that coaching is not just for the coachee. Coaching promotes organizational learning and learning on the part of the manager. In that sense, it is the coachee's obligation to engage in coaching, at least to a degree, regardless of career stage.

Coachability: Treat Each Employee as an Individual

This exploration of the factors that promote or inhibit an individual's ability to engage with a manager in a coaching relationship may have raised more questions than answers for the reader. Although we can describe the factors that suggest a high degree of coachability, and we can describe some commonly seen barriers to coachability, ultimately, the best coaching managers don't use a formula or cookbook. They treat each employee as an individual. They are likely to try a variety of approaches to an employee's development before concluding that an employee is beyond help or is in the wrong job.

So is Roger coachable? We actually think he might be.

Stopping the Action and Starting a Coaching Dialogue

7

In this chapter, we describe the following:

- How coaching managers help employees seize valuable learning opportunities

- Techniques for stopping the action and starting a coaching dialogue that results in the employee taking ownership for learning

In the coaching-friendly context, people seize learning and coaching opportunities both formally and informally, whenever they can. Most likely, your work is fast-paced, and your business unit is filled with people who incessantly focus on action. They need to get it done, *now.* Somehow, you have to find a way to stop that action, if only briefly, and engage potential coachees in a useful coaching dialogue.

We emphasize here that we've chosen the name of this aspect of the developmental coaching process carefully. In follow-up interviews with those who have had successful executive coaching experiences we have heard that the most valuable thing the coach did was to schedule an appointment that required the coachee to stop the action and reflect on what was happening (Hunt, 2004). Executive coaching is of course different from the coaching that managers provide to their teams. However, the underlying learning process is not different. The coach has to, often actively, "hit the brakes" on the fast pace of those who are doing important and challenging work. Only when the work comes to even a brief halt can the individuals engage in meaningful reflection. This may be the toughest job that the coaching manager faces.

We list the steps in the process in Box 7.1 and will review them here. Some coaching managers follow the steps in a fairly linear way. They may stop the action by holding a scheduled coaching session. Planned meetings are particularly useful for employees who would like to bring up a complicated issue or an issue that couldn't be dealt with in a more timely fashion because of circumstances (e.g., an issue from this morning or last year). Planned meetings are also important for those who travel or whose schedules are so frantic that if they don't create a structure to protect a few minutes of their day, it won't happen.

BOX 7.1   Stopping the Action and Starting the Dialogue

1. Maintain a coaching mind-set.

   • Make sure you are ready to coach, not evaluate or appraise performance.

2. Look for useful coaching opportunities before action, after action, and/or at natural stopping points during an action.

   • Consider the learning potential of the situation at hand.

     – Does the situation involve a challenge for the employee?
     – Is it important to the employee?
     – Is it important to the organization?

3. Assess the timing.

   • Is the employee able to engage with you now about this issue or topic?

     – Can you and the employee make adequate time for the dialogue?
     – Is the employee in a receptive frame of mind or emotional state?

4. Take a minute to establish rapport (even if you know the coachee extremely well).

5. Ask reflective questions, listen, and probe for understanding.

   • When appropriate, ask follow-up questions.

     – While being empathic, help employees think about their roles, their intent, and their actions.
     – Try to help the employee avoid blaming others.

6. Help the employee define and take ownership of the real issue, challenge, or problem about which the employee needs to learn more.

   • Avoid providing premature or gratuitous feedback.
   • Avoid giving advice or jumping in with the solution.

7. Ask the employee what he or she would find useful as a next step, unless you feel that, on the basis of the issue or the potential costs of failure, you need to direct the employee to a next step.

- The employee may be ready, on the basis of self-reflection only, to try out a new approach or idea.
- The employee might find it useful for you to provide feedback on the spot.
- The employee might find it helpful to get more data about his or her performance or the issue at hand.

The reality is that most managers don't physically spend a lot of time in the same space as their employees, even those who practice "management by walking around" (MBWA). Some managers, such as those supervising employees at some distance, may spend very little time indeed. As we discussed in Chapter 4, making yourself accessible invites employees to bring learning issues to you. (Frequently, if conditions are right, they will in fact stop the action themselves.) Given the problems that we all face in making ourselves accessible to one another for any kind of business, most of our coaching managers report that they do create some formal, structured time for coaching to create accessibility. This usually takes place in person, though for some managers, routine scheduled coaching sessions take place by phone.

However, even managers who coach in a scheduled way tell us that they also look for impromptu coaching opportunities, the timing of which may not always fit the schedule. Developing effectiveness at spotting and working with good coaching opportunities can take some practice. Given that most managers have very little time, we believe that the ability to take advantage of impromptu and immediate coaching opportunities can be of enormous help to both you and your employees. When you are able to spot and make use of naturally occurring learning opportunities, the learning can potentially be immediately integrated with the work at hand. The employee can go out and test new ideas in a very timely fashion.

The coaching dialogue we describe in this chapter can be used to help extract learning from such spontaneous coaching opportunities, or it can be used in scheduled coaching meetings. The coaching dialogue, whether impromptu or formal, should also result in the employee's defining what he or she wants or needs to work on so that the employee takes psychological ownership for the learning process.

We'll walk through the steps involved in stopping the action and creating a coaching dialogue by seeing how they could be helpful in the case of Aron.

At the end of the chapter, we will present two other case examples and discuss what our approach to stopping the action and creating a dialogue might be in those situations as well.

Case 7.1: Aron, the Struggling Team Leader

Aron has been a team leader at the company for the past 3 months. He is very good technically, but his interpersonal skills leave something to be desired. Historically, Aron has been quick to jump into a discussion and always seems to have the right answer. The impact of this, of course, is that people tend to then keep their own ideas to themselves. Team members in the past reported that he was intellectually intimidating—not a bad guy, and certainly someone who was very strong in his technical area, but occasionally sarcastic and even abrasive. His manager has discussed this with Aron several times. Aron recognized that this was a problem and has been trying hard to slow down and encourage others to share their ideas. Aron said he understood and would try to work on his behavior. In light of that pledge, his manager decided to put him into the team leader role, with some coaching as support.

The feedback his manager has received more recently from the rest of his group members suggests that Aron is really trying to work on the problem, but his solution isn't necessarily making things better. (It isn't unusual for people to "overcorrect" while trying to change their behavior.) Now, instead of jumping in first, he becomes silent. He has been trying to follow the old adage "If you can't say something nice, don't say anything at all." Unfortunately, his new style confuses people. They are used to the old Aron, someone who took a strong position and held it regardless. Aron is generally somewhat quiet. Now, people don't know when he is being quiet because he is upset, because he's keeping his ideas to himself, or because he is just being himself. The net result of all this is that people sometimes still find him to be intimidating, even if less abrasive.

However, Aron is a well-intentioned, highly motivated individual. When he's not under stress, he handles himself well and genuinely tries to do the right thing. He wants his manager to help because his aspiration is to use his current assignment to prepare himself for possible promotion to a director-level position. His manager came to Aron's team meeting to do a brief presentation on a high-level strategy issue. The manager chose to stay at the team meeting after he finished his presentation because he knew it would give him a chance to watch Aron in action. When a difficult issue involving another group came up for discussion, Aron's body language and nonresponsiveness made the manager very uncomfortable. When one team member spoke to Aron, he didn't really respond; he just wrote down the team member's comments and went on to the next subject. Similar interactions occurred throughout the meeting. Team members didn't follow up on one another's comments. There was no debate. Few new ideas were generated. They also didn't seem to be having any fun. It seemed clear to the manager that Aron's meeting wasn't that productive. (The manager didn't believe that the team was being particularly quiet in response to his presence. He knew them all fairly well and knew that they were comfortable with him.)

After the meeting broke up, Aron walked toward his manager and said (so that no one else could hear), "See what I mean? I can't get anything out of these people." He seemed frustrated and started to walk back to his office.

Seizing a Coaching Opportunity With a Coaching Mind-Set

Several factors should be considered when assessing whether or not a good coaching opportunity is at hand. First of all, is the coaching manager thinking about the potential for learning that is inherent in the situation? Let's say that most of the people on Aron's team were about to go on vacation. This could readily explain their lack of involvement in the meeting and obscure the issue of whether or not Aron played a role in their behavior. In this case, however, there were no such extraneous forces at play. Aron was caught up in the action and didn't realize how he was coming across. Though there was no emotional outburst, the manager is concerned about Aron's new, more passive approach to dealing with stressful discussions, knowing that Aron is still having trouble dealing with team discussions that become tense. He knows that Aron is working on the problem, but he also knows that there may be more work to be done.

Being Vigilant for Learning Opportunities

In addition to an attitude of helpfulness, as we discussed in Chapter 5, the coaching mind-set also involves being vigilant for learning opportunities, being able to quickly relate them to the employee's needs, and then having some idea how you might intervene. Coaching doesn't have to take a lot of time if the manager is mentally prepared.

As part of this vigilance, coaching managers also have to be vigilant about their own agendas. Are they ready to coach, or are they ready to slip into the appraisal of performance for the purposes of evaluation? Let's say that in this case, the manager is increasingly concerned about members of Aron's team leaving the company. These are highly valued employees. The manager sees Aron behaving in a way that could cause the employees to disengage even more. The manager might feel a sudden surge of anger directed at Aron because of his behavior. The manager has told Aron a dozen times to be more responsive to his people. Perhaps this time, the manager feels as though his patience has run out and comes to believe that Aron isn't going to "get it," no matter what anyone says. The next stop for Aron might then be a formal performance improvement plan.

The coaching mind-set requires that a decision be made at that point. What direction should the manager take? He may be justified in treating Aron's behavior as a serious performance problem and begin a disciplinary action. If, indeed, the manager has tried to coach him on this kind of behavior a dozen times, that may be the proper direction to take. It may be helpful, if emotions are running high, for the coaching manager to do nothing immediately but reflect on what he sees and perhaps consult with others as well.

Assessing the Importance of the Opportunity

Let's assume that the manager decided that Aron was coachable and that the situation did not warrant the use of a more evaluative management tool, such as a performance improvement plan. How should the manager assess such opportunities to help Aron become a more effective team leader? Learning opportunities can come along at any time, but they predictably emerge at "punctuation marks" of life: (a) at the beginning of an activity or a new job, (b) when a result occurs that allows for the assessment of whether or not things are going in the right direction, (c) when something novel is interjected into a situation, and (d) on completion of a task or a logical unit of work, even though the larger task may not have been completed. When the work is moving along and the task involves maintenance of a well-understood process, there may be fewer important learning opportunities. Related to this, the potential for learning is likely to be greater in a situation that is challenging and takes the individual to the limits of his or her current knowledge and capabilities (Hicks & Peterson, 1997).

However, assessing the importance and therefore the learning potential of even a challenging situation also involves consideration of the level of interest the employee has in learning from that situation. The degree to which an individual is invested in learning a particular concept or skill can vary considerably from situation to situation. Alan Clardy (2000) described three different types of learner-directed learning projects, as follows.

In the *induced* learning project, the individual employee has to deal with an organizationally imposed challenge and must learn to adapt to that challenge.

The context provides the potential for learning. The employee could develop a great deal from engaging in the challenge, but this was not a challenge that she chose. The individual employee may under such circumstances be more interested in compliance. "Let's get this over with, shall we?" Simple direction rather than developmental coaching may be the most appropriate guidance from the manager in such a situation: "This is the way you have to fill out your expense forms; we all have to do it this way, so let's get onboard and do it right."

In a *voluntary* learning project, the individual employee, curious about something, digs into a problem with no organizational prodding. The employee's motivation to learn is probably high, though there may or may not be a payoff for the organization. Entrepreneurial employees in particular may stumble on an interesting idea and spend a great deal of time on it, sometimes annoying their managers in the process. The reality is that a manager can't necessarily be expected to respond to every employee idea, particularly if those ideas are tangential to the work of his or her team.

Probably the greatest learning potential exists when the individual's motivation meets the organization's needs head-on. The individual employee wants to learn how to be successful in a job that the organization needs him or her to do. In such a *synergistic* learning project, maximum gain to both parties meets maximum challenge under circumstances of maximum motivation. This is an important situation from the employee's perspective. It is also an important situation from the organization's perspective. The learning potential is enormous.

Note two points with regard to learning potential. We state again that if you have been relatively careful in hiring, employees are more likely to want to take on the challenge in which the organization needs them to engage, making synergistic learning projects more likely to occur. However, the employee also has to know what that challenge is! Consider again the Gallup study of 12 core elements linked to productivity, profitability, and retention (Buckingham & Coffman, 1999). Core element number one is knowledge of "what is expected of me." Employees need to know, at least generally, what they need to learn.

Let's look at a simple example. If employees know that the firm has determined that sales associates need to become more adept at showing how the firm's products can integrate with those of its competitors, they will likely be motivated to learn about the technical issues that must be addressed in such an integration. If employees don't know what the firm wants, it will be harder for them to look for appropriate learning opportunities on their own.

One of the concerns that managers have when they begin to coach is that they will be perceived as "micromanaging" their employees. We have rarely heard this complaint from employees when the manager focuses his or her coaching efforts on important aspects of the employee's actions or behavior. If the manager has a sense of what the employee is trying to achieve and the challenges the employee faces, he or she will be much better positioned to intervene with coaching in important situations.

This situation seems to have a great deal of learning potential for Aron. From his perspective, it is synergistic. He wants to learn, and it is important to the organization that he be successful. The situation also seems to represent a significant challenge for Aron because it calls on him to develop new interpersonal skills—not an easy thing to do. This situation is important, then, and worthy of intervention.

Is the Timing Right?

Just because the situation has a high learning potential doesn't mean that a focus on learning will necessarily be appropriate. The dictum to stop the action and seize the opportunity suggests that Aron's manager would do well to ask Aron to talk right after the meeting. His manager could immediately begin the process of trying to establish a coaching dialogue.

However, let's say that Aron is ill that day. He may not feel up to talking about what just happened. Perhaps he has no time because he must hurry off to a meeting with the CEO. If so, he may be so anxious about the next meeting that he won't be able to concentrate on learning from the most recent one. Immediacy is important. If you wait too long to intervene, you can lose the benefits of immediacy: good data about what just happened, clear recall of those data, and the helpful residue of emotions that go along with the sense of being challenged. If Aron is stressed about other things, his manager's interest in discussing the matter with him right away may come across as a criticism. Immediacy isn't always possible. (And in most, though not all, cases, the coaching manager and coachee will get another chance. Unresolved problems and learning issues tend to recur.)

In this case, Aron is annoyed, but this doesn't seem to be a major problem. He doesn't have anything else pressing, and his manager has the time. Because he and Aron have talked about this issue previously, the manager anticipates that it will take about 15 minutes to talk with Aron about what has transpired. If the discussion is going to be difficult or complex, they may need to talk for 30 minutes or an hour. In any case, the coaching manager needs to make a rough estimate of how much time the discussion might take (you'll never know for sure) and whether or not that is realistic for both parties. If the manager and/or the employee don't have the time now, at least they can schedule a follow-up meeting. If the follow-up meeting is scheduled right away, even though it may not take place for several days, both parties know the issues and may still be able to draw on their experiences from the meeting for learning.

Establish or Reestablish Rapport

If the coaching manager and employee haven't done so already, they could make good use of a few minutes of small talk, just to establish rapport and comfort. The degree to which the manager needs to attend to rapport has to do with the nature of his or her relationship with the employee. If the relationship is solid, particularly if the two have been working on a particular issue already, as is the case with Aron and his manager, it may feel right to jump in and start the coaching dialogue right away. However, we suggest that the coaching manager make it clear that he or she would like to talk about what has just happened (or that recent situation, etc.) if this has not already been established. If the employee is expecting a social chat, the manager may need to signal that he or she would like to talk about something important.

In this case, Aron's manager said: "Thanks for inviting me to the meeting, Aron; it saved me a lot of time, not having to pursue everyone on your team to talk about this new strategy. It was also good for me to get a sense of how you and the team are doing, since we've been talking about that in our meetings. Do you have a few minutes to debrief?" Aron responded in the affirmative out of his frustration with the team, his wish that he could do something to improve their ability to communicate with one another, and the knowledge that his ability to manage the team is important to his career. We can guess that he was also a bit nervous having his boss in the room and wanted to appear cooperative (note that even when people want to learn, impression management is still a concern).

Aron's manager, then, actually asked permission to stop the action. Granted, it might have been hard for Aron to say no at that point, but his manager was purposefully respectful of Aron and his time. His tone of voice also signaled that he recognized that this was a tough issue for Aron and that he wanted to help. In asking for permission, however, he also asked Aron for his active participation in what Aron had come to understand was a coaching or learning discussion. If Aron had been ill, had another major challenge coming up in the next few minutes, or was so angry he couldn't talk about it, he would have had an out.

Ask Reflective Questions, Listen for Understanding

As we have already stated, coaching, particularly developmental coaching, is not just feedback! We can't emphasize this enough. From our consultation and training experiences, we have come to understand that many well-meaning managers believe that when they give feedback, they are coaching. Certainly feedback is an important part of coaching. Furthermore, managers who provide carefully thought-through feedback do a lot better by their employees than those who don't. Nevertheless, feedback by itself, no matter how immediate, sometimes backfires. A story from one of our managers illustrates the point.

She was working with a high-potential employee who had a habit of over-committing. The employee, a very talented but somewhat scattered young man, was motivated to do the right thing for his company and his own career. However, he seemed to have a characterological tendency to say yes when he should have said no. Whenever the manager caught him doing that, she would try immediately to give him balanced feedback about his having taken on yet another commitment that he might not be able to honor.

The problem is the employee's role involved highly visible customer service tasks. He thought that he probably shouldn't be saying no too often and quickly defended his position. His manager ended up feeling as though "he just wasn't listening; he was just defending his actions," which was true. However, the employee felt that he should defend his actions. He hadn't stopped to think for himself about decision-making rules that might govern when to say yes and when to say no. He hadn't really thought through the impact of his behavior. Perhaps most important, he took no ownership for the issue. He felt that his boss was wrong, that his boss didn't understand him, and ultimately that he was being micromanaged. His manager had taken ownership of the problem. Two highly motivated individuals had created a non-coaching-friendly context in their relationship. Advocacy of one's position, no matter how carefully thought out and how caringly delivered, doesn't necessarily support learning. Feedback in advance of an initial self-reflection on the part of the learner is advocacy. It is very close to the "fix 'em" model of coaching discussed in Chapter 5.

In the 7 years since we wrote the first edition of this book, we have come to truly appreciate the absolute power of the urge to "fix 'em" and jump right to feedback. It is absolutely addictive. It is so difficult to keep one's mouth shut when one knows the right answer, it seems (of course, we've got the same problem!). We have seen very well-intentioned people in our on-campus coaching program for students be told specifically, "Don't start with feedback; make sure you give them a chance to talk first," and within hours of receiving such instructions, they start giving away feedback like it's going out of style. Of course, some of those folks are unable to take on a coaching mind-set, ever. Some have just slipped back into the "fix 'em" mode. You can't "fix 'em." You're not that powerful. Only the coachee can fix him- or herself and, even then, only if he or she chooses to do so. You can help. (If that fails, you can utilize disciplinary tools to resolve the problem.) Relax and see what you can learn.

As a coaching manager, there is a power differential between you and your employees. To a surprising degree, they want to please you or at least stay out of harm's way in their relationship with you. If you signal that you have the right answer, the employee's natural response may be to acquiesce to your point of view. After all, you seem wiser, have a position of authority, and may even be older. To understand this problem more thoroughly, it is useful to consider the definition of the word *dialogue*.

Drawing on the work of David Bohm, Peter Senge (1990) calls our attention to the distinction between a discussion and a dialogue. In a *discussion*, the participants are trying to persuade one another of the correctness of their point of view. Discussion represents the most common form of interaction for most of us when we talk about issues of importance. Aron's manager could have started the coaching session by pointing out to Aron that his body language tends to be intimidating and that the impact of his intimidating style is that his team is unwilling to risk being open with him. A cursory reading of the case would suggest such a scenario.

How might one expect Aron to respond if confronted with that kind of feedback? He might well become defensive. He might talk about how much pressure he's under to achieve results and insist that his team should start acting like adults and tell him whether he's coming across inappropriately. We can guess where such a discussion might lead. Aron's manager might come back with a more direct confrontation, perhaps offering several examples. Aron, being human, might feel the need to deflect each example. Aron has a point of view, which in fact is quite valid. Likewise, Aron's boss has some useful insight as to the dynamics taking place between Aron and his team.

In a *dialogue*, however, the parties attempt to engage in an interaction that can help explore the underlying dynamics, assumptions, or perceptions that serve to support whatever behavior is taking place on the surface. The first task of the coaching manager, then, is to encourage the coachee to explore his or her own perceptions of or assumptions about what has transpired. If Aron can be honest with himself (and in a coaching-friendly context, one hopes this is possible), then he can explore his own behavior and the factors that drive the behavior. We illustrate this below.

The coaching managers in our research report that the easiest way to create a dialogue is to ask questions while withholding criticism, feedback, or advice. A properly phrased question can encourage both parties to think about what has happened without making either feel defensive.

Some managers are reluctant to ask questions. They may not believe that employees will honestly or accurately appraise what they have done or be open about the assumptions that guided their actions. Of course, if the employee has reason to be defensive—if the context is not coaching-friendly—this is likely to be the case. If the context is coaching-friendly, a question can offer a powerful invitation to reflect on what has happened, why, and what might be done differently next time.

Given that most interactions in business are probably more aptly characterized as discussions (the advocacy of a position), we accept that asking questions instead of telling others what to do may be quite a change for the average manager. Nevertheless, the feedback we have received is that a good question is often far more powerful than a great directive. Indeed, research strongly suggests that the behavior of managers who are seen by others as creating the most learning in their organizations includes the frequent use of questions that encourage employees to think for themselves about the issues at hand (Ellinger, Watkins, & Bostrom, 1999).

Examples of useful dialogue-building questions can be found in Box 7.2. These questions are all intended to encourage individuals (or a team, as the case may be) to think about what just happened and about the role they played in it. Although employees may need to talk about their context or the other people involved, they fundamentally have little control over others. They can learn the most from reflecting on themselves, their actions, their assumptions, their goals, and the outcomes that occurred in response.

BOX 7.2   Basic Introductory Questions Useful for Creating a Coaching Dialogue

How did it go for you today?

- Follow-up probes: Tell me about it. What happened then? Let's go over the details.

What did you see taking place?

- This question is more specific than the previous question and encourages coachees to focus specifically on their own observations, not the manager's. It offers an implicit validation that the employee's point of view is important.

What were you trying to accomplish?

- This question encourages coachees to reflect on their intent in a given situation.
- Follow-up probes: How did that work? Can you tell me more about what you did there? What did they do next? What kind of results did that yield?

- Questions about intent can be very useful for well-motivated or assertive/aggressive learners. For those individuals who push too hard, for instance, a useful follow-up question might be "How do you think others responded to you? How did others see your actions?"

A debriefing series for use in helping an employee think about a process:

- What do you think you need to keep doing?
- What do you think you need to start doing?
- What do you think you need to stop doing?

A debriefing series for use after a project (courtesy of the U.S. Army's after-action review [Garvin, 2000]):

- What did we (you) set out to do?
- What did we (you) actually do?
- Why was there a difference?

Questions to avoid:

- Questions that suggest blame.
- Questions that encourage the learner to dig into the "why" before you both have a clear picture of what happened.

Aron's manager posed the simple question "How did it go for you in there?" Because the two of them had been working on Aron's team leadership skills, Aron was ready to respond with his own perceptions of what had taken place. He talked of his frustration and how the team didn't seem to be responding to his efforts. His manager then followed up with "What kind of response were you hoping for?" Aron quickly responded, "I want them to offer some suggestions that will help us move forward again."

With a little prodding in the form of a follow-up question from his manager, Aron began to talk about what he'd recently learned about the group's previous leader. That individual had been even more directive than Aron. The team had dealt with him by being passive, just following orders. This was new information for Aron's manager. It gave him a clearer sense of just how difficult the situation was going to be for Aron. Aron not only had to learn how to alter his own management style; he also had to learn to deal with a team that had already been trained by a previous team leader to be passive. Aron finished his initial reflection by stating, "I somehow think that knowing this, knowing how they have learned to treat team leaders, has made me a bit defeatist. I'm trying not to talk over them or tell them what to do. Maybe I've taken it a bit too far. Clearly, I'm going to have to do something different to get them to work with me."

In a coaching dialogue, both participants—not just the coachee—frequently report that they learned something. Yes, the coachee has a chance to step back and examine his or her actions from a somewhat dispassionate perspective. The coaching manager, however, learns more about the coachee and his or her challenges. In this case, the manager learned that though he may have assumed that Aron was solely responsible for the poor quality of the interaction in the team meeting, the situation is more complicated than that. It is as if both employee and coaching manager get a chance together to rerun an imaginary but, ideally, realistic mental video of what has just taken place. Such is the nature of reflection. Reflecting on an event and pondering what has happened, carefully and persistently, allows the individual learner to try and make sense of what has happened and to give it meaning (Daudelin, 1996). The added benefit the coaching manager brings to the process is a sense of connectedness. Learning is a social activity. The presence of another person implies that what is taking place is important, offers encouragement, and at times provides another perspective (Seibert, 1999).

The coaching dialogue will come to a quick end, however, if the coaching manager doesn't listen. We think of listening as one of the most critical components of developmental coaching because it supports individuals' efforts to reflect more deeply on their goals, assumptions, and actions. The coaching manager needs to demonstrate listening with behaviors such as holding eye contact (when culturally appropriate), not talking, summarizing what has been said, asking clarifying questions, and following up on what the coachee has said.

Failure to listen on the part of the coaching manager encourages the dialogue to evolve into a discussion in which the parties return to advocating the position. One of the most common assumptions on the part of the manager that can interfere with listening is that employees are making excuses when they say they are responsible for only part of the problem the manager may have observed. When the manager isn't ready to listen to and deal with the complexity of a situation such as Aron's, advocacy and defensiveness almost invariably emerge, and the potential for learning is diminished.

Researchers tell us that a sense of autonomy on the part of the learner is necessary if learning from reflection is to take place (Seibert, 1999). Coachees need the chance to stop and think for themselves before managers interject their thoughts. The challenge for coaching managers is to remain engaged with employees and at the same time not rob them of the opportunity to independently make sense of what is going on.

On Learning to Ask Useful Questions

Given that most of those in responsible business and organizational positions feel like they're getting paid not for asking questions but rather for answering them, it's no surprise that this business of asking questions is a real challenge. Since we wrote the first edition, we've found that questions and complaints about how difficult it can be to ask useful questions have been quite common. If you're struggling with this, let us begin by taking a "coaching manager" approach and asking you a question: What in your view is the problem? Is it, in fact, lack of experience? Is it attitudinal? Is it something about your own comfort level or comfort zone that is in play here? Is it the way you come across to others when you ask questions? All of these can be important to consider. Let's look at them a bit more deeply.

Most of us in management education in the United States at least were trained in the Socratic method of teaching. Classically, we ask students to read a case or some text and then come into class prepared for a case discussion. We then ask them questions intended not only to raise key facts from the case but also to explore how different members of the class might interpret and then act upon those facts. Differences of opinion surface, in a good class session, which then helps students see the value of exploring multiple perspectives when trying to solve a business problem. A great case teacher, like a great counselor, therapist, or consultant, can accomplish much without ever offering a declarative statement.

When one sees great case teachers in action, it's obvious that they are disciplined. They don't fall into the trap of ending the discussion early by offering the right answer. (Students are perhaps even more vulnerable to such a tendency than employees are.) The "right answer" delivered from on high can curtail the learning opportunity. This is enormously frustrating for some students. They want the right answer. Discipline is required to keep them thinking (assuming they are ready and have the right preparation for such tough discussions).

They are also practiced. If you ask them how they came to be so effective, they will tell you that with practice they have developed a greater ability to "think on their feet." When conducting a case discussion in which one opens the class to the ideas of class participants, one never really knows where things are going to go. The teacher, like the coaching manager, is not in full control of the exchange, and that's a good thing. Practice helps you realize that you can depend on the admissions office, or the hiring process in your case, to get the right people in the right seats.

Practice also helps you learn how to do the following on an impromptu basis:

- Ask questions that are open-ended but that are not so general as to be without use.
- Avoid questions that call for a closed-ended or "yes versus no" type of response. Closed-ended questions resolve issues. They are useful when trying to establish the presence of a final agreement, for instance, but not as useful when exploring options.
- Use reflective listening techniques. We know that some people bristle at the idea of "parroting" back what someone has said. Largely, we disagree with those folks. Reflective listening, restating an individual's comments so as to confirm an understanding of what was said, gives both individuals time to think, in addition to ensuring shared understanding. Reflection requires thought, which brings us to our final points about practice.
- Ask probing questions. You don't have to think up every new question. You need to listen and then ask questions that deepen your understanding of what the coachee has just said. Remember that when we are listening, if we're not careful, we're actually formulating a response to what the other party has said. Try not to fall into that particular trap. Slow yourself down, listen to everything that has been said to you, and consider what you don't know. Follow the trail.
- Tolerate silence. Give the person you're talking with 3 to 5 seconds before jumping in to fill the silence. See what happens; as we've already implied, you are very likely to learn something when you do.

Exercise 7.1   Learning to Ask Questions— A Simple Exercise

You can do this exercise with anyone unless he or she has reason to distrust you. You can do this with your spouse, your friend, a direct report, and even your boss. Here's the exercise.

1. Find a partner. You and your partner are to each think about an issue around which you'd like some coaching. The issue should be one you are prepared to share with your partner.

2. Each of you will have 5 minutes in the role of coach and 5 minutes in the role of coachee. Appoint a timekeeper.

3. When you are in the coachee role, begin by explaining your issue.

4. In the coach role, your job is to try and be helpful to your partner. There's just one small rule we ask you to follow. You're not allowed to make any statement that ends in anything other than a question mark. No periods or exclamation points allowed.

5. You should then debrief. As the coach, talk about what you felt like and the challenges you experienced when trying not to make a statement. As the coachee, report on whether or not you actually received help from the process. We think you'll both be quite surprised.

We've done this exercise with quite a few teams and classes, across an amazing age range. The results are always the same. If you read this book, you should be well positioned to predict how people will respond. We'll give you one hint; most coachees are surprised to find that just 5 minutes of dialogue allowed them to feel some sense of progress toward the resolution of their problem. Dialogue can really work!

Our point here, though, is that we can't offer you a cookbook that will help you build your skills in dialogue. Practice is key. Feedback from others can help.

As we've implied here, your attitude and your actions are intertwined when it comes to your ability to ask useful questions. We've mentioned the fact that when you ask a question, unless it is a leading question ("Isn't it true that you stole that money?" is actually not a question but an accusation that ends in a question mark), you are sharing responsibility for a dialogue with someone else, sharing control. Being in control has helped you get things done in the past. Sharing control can lead to a bit of anxiety. Managing that anxiety then is a part of the challenge of being a good participant in a dialogue. Again, practice and careful attention to the setup for coaching can help mitigate that anxiety.

Before leaving this topic, however, we should mention one other factor related to the fact that the task of creating a coaching dialogue may take you outside your comfort zone. We've known a number of well-intentioned managers who embraced the model described here but were betrayed by their body language, their tone of voice, and other aspects of their presentation of which they were not aware. They knew that a dialogue could be valuable, but when they tried to institute such a dialogue they looked pained, or perhaps came across as though they were being evaluative, even when they weren't. That is a truly unfortunate outcome, but it doesn't have to scuttle your efforts completely.

Step 1 is to develop an awareness of the tendency. If you know you look more like a state prosecutor than a manager when you ask a question, let others know you're aware and that this is unintended. Make it clear that it's just your style, not your plan. You may also try to work on the behavior a bit. Once you have awareness of the behavior, you may need feedback to help you modulate your change effort. The problem with behavioral issues such as these is precisely the fact that they can be so divorced from your intent. You don't see it, and you don't intend it, but others do. You need an extra pair of eyes to help you see how you impact others.

Help the Employee Define and Take Ownership of the Real Issue

Having ventilated his feelings a bit and interjected this new information about his team into the discussion, Aron felt better. However, he still had not clearly articulated how his actions helped or hurt his efforts to be an effective team leader. Interspersed with an occasional "That is frustrating," his manager kept asking questions, encouraging Aron to think about what he was trying to accomplish and what he might need to do differently. He accepted that Aron was indeed not talking over people but kept encouraging him to think about whether or not he was doing anything that might still be getting in the way of his effort to generate more useful interaction in the team meetings. After several minutes, Aron said, "I know I look stiff to them. My wife has told me the same thing. I get that way now especially when I'm frustrated. Others have told me I stop looking at people, you know, making eye contact. It's better than saying something sarcastic, I suppose, but I become very quiet. That probably isn't helping."

Aron's self-assessment fit with his manager's observation. However, the manager still had to be careful not to step in and either define the problem for Aron or start giving advice that Aron might not be able to follow. Aron is well motivated. However, it isn't easy to change one's leadership style. Whatever action he may plan to take next time to improve the situation, he'll probably be committed to the tough work of following through on the plan if it is his idea or if it will help him achieve a goal that is important to him. And as is often the case in a coaching-friendly context, Aron recognized the problem. There was no need for the manager to offer additional feedback to correct his perception. The manager said, "What you're saying makes sense to me." The manager then used a follow-up question to help Aron plan his next series of actions: "If you are right, what do you think you should do?"

Aron was used to such questions from his manager and found them helpful. He said, "Clearly, I need to keep not interrupting and not go back to dictating solutions. I can't go back to that. I think I need to be more patient, though. The other thing I need to do is change the way I respond to them. I have to watch the body language and try to do something to let them know that I do want to hear them out. I have to keep reminding myself that this is going to take some time. If I don't get so frustrated, it should be easier to do something other than frown. That will be tough for me, but I'm sure that I'm sending the wrong message. I guess what I need to do differently is raise this as an issue. I'll put it out there that I'm trying to build a more effective team. I realize their old manager was something of an autocrat, and I could be one too. I'm trying not to do that. I need them to help . . . Something like that."

Several forces are at work here, and Aron's last comments address them all for the most part. Aron's body language during the team meeting sent the wrong message. He can work on changing that. However, underlying his behavior was his frustration. His frustration emerged because his team wasn't able to meet him halfway. He's pulled back, but they haven't responded. Now he is more aware that it will take time for his team to develop a better style of interacting in the meetings. Aron's solution represents an explicit acknowledgment of what he can do to further a change process for his team as well as for himself. Most important, Aron owns the problem and the solution. Granted, it isn't all of his making, but he sees his own role and is developing a preliminary plan for doing something differently. He is more aware of the role his attitude is playing in the situation and wants to work harder on applying an important social skill: smiling.

Will this work? We don't know. Aron will have to try it and see. Real change takes time. Aron will probably have to ease into the new behaviors. It may be quite uncomfortable for everyone if Aron finds himself smiling throughout the entire next team meeting. The real payoff will be not in whether or not Aron smiles but in whether or not his behavior helps move the group toward more effective communications.

Aron's manager did not have to do much more than stop the action, encourage Aron to reflect on his own behavior by asking the appropriate questions, and control his own impulse to jump in and "fix" the situation. The connections in Aron's mind between his own actions and outcomes in his interaction with his team became clearer in the process. Significant learning has taken place.

Follow-Up: Ask the Employee About Useful Next Steps

The interaction we have highlighted here represents one piece of an ongoing coaching dialogue between Aron and his manager. We can assume that they will continue capturing coaching moments such as this as they move ahead. However, it will probably be very useful for Aron and his manager to discuss explicitly what kind of follow-up might promote continued progress. Aron told his manager that he was meeting with the team again the next day. He was going to pay close attention to how he was coming across. He wanted to try and be at least a little more patient with the team and be a bit more friendly. He wanted to raise the issue with them, as he and his manager had discussed. He promised his manager that he'd let him know how it went. Aron's manager believed, on the basis of their previous efforts, that Aron would indeed observe his behavior more closely and report back to him.

Alternatively, Aron might have found it helpful to have his manager sit in on another team meeting or even talk with members of the team himself. Aron's manager would then have to provide balanced feedback, holding up the mirror to give Aron more information about his behavior. Note that the step of providing formal feedback to Aron would take place as part of a process in which Aron was actively engaged.

What if Aron did not want to actively engage in the coaching process? We remind you again that as Aron's manager, you would probably have to nurture his participation by creating a coaching-friendly context. A high level of openness, honesty, and vulnerability on Aron's part characterizes the dialogue described here. Aron has to truly believe that his learning and his success are important priorities for his manager. He also has to get used to the idea that every so often, the action will stop, and reflection and learning will be prioritized.

Practice Cases: Stopping the Action and Starting the Dialogue

In the following cases, consider whether or not it would potentially be useful to stop the action and create a coaching dialogue. If so, what questions might you use to start the dialogue? Read the case first and then read our commentary. These cases are disguised; they are based on scenarios provided to us by human resource and leadership development managers from firms we provided with training in developmental coaching as part of an executive education program.

Case 7.2: Is John Headed for Burnout?

John has been a project manager at a company for the past 2 years. His projects are completed on time and on budget. He is quite gifted technically. He is also very nice when dealing with others—too nice, in fact. He is successful because he is doing much more than his share of the work. He won't push back on his colleagues, delegate more, or hold them accountable for scheduling and workload. Recently, he was looking tired and complained of a cold that wouldn't go away. John is a very proud individual, and he wants to get ahead at the company. But his manager also knows that he'll burn out at this rate. His work style would cause even more trouble at the senior management level to which John aspires. His manager sent John an e-mail asking him to meet for lunch. John sent back a very nicely worded response, thanking the manager but stating that he just didn't have the time right now; he was up to his elbows in work and totally stressed. Perhaps he could call his manager when he got back from the customer site next week? His manager wondered whether or not she should walk down to his office and have a chat with him.

Commentary: This is a difficult situation that many managers know well. One of your most valued resources, a dedicated manager, is probably working himself beyond a level that is wise for him or for the company. Of course, the company is at least partly to blame. The question here is whether or not there is learning potential in the situation, and if there is, is the timing right to stop the action? If the manager decides to stop the action, how can she begin a useful dialogue?

We have had participants in executive education programs take this case in two directions. Is John going to be able to learn from a coaching intervention at this point? The answer may be no. If he is so consumed with the needs of his current client, it may be very difficult to create a learning opportunity no matter how important the situation might be. Clearly, however, some type of intervention is warranted. We would suggest that the manager let John know that even though the time isn't right, it is important that the two of them talk and arrange a meeting after his return. The coaching manager in this case has to remember that she can't necessarily fix the problem all at once. She could order John to take a break. Would any learning take place under such a circumstance? Probably not. It isn't clear that John wants or feels the need to change. He is not taking any ownership of the problem at this point. (If the meeting is delayed, the manager should take a few minutes to jot down her thoughts and concerns so that her memories will be fresh when they do meet.)

Alternatively, let's say that the manager was aware that John actually had some health or family problems. She might then direct him to slow down a bit, thinking that he would at least comply with a directive. The manager could then have a follow-up coaching dialogue to explore John's interest in changing his management style.

If the manager chose to talk with him that same day, we would recommend that she be respectful of the fact that John had already declined the opportunity to talk. An opening comment such as "John, I know you're busy, but I think this is important" might convey that sense of respect. The manager could undertake the task by asking questions (remember, John already knows how stressed out he is and doesn't need feedback on that point) to help him express what he is trying to do and consider whether or not another approach might help. She would probably know fairly quickly whether or not John was ready to stop the action and reflect on his behavior.

Case 7.3: Sara, the Frustrated Superstar

Sara is one of the best account managers on the staff. In her 2 years with the firm, she has consistently performed at or above the level of other "best performers" in the company. She likes the company but fears that it will take forever for her to move up the ranks to program manager. Her manager knows from previous discussions with her that she aspires to a leadership position and wants to have a big impact. (Her work is global, but she and her manager talk by phone for an hour each week and meet when she is in town. She understands her manager's approach to coaching and has made good use of it in the past.)

Sara has expressed some of her frustration with how long it takes to move up at the firm. However, her manager also knows that she has a lot to learn about the challenges of sustaining long-term client relationships through difficult times. She is technologically savvy and good with people but doesn't have a deeper feel for the economic drivers in customer relationships. Her inexperience in this area clearly influenced the results of the project she completed yesterday. Her work was timely and effective, but her failure to mobilize the right team to help her led to some significant cost overruns. The firm will make very little money as a result. Sara has asked to speak with her manager about the project and her career.

Commentary: This is an important learning opportunity. The timing is right as well. The project is coming to an end, and Sara has asked to speak with her manager. The tricky problem for the manager is his awareness of her frustration and her desire to move ahead quickly. This is not an unusual problem for a manager with bright, ambitious employees. Such employees are likely to be very action oriented. However, this manager is acutely aware that there are important issues about which his employee must learn more before she can advance.

We would recommend the manager begin by reestablishing rapport (chatting a bit) and letting Sara know that there are a few items to be discussed, while making it clear that he wants to hear her agenda first. If her career concerns and her desire to move up are paramount in her mind, it makes sense to deal with those first, by thoroughly hearing her out. By listening in-depth, the manager allows her to take full ownership for her goals and the steps it will take to reach them.

It would then be helpful to outline to Sara exactly what is required for promotion to the next level (thus defining success) and begin to create the dialogue by asking her how she feels she is doing in relation to those promotion criteria. If Sara and her manager have established an effective coaching relationship, she may be able to talk about the problems she is having in building her own team and in paying more attention to the economic issues in her work. However, it is important that the manager not use the problems on Sara's most recent project as a weapon against her. Rather than telling her "You're obviously still having problems," the manager can put the onus on Sara by opening a dialogue about her own assessment of her strengths and weaknesses in relation to each competency she is required to master before being promoted. Once Sara has had a chance to offer her own perspective, the manager is in a better position to provide specific feedback to her with regard to the perceptions of others in relation to each criterion. We have been enormously impressed over the years with how frequently coachees have insight into their shortcomings. The question for them is whether or not they can effectively discuss those shortcomings without undermining their careers.

The goal here is not to "talk some sense into" Sara or to frustrate her perhaps overzealous career planning. It is, rather, to encourage her to stop and begin to think out loud about how she is doing in relation to her goals. If she is used to the process of reflecting on her work, even someone as aggressively ambitious as Sara will be able to use the opportunity to consider her career goals and the progress she is making toward achieving them. Action-oriented people can have a tough time with the idea of "stopping the action." One of the greatest benefits of developmental coaching is that it helps them learn this invaluable skill.

Stopping Time and the Coaching Dialogue

A video captures the story, the ongoing narrative. A still image, though, stops our attention and helps us dig more deeply into a specific moment in time. The coaching dialogue in that sense is a bit more like still photography. It makes it possible for us to look at the record, at least to an extent, our assumptions about what happened, and our feelings about what happened before we move along to the next task. As with all aspects of the developmental coaching model, you don't have to be perfect to be helpful. The question here is, for just a moment, whether or not you can slow time so that learning can take place.

The Coaching Mirror

8

In this chapter, you will learn the following:

- How to help your coachees see themselves and their actions more clearly by improving your own ability to observe, to create a "coaching mirror"

- How to focus your observations on what is important for the business, for you, and for your coachees

- Ideas for managing natural perception filters that impair your ability to observe

In this chapter, we describe a concept that we call the "coaching mirror." We like the metaphor of the mirror for several reasons. First, it signifies the importance of stopping to reflect on what is happening, an idea we described in detail in Chapter 7. Perhaps more important, we have found the notion of the mirror to be of enormous value in teaching managers about the somewhat abused concept of feedback, to be discussed in the next chapter. A mirror can send us a powerful message, but it can't change us. Feedback at its best is offered as a tool that recipients can use to help them achieve goals to which they are committed.

This makes feedback sound somewhat impotent, as tools for change go. However, the coaching manager can greatly enhance the power of the feedback in two ways. First, the manager can help the coachee focus on what is truly important. Second, the manager can provide the feedback in a way that makes it as useful as possible. We've already discussed the need to define success (as clearly as possible). Coaching relies on a shared understanding of what your team or organization is trying to accomplish. That shared understanding can be reinforced by observations of how the most successful performers contribute to the unit's overall effectiveness. In this chapter, we focus on observation, how to observe what you've already defined as important. In the next chapter, we discuss how you can turn those observations into useful, balanced feedback.

As you move through these chapters, keep the idea of a mirror in mind. Most of you have seen "fun house" mirrors, the kind that distort your image, making you too heavy—or, better yet, too thin. The best mirrors are quite accurate. They serve to augment what individuals looking in the mirror can see on their own. But does one look in the mirror tell the whole story? You and your coachee have selected the competencies that are most important for you to help your employee develop. Now your task is to be able to help the employee build a clear picture of what his or her performance is in relation to those competencies. That turns out to be more difficult than one might think.

How many times have you been evaluated by a boss on the basis of what you felt were erroneous data? We guess too many times to remember. Unfortunately, human beings, at least in our culture, tend to defensively conclude that information they don't like is inaccurate. We're a defensive lot, and sometimes it seems as though we have a lot to defend ourselves against.

A friend of ours happens to work as a field supervisor in the road construction industry. He tells of a common experience suffered by the workers who build roads in all sorts of bad weather. They may come on the job at 6 or 7 a.m. and work hard until 9:30 a.m. or so, at which time they, deservedly, take a coffee break. Some drivers (annoyed taxpayers probably) passing by the site during the 9:30 to 9:45 time frame will frequently yell, curse, or make obscene gestures at the "lazy government workers who do nothing all day long except waste good taxpayer dollars." At 9:45, the workers go back to work, doubtless feeling unappreciated, to say the least, for their toil on behalf of the public.

The drivers see, accurately at that point in time, a group of construction workers who are not working. But they are missing the picture as a whole. What appears to be an accurate perception of what a group of people is doing at that particular time is actually quite inaccurate. To make matters worse, as the drivers drive off, they leave with confirmation of their previously held beliefs: People who work for the government engage in loafing. Consequently, they are likely to make this assumption with an even greater sense of conviction the next time the occasion arises. The drivers have seen a "snapshot," which can leave them with assumptions that are not representative of the more complete and ongoing "movie."

One of the most helpful things that the coaching manager can do for an employee is to provide accurate and useful performance feedback. Feedback alone may be enough for a coachee to improve his or her performance, if it is "high-quality" feedback. This is particularly true when the coachee is working on skills such as leadership and teamwork; when people try to self-assess their effectiveness in these interpersonal areas, they are often poor judges of their own behavior and are prone to inaccurate self-assessment (Clark & Clark, 1996). Once they know how they are coming across to others, however, many people will try to improve their performance accordingly.

Effective feedback is possible only when it is based on *accurate observation (or other kinds of performance data)*. As the saying goes, "garbage in, garbage out." If the coaching manager has bad data, the feedback will be flawed, and the result will be a lack of learning and even greater defensiveness on the part of the employee. You don't want your employees feeling like the road construction workers just described.

The challenges of gathering good performance data are relatively well understood by industrial and organizational psychologists. We'll review those challenges briefly before reorganizing them in a fashion more consistent with recent work from the field of organizational learning. We will demonstrate how a conceptual tool called the "ladder of inference" (Argyris, Putnam, & Smith, 1985; Ross, 1994) has been particularly valuable to the participants in our coach training programs. We'll then examine the various means that coaching managers have at their disposal for gathering information about employees' performance and offer some suggestions, as well as a few critiques.

As the story of our hapless road construction workers illustrates, even eyewitness observation is not necessarily accurate. Nevertheless, we propose that in-person observation is the standard against which other data-gathering methods should be judged. We realize that this is a high and difficult-to-achieve standard, particularly in a "virtual world" in which team members operate at a distance from one another and the pace of change is rapid. Viewed in this light, most other methods of data gathering, such as the use of multirater or 360-degree feedback, appear to be useful, though with a few cautionary notes.

Regardless of the source, however, performance data should be viewed by the coaching manager with a certain tentativeness. What you think you see or the reports that you get from others about a particular employee represent at best a series of snapshots. Unless you can follow the employee around day in and day out, you will end up with a photo album, not a video. It is important to keep that point in mind. What is the coaching manager to do, then, when confronted with the unreliability of performance data? The answer, we believe, is not to place the burden for making the data more reliable completely on your shoulders, but to share that burden with the employee.

While coaching, the manager isn't a judge and jury but is, rather, a facilitator of learning. We stress this perspective because it is different from the traditional model of coaching that is linked to performance appraisal. While conducting a performance appraisal, the manager is like an umpire, calling the pitches as "balls" and "strikes." (And as in baseball, arguing with the umpire can get you kicked out of the game.) Managers use the power of their position to take a stand behind their observations, and employees are often left with no choice but to acquiesce. Under these circumstances, the employee may not be motivated to participate as a "co-investigator" in the process of developing good performance data to aid in the appraisal process. The employee will likely be motivated to give the manager data that put the best possible light on his or her performance.

This kind of interaction may be understandable but should not be confused with coaching, a process that focuses on learning. In a coaching process designed to facilitate learning, both the coach and the employee are responsible for getting the best possible information on which to base their assessments. In a coaching-friendly context, the coachee will be motivated to help fill in the gaps in the photo album so that the manager can help him or her learn.

Why Are Performance Data, Even Observational Data, Suspect?

In the discussion that follows, we'll leave out the problems associated with organizational politics or incentive systems that encourage managers to consciously present a distorted picture of an employee's performance. Such contextual factors really should be addressed in considering whether or not the manager has created a coaching-friendly context. Our focus here is on the challenges that even well-intentioned and properly motivated managers face when they try to assess how someone else is doing. This is a problem of perception.

Human perception is influenced by a variety of factors. If you just stop to think about your own effectiveness when observing someone else, several challenges come immediately to mind. First, do you have the right kind of access to the person you are observing? The up-close view can be quite different from the view in the grandstands. Second, what was the physical context like? Was there plenty of light? Could you hear well? Could you see well? Third, how were you feeling at the time? Were you distracted by other thoughts? Were you stressed or unhappy? Fourth, did you have the time to stop and record what you saw, or are you relying on memories that are several days old? Fifth, how well do you really know the other person? Do you have something in common with that person? Do commonalities or differences tend to make your observations more accurate or less accurate? Sixth, how do you feel about the person? If you dislike him or her, your observations, particularly your interpretations of what you see, may well be biased. Seventh, how has the person done in the past? If you have seen someone fail repeatedly at a particular task, you're likely to be expecting that person to fail again, and this expectation may actually influence what you see.

We could go on. What becomes clear while reviewing the variety of factors that can influence our observation of another is how many things can go wrong. Human resource management specialists have defined the following six sources of observer error, which are worth taking into consideration (Dessler, 1999).

The first source of error stems from a *lack of clear standards*. Employee and manager don't know what should be observed. We discuss this in detail in Chapter 3. If you don't know what you're looking for, it is very unlikely that you'll be able to describe it accurately.

The *halo effect* is one of the most common factors that shape the perception one person has of another. Friendly people, attractive people, cooperative people, and people who are effective in one aspect of life are likely to be judged as more effective in other aspects of life. A great scientist may be thought of as a great leader even though his or her leadership skills are lacking. Observers tend to give people who demonstrate a desirable characteristic much greater leeway when it comes to evaluating other characteristics or behaviors. We give them a "halo." We also give them a halo if their most recent work was excellent despite the fact that every other performance was not. This creates a real challenge at appraisal time. Unfortunately, people on whom a halo has been bestowed sometimes come to believe that they deserve it.

Three additional sources of error reflect the specific attitude of the observer. Observers may have a tendency to rate everyone as average, with very few exceptions (the *central tendency* effect), or they may be consistently strict (*tough*) or consistently lenient (*supportive*). In these cases, the observer's attitude shapes what he or she sees. For example, "I never give anyone the top rating; I just don't believe in it" is the cry of the tough manager.

Finally, various forms of socially constructed or cognitively *biased perceptions* can influence what observers think they see while observing others. Age, sex, race, sexual orientation, occupation, and ethnicity all serve to define an individual as a member of a particular group. If we expect stereotypical behavior from members of a particular identifiable group, we are more likely to see the expected behavior. We are also less likely to see behavior that runs counter to the stereotypes we hold. If you hold the assumption, for instance, that scientists don't make effective managers, you may be more likely to see the failings in a scientist/manager and less likely to see the strengths and potential strengths. In reality, each individual is unique, and it is typically a mistake, from a coaching perspective, to judge individual performance on the basis of biases one might have about a *group* of individuals.

A coaching manager in a high-tech company told of his effort to help one of his team leaders do a better job at getting his team on the right track. The leader invited the manager to sit in on a few team meetings. The manager saw one particular woman in the group, an engineer, who seemed to be having a very difficult time making eye contact with, or even looking at, any of the men in the group. The situation appeared to be quite tense. This concerned the manager because he had become increasingly worried that his division was not a hospitable place for women to work.

He also was concerned that the team leader seemed to be doing nothing about the situation. When they held a brief coaching dialogue after the team meeting, the coaching manager who had observed the meeting asked about the situation and expressed some concern about what he had seen: "Isn't there something more that the team leader should do about this to help the team manage diversity?"

The stunned team leader expressed some confusion for a moment and then reported that he had talked with all three of the team members who had worked together recently. The problem had nothing to do with a gender issue on the team. Both of the men had happened to have major performance problems during their last project, and the woman had had to pick up the slack for their ineffectiveness. She had confronted them in the last meeting and gotten nowhere. She was completely frustrated with their work, and her frustration was palpable. The real problem for the team leader and for the team was managing conflict and poor performance. The coaching manager, being well-intentioned, had assumed that a gender issue existed, on the basis of the gender of the individuals involved and the behavior he had found himself attending to. Bias causes us to make assumptions about the meaning of what we see. In fact, all of the sources of error create a tendency to assume or to make inferences that cause us to misinterpret what little data we actually have to work with in many instances.

The Real Problem: Our Tendency to Draw Inferences From Selected Data

In our efforts to formulate a means of helping coaching managers deal with the human tendency to distort the reality of what we see, we have sought out simple solutions. The root problem seems to involve a comingling of data with what may be inappropriate interpretations of those data. Unfortunately, this mixing of data and interpretation seems to occur automatically. It can take place very quickly, can be hard to spot, and can be self-confirming. Like the driver who spots the tired construction worker taking a well-deserved break and leaves the scene feeling more convinced than ever that those who build roads are really goofing off, we look for what we believe to be the case. Next time, we'll be very likely to find it.

Ross (1994) describes this as the problem of self-generating beliefs:

> We live in a world of self-generating beliefs which remain largely untested. We adopt those beliefs because they are based on conclusions that are inferred from what we observe, plus our past experience. Our ability to achieve the results we truly desire is eroded by our feelings that:
>
> - Our beliefs are the truth
> - The truth is obvious
> - Our beliefs are based on real data
> - The data that we select are the real data (p. 242)

This phenomenon is aptly captured by the title "ladder of inference" (Ross, 1994) because it describes how we quickly move "up" the ladder. The steps up the ladder of inference are presented in Box 8.1. Several of the steps are particularly worthy of discussion in the context of the coaching manager.

BOX 8.1   **The Ladder of Inference**

Step 7. I take actions based on my beliefs.

Step 6. I adopt beliefs about the world.

Step 5. I draw conclusions.

Step 4. I make assumptions based on the meaning that I added.

Step 3. I add meaning to what I see (cultural and personal).

Step 2. I select data from what I observe.

Step 1. I observe data and events.

SOURCE: Adapted from Ross (1994, p. 243).

The first step on the ladder involves observation. Accurate observation, much as a video camera might provide, is the goal. However, as we've already said, you can't observe everything, and if you did, you'd have too much data to actually help the employee. On the second step, the observer has to select the data on which to focus. (This again refers to "Defining Success," as we discussed in Chapter 3.) If, however, you have not decided in consultation with others what is important and made it common knowledge, you'll immediately find yourself moving up the ladder of inference and out of control. The reason for this is that everyone, including you, will have an opinion about what is important and impose that opinion on the choices he or she makes about which data to select.

The third step up the ladder involves the imposition of meaning on the data you have already decided to select. This is the basic inferential step, though you should note that meaning isn't imposed on everything the other person does; it is imposed selectively on what you have consciously or unconsciously chosen to pay attention to. In our previous example, the coaching manager visited a team meeting. He made note of the behavior of a female team member and didn't pay as much attention to the behavior of the males on the team. He then made an inference about the meaning of her behavior. He focused on her because he had, for other reasons, been sensitized to the problems of women in his organization. He was observing the men in the group less intently and didn't even note that they were looking down most of the time, avoiding eye contact with everyone else in the group.

Fortunately, as an effective coach, he tested this assumption in his dialogue with the team leader. He discovered that he had been wrong; something else was actually going on. However, let's assume for the moment that he had not tested his assumption. He might have drawn the conclusion that the firm, or at least this team, was inhospitable to women and then taken actions on the basis of this conclusion. The real problems of the group would have been ignored. His focus would have drawn attention to issues of gender and diversity and, ironically, might have left the female engineer feeling unsupported (she wanted the other two, who just happened to be men, to be dealt with).

Our coaching managers have consistently told us that learning to work with the ladder of inference has been of enormous value. Note that we say "work with." We can't pretend that we can avoid the ladder of inference. Rather, our coaching managers have suggested that a two-step process in which observation and inference are captured helps them keep track of both and consciously manage the relationship between the two.

We now use a simple observation sheet to aid in making the distinction, presented in the exercise in Box 8.2. The format is based on the work of Chris Argyris (Argyris & Schon, 1978), who developed the use of a left-column/right-column case study tool (for a different though similar purpose). We ask coaching managers to draw a line down the middle of a piece of paper. On the left side of the line, write down what is actually observed. On the right side of the paper, record thoughts, feelings, reactions, or ideas about what is observed. We encourage coaching managers to capture both sides because the feelings, ideas, or hunches that are recorded on the right side, although they are the building blocks from which inferences are drawn, can also be useful.

BOX 8.2   Exercise: Observation and Inference

Make an observation sheet like the one illustrated here. Note that the left-hand column includes actual behavioral observations. The right-hand column includes your thoughts, reactions, hunches, hypotheses, and feelings about what you see. Keep the two rigidly separate. We use an example from a coach training program to illustrate. Use the observation sheet the next time you get a chance to observe one of your direct reports in action. Does it help you to organize your thinking in this way? Which side is likely to be most useful as a source of performance feedback to the employee?

• John entered the room, fixed his eyes on his notebook, and didn't look at the other members of the team seated around the table.	• He's angry. Something has gone wrong. This isn't the way to send a message to his troops.
• Several members of the team began to make small talk.	• I think they must have been uncomfortable.
• John interrupted their chatting and said, "We have to get on with this meeting. I have some important new numbers from the CFO that you'd better be aware of."	• Again, he sounds angry, or in a hurry. He needs to let them socialize a bit if he wants them to work well together.
• John then talked about the report from the CFO. He used an overhead with a lot of writing on it. It was hard to see. He read the facts and figures on the overhead in a monotone, still not looking at the group.	• He's not conveying that this is important, interesting, or urgent. He's losing them.
• Team members started to shuffle paper while he was talking.	• He's lost them, and I don't think he'll get them back like this. He's not coming across like a leader.

Discussion: Let's say that your hypotheses on the right-hand side were actually correct. (Again, we encourage you not to ignore your feelings and hunches because such reactions may represent important sources of data, particularly on the impact of the employee's behavior.) You might present this to your coachee by saying, "When you did 'this,' I felt 'that.'" Consider the problems associated with providing feedback that is based solely on the data of the right-hand column. Such data are hard-hitting, if not quite critical and evaluative in nature. They are also loaded with a series of inferences. The inferences include but aren't limited to the following:

- John is angry.
- The team is uncomfortable.
- John is angry, again.
- The team members will work together more effectively if they have a chance to socialize.
- His team won't hear his message as being important.
- He has lost his leadership relationship with his team.

All inferences may be accurate—but they may also be inaccurate. It is imperative that the coaching manager understand the difference before using data from the right-hand column. If you, when coaching, believe that these data represent more of a "maybe" than a sure thing, you will ideally use them in a different way: to help you formulate questions, next steps, areas to explore, or possibilities to consider. Data from the left-hand side can be used "as is," as accurate reflections of what you saw in the meeting. The only problem with the data from the left-hand side is that they represent a "snapshot." John may be ill, he may be having a bad day, or he may be behaving differently for a variety of reasons.

One coach, using this technique, described an observation that she made of an employee new to her group, in a very important meeting: "I just didn't like this guy." This rather intense emotional reaction ultimately proved to be an important source of data. What she realized in retrospect but couldn't put her finger on at the time was that the employee, someone from a country and culture different from her own, had made several subtle remarks to a customer in the meeting that struck her as very arrogant. This was particularly troubling given the sensitive and political nature of his work.

Other managers in the very same meeting who had overheard his remarks and with whom she later consulted didn't recall having the same reaction. No one could recall what he actually said. They did, however, feel that he might be having some communication problems because of his cultural background that could give others the wrong impression and ultimately interfere with his performance. They were also making inferences about his behavior, but their inferences were strikingly different from the manager's. She resolved at the next meeting to listen more carefully to what the employee was actually saying and to get some real data before jumping to any conclusions.

Using the additional data, she reflected on her relationship with the employee. She began to consider the possibility that she was having difficulty understanding his cultural framework. She felt that she should get to know him better before intervening so that she could have a clearer sense of what was going on. If she had given him feedback about what appeared to be an arrogant personal style when the issue was really something quite different, she might have provoked considerable defensiveness on the employee's part. She caught herself on the upper rungs of the ladder of inference and forced herself back down to the ground level: the data of observation. Although her emotional reaction does matter, she'll have to wait until she actually talks with the employee to get a clearer sense of the origin of that reaction. It matters, but it is not the place to begin.

Error and Expectations:
What You See Is What You Get

The "Pygmalion effect," also known as the *self-fulfilling prophecy*, is well understood in education and management (Livingston, 1988). Research has shown that children who are expected by their teachers to succeed *are* more likely to succeed. Employees who are expected by their managers to succeed seem to be more likely to succeed as well. Conversely, the reverse can occur. In the "set-up-to-fail syndrome," the manager's expectations of poor performance can resonate with an employee's lack of confidence or timidity, resulting in performance problems (Manzoni & Barsoux, 1998). Both of these outcomes, the good employee doing even better or the marginal employee doing even worse, have to do in part with expectations in the relationship between the employee and the manager. The coaching manager who expresses a belief that the employee "can do it" may find that in an effort to live up to the manager's expectations, the employee actually does it.

The expectations the manager brings to a relationship with an employee are determined in part by how he or she manages the ladder of inference. As we've already come to understand, research on self-fulfilling prophecies, good and bad, suggests that expectations can influence perception. If you expect a problem, you are far more likely to be looking for one and to find data that support your theory that one exists. (This is one reason that employees are aware of the importance of impression management.) If you are aware of this possibility, then you're much more likely to master the discipline of keeping inference and observation separate.

We encourage you to give the exercise in Box 8.2 a try. You can do this exercise while watching a video with your family, sitting in a fast-food restaurant, or watching a team at work. Try the exercise first, though, with someone else present who is watching the same event or group of people that you are watching. Choose your target and document what you see on the left side of the column; record your theories, ideas, or emotional reactions on the right side. Then, stop and discuss what you have seen with your partner. Did you and your partner see the same things?

When we ask two coaching managers to go through this exercise, we often find that they offer significantly different reports. The reasons for this have to do with the fact that, as stated above, inferences are based on observation, but they are also based on the perceptions and background of the observer. Sometimes the observer's "hot buttons" are very potent, leading to quick and erroneous inference making.

We encourage you to start thinking about your own issues, concerns, or "hot buttons." What kinds of people and situations tend to lead you to distort what you see? What kind of inferences do you tend to make? Be honest with yourself. Whom do you like? Whom don't you like? What groups of people do you have a difficult time getting to know, and what groups are you more comfortable with? What tasks do you enjoy observing, and what tasks do you not enjoy observing?

The ladder of inference is a good tool for keeping an eye on the distinction between data and inference, but it is also a good tool for learning about yourself. The best coaching managers are very self-aware. They know what kinds of issues are likely to encourage them to distort what they see. The emotionally sensitive or team-oriented manager might mistakenly see the task orientation of an employee as a manifestation of poor interpersonal skills. The "big picture" coaching manager might see an employee's focus on the details as a roadblock to change. We make one helpful suggestion in this regard. Personal style assessment instruments, such as the DISC methodology or the Myers-Briggs Type Indicator,[1] can often be helpful to managers who want to better understand their own "default" response as they move up and down the ladder of inference. Knowing something about

---

[1] The Myers-Briggs Type Indicator is a registered trademark of Consulting Psychologists Press.

your personality allows you to understand an important source of diversity in the world, the diversity of personal styles.

Getting the Most From Direct Observation and Other Approaches to Gathering Performance Data

So far, we have explored the problems of data versus inference in some detail but only as they apply to direct visual observation of the employee by the coaching manager. When the coaching manager is forced to rely on data from sources other than direct observation, it stands to reason that the potential for the ladder of inference to distort the data increases significantly. Likewise, data-gathering methods that rely on the reports of others (verbal or written reports, survey instruments, or multirater feedback instruments that ask various stakeholders to rate or comment on the effectiveness of a particular employee) may engage more people in climbing the ladder of inference as well.

Strangely, apparently robust methodologies, such as the manager's interviewing others who work with the employee or using well-designed multirater or 360-degree feedback, may actually give the manager enough data to make a fairly accurate appraisal rating of an employee—but such data won't necessarily be good enough for coaching purposes. When coaching managers interview other employees or customers who work with coachees, they may find themselves hearing inferences or generalizations instead of data. "We're very satisfied with her performance" may be an important statement about an employee, coming from a customer. However, as a coaching manager you'd also like to know what the person is doing that is in fact yielding that sense of satisfaction.

Likewise, feedback data provided by formal multirater feedback systems can also push people up the ladder of inference. The reasons are simple. Multirater feedback surveys ask general questions, such as "Does the employee display effective listening in team meetings?" This question asks for a conclusion about a pattern of behavior, not an example or examples. Although most multirater reports have a section for qualitative narrative comments from people filling out surveys, if the respondents are untrained, they are more likely to provide general statements than specific examples. If employees are to truly see themselves clearly, they need accurate mirrors with the details included.

What are the implications of this state of affairs? We have to be practical. The coaching manager will often have to make do with the available information. First, we present some practical guidelines for coaching managers, and then we discuss how the coachee can help (see Box 8.3).

BOX 8.3   **Getting the Most From Various Sources of Performance Data**

1. Always strive for specific examples of work. This is easiest to do when the source of data is your direct observation as the coaching manager. It is the standard against which all other sources of data must be judged.

2. Keep in mind that even observation can be limited by inference and even a specific example represents a "snapshot," not a "video."

3. Always follow up on formal and informal multirater feedback assessment activities. Get specific examples from the people involved to reflect the generalizations that are offered by the feedback report.

4. Be cautious of how you interpret unsolicited feedback provided by others that is delivered by e-mail or by hearsay.

5. Differentiate feedback from interpretation. Understand your own ladder of inference.

6. Enlist the coachee in producing the "video" and in taking responsibility for thinking about how individual "snapshot" observations fit into the pattern that he or she is monitoring.

Seek specific examples. This is true regardless of whether or not the employee is self-assessing his or her performance, the coaching manager is providing feedback based on observation, the coaching manager has interviewed others who work with the employee, or the coaching manager and/or employee are following up on a formal multirater assessment. Direct observation, then, must be considered the standard by which all other sources of performance data are judged. Direct observation offers specific examples of work.

Keep in mind that specific examples represent one "snapshot," not a "video" of the employee's life. Do the specific examples represent part of a pattern, or are they unrepresentative of the employee's ongoing performance?

After a formal multirater feedback process in which the employee has received a report, there must be a follow-up. Employees should go back to those who filled out surveys describing their performance. Typically, the feedback report includes the observations of the person's boss, peers, and direct reports, if appropriate. After thanking those people, employees should ask for input in a positive way—for example, a description in general terms of what appear to be their strengths and their weaknesses. They should then ask for specific examples of times when they have not performed at their best, according to the general feedback from their multirater report. They should listen and not become defensive or attack. Employees can bring these data back to their discussions with coaching managers. Unfortunately, they will probably have to accept the fact that every individual who filled out a survey form may not actually remember or be inclined to offer specific examples. Multirater feedback reports, especially those that are well constructed, can be of enormous value. However, almost all authors of commercially available multirater feedback programs recommend exactly what we have described here. Multirater feedback reports are designed to suggest strengths or developmental needs, but they are only the first step. The real work and payoff are in the follow-up.

Be careful about using unsolicited feedback, particularly if it is delivered by e-mail. Our concern here is that impromptu and unsolicited feedback may be of low quality and may draw heavily on inference. E-mails can be sent impulsively, before the sender has had time to think through whatever is provoking the feedback. Unfortunately, if someone has critical feedback about an employee, he or she may feel very angry and therefore be motivated to retaliate against the employee. We recommend that, unless it is exceptionally clear, unsolicited feedback or feedback offered by e-mail be seen as an opportunity for an in-person discussion, or at least a phone call, so that the coaching manager can ask questions to help clarify the data being offered.

Using the methodology of the ladder of inference, be sure to differentiate feedback based on observation from ideas, hunches, or generalizations about the coachee's actions. Your ideas, hunches, and gut reactions may be very valuable. They may tell you something about how others are reacting to the behavior of the coachee, something about the question of impact. So don't discard them. Distinguish them from observation. We discuss this in Chapter 9 as representing interpretations of feedback. Interpretations made without consulting the coachee are based on inference. You may have good data that accurately describe someone's behavior, but you don't know why this person is behaving the way he or she does. Our coaching managers stress the importance of keeping an open mind.

The Coachee's Role

The coachee needs to be an active participant in the coaching process. He or she must keep track of the learning goal, results to date, feedback from others, and thoughts about what needs to happen next. Keeping with our metaphor of the "snapshot," the coachee must keep charge of the "photo album." This allows the coachee to make effective use of the observations of others, even if those observations are one-time events. When it comes to learning, the coachee, not the coaching manager, is in the driver's seat. The employee may choose to make a great deal out of an individual observation. On the other hand, some employees would ignore a "video review" of their work even if Steven Spielberg had directed it!

We had an interchange relevant to this type of observation with Adam, a participant in an executive education program that we were running. Adam was already well-known to us. He is a high-potential manager possessing enormous enthusiasm and unbridled assertiveness. His behavior can at times resemble that of a good-natured "bull in a china shop." In the classroom, as teachers, we noticed that Adam was exercising enormous and uncharacteristic self-control. Every time he would appear ready to jump into a discussion (without raising his hand), he seemed to catch himself, settle down, and try to listen to what others were saying. Curious about this, we asked him about his actions in the classroom (not wanting to give away our enormous sense of relief!).

Adam explained that about 4 months before, he had participated in an important cross-functional task force with a number of senior-level marketing managers from throughout his company. The vice president for human resources happened to be at the meeting. The two had never met, but he asked Adam to join him for a cup of coffee after the meeting. Curious, and eager to make a high-level contact, Adam accepted. The vice president took his time and got to know Adam a bit. He asked Adam about his career goals and how he felt about his participation on the task force. Evidently satisfied that Adam was interested in improving his performance, he then offered to give Adam some feedback he thought might help.

He explained that he saw Adam's comments in the meeting as being very much on target and that he clearly had a bright future with the firm, words that Adam was happy to hear. However, the vice president then said that, in his enthusiasm, Adam had interrupted several important people from other parts of the firm, and this limited his ability to build influence with those key players. Adam was perturbed but felt he had to agree with the vice president's observations. He could see it himself. He knew that, out of his enthusiasm, he sometimes inadvertently ignored the needs or feelings of others. No one had ever directly offered that feedback in such a powerful way, however.

Four months later, as we could see in our classroom, Adam was continuing to work on the issues raised by the vice president of human resources. (The two had not met since.) Adam expressed gratitude about the fact that the vice president was nice enough to be observant and then take him aside to give him the feedback in a way that was helpful. Adam explained that he'd been trying to monitor his behavior because he knew he had to change. He had lofty aspirations and didn't want to get in his own way. He went on to say that some days, he was pretty good at monitoring how he was doing; other days, he was not so good. He was glad that his efforts in our classroom had been noted.

Adam is the keeper of his own "photo album" of ideas and observations about his performance. The vice president is certainly in no position to keep track of Adam's performance. Perhaps his manager is in no position to do so, either—but Adam is. He is aware of what he needs to learn and is in charge of that effort.

The Coaching Manager as Observer: Promoting Learning and Performance, From the Sidelines

It isn't easy to be a good observer, even if you are properly motivated. In our coach training programs we ask our participants to observe groups in action for as long as 90 minutes. That's only 1.5 hours, but actually it's a very long time. It is intellectually, physically, and even emotionally demanding. It is easy to make inferences and difficult to organize your thinking to focus on data rather than interpretation. It is difficult to watch an employee without thinking in an evaluative way. Perhaps just as challenging, managers like to take action. Observation can feel very passive and unproductive. As we've described, sometimes people find it almost intolerable. Nevertheless, the discipline of observing (or getting observation from others), not imposing your own inferences, and then packaging the data in a useful way for feedback to the employee is hard work. It is one aspect of the work of leadership.

Providing Balanced and Helpful Feedback

9

In this chapter, you will learn about the following:

- The benefits of feedback

- The problems associated with feedback and "management by guilt"

- The basics of providing balanced feedback

- The factors that shape an employee's emotional reaction to feedback, and how the employee's reaction affects his or her ability to learn from feedback

- The tactics you can take to maximize the value of feedback

Feedback is often thought of as the foundation for all coaching—indeed, for all development. As we've stated, although we do believe it is important, it is only one component of the coaching model we have described. According to most research on learning, feedback offered without the support of the other aspects of the model may not be all that helpful. To be useful for developmental purposes, feedback should target what the employee is trying to learn about. Feedback must also be delivered to the employee in a "helpful" way and in a fashion with which the employee can work. Finally, and perhaps most important, feedback must be delivered by a coaching manager who is aware of (a) the power of the emotional impact that can accompany feedback and (b) how the coachee's reactions can shape his or her ability to learn from the feedback.

The Benefits of Feedback

Although feedback as a learning tool is not without its problems, as we'll discuss below, when feedback is effectively directed at an employee's learning goals and offered in the context of a model of coaching that includes self-assessment and is preceded by a coaching dialogue, the benefits can be substantial. As such, developing skill in effectively providing feedback to employees should be considered an important goal for all coaching managers. Research on feedback shows that the following are just a few of the most important benefits of providing feedback, particularly to employees who are interested in their own learning and development (London, 1997):

- Feedback helps keep goal-directed behavior on course. Keeping employees informed about progress as they attend to change or pursue any goal helps them see how far they have come and how far they have to go.
- Feedback helps employees set new and more aggressive goals. On the basis of the feedback they receive, they see what they have accomplished. Those who are motivated will want to push on further.
- Positive feedback, when appropriate, helps employees feel that they have achieved even when their achievement doesn't lead to a material result, such as project completion or a pay raise.
- Motivation theory and research also show that feedback can serve to enhance motivation because employees understand what it takes to be successful. They know the rules of the road. The employee who can say "Now I know how to get there" is more likely to make the attempt.
- Feedback helps employees develop a greater ability to detect errors on their own. When coupled with self-assessment, feedback helps us better judge our own actions because our ability to observe ourselves has been calibrated by comparison with the feedback of others.
- Related to the last point, feedback also helps employees see what they need to learn. They have a clearer sense of their own weaknesses or learning gaps. Their ability to take charge of their own development is enhanced.
- People who are used to getting feedback tend to seek it out. Effective provision of feedback by a manager is one of the most important tactics for creating a coaching-friendly context and the "market for coaching" that should be the goal of every coaching manager.
- Frequent feedback also serves to eliminate most of the conflicts we've discussed between performance appraisal and developmental coaching. As many of our coaching managers have told us, "If the employee is surprised in the performance appraisal meeting about any serious problem with his or her performance, I've failed to give them feedback along the way."
- Finally, feedback helps employees develop what is called a *career identity*: "I know that I'm good at this because my manager told me." Feedback shapes

how employees see themselves. One of the authors of this book can point to two specific instances of positive feedback from senior managers, early in his career, which helped crystallize a view of himself and his abilities that survives some 25 years later. Feedback to employees about their strengths communicates to them that they can make a contribution that will be valued by others.

The Problem With Feedback

Unfortunately, feedback does not always result in such positive outcomes, a fact of life of which we are all too aware. A review of the research on feedback to date has shown that, overall, feedback has only a moderately positive impact on performance (Kluger & DeNisi, 1996). Feedback that focuses on personal characteristics ("You are a slow worker") rather than on tasks and behavior ("You took 7 extra minutes at Step 3") and is delivered in a way that threatens an employee's self-esteem ("You're just not as good as the rest of them") appears to significantly undermine its usefulness. Overly negative, personal, or overly general feedback is discouraging from a motivational standpoint and is also not helpful from a learning or performance-improvement standpoint. Such feedback leaves the receiver feeling angry and less likely to communicate with his or her manager in the future.

There are also more nuanced challenges associated with feedback. Those of you who have had training in providing feedback have undoubtedly been encouraged to make feedback as specific as possible. We've certainly taught that specificity is important in providing feedback, and as we saw in the previous chapter, specificity is not always easy to generate. (We'll now start sounding like diet experts who are about to explain to you that things are more complicated than might be helpful.) Feedback that is quite specific, however, is now thought to have varying impacts on the receiver of the feedback when the full range of responses is considered.

Highly specific feedback may promote improved performance when things are going well but not promote performance improvements when things are not going so well or when a substantial change in direction is necessary (Goodman & Wood, 2004). Feedback research in this area suggests that highly specific feedback may provoke temporary performance improvements but may not encourage exploration across a broader range of possibilities (Goodman, Wood, & Hendricks, 2004). Further, some researchers suggest, in line with what may be common sense, that negative feedback may in fact provoke more attention to managing one's self-concept and impression management than to task performance improvement (Vancouver & Tischner, 2004). One additional not terribly surprising finding is that cultural variables, such as participation in collectivist versus individualist societies, can have a significant impact on whether or not an individual makes appropriate use of feedback or finds that he or she must exert time and energy mitigating the impact of the feedback (Milliman, Taylor, & Czaplewski, 2002).

So what are the implications of the growing body of work that insists that we take another look at our underlying assumptions about feedback? We suggest that the literature makes it clear that feedback, by itself, is unlikely to result in performance improvement, or if it does lead to such a result, our ability to expect a repeat performance improvement the next time we provide feedback may be limited. Linking feedback with a deeper understanding of the learning process and other developmental interventions, however, may help mitigate some of the more negative aspects of feedback while at the same time providing an opportunity to harness its potential power.

So we shouldn't give up on feedback just because it's a more sophisticated instrument than we might have assumed. Practical experience suggests that even poorly delivered feedback might be better than none at all. In other words, are there negative impacts that we should anticipate if no feedback is provided? The answer of course is yes. If one asks employees about their "worst feedback experiences" one is likely to hear something like the following:

- "The worst feedback I ever got was the feedback I never got." The employee who is left out in the dark, getting only some sense of how he or she is doing on the yearly performance appraisal day, has a legitimate complaint. Not knowing how you are doing creates a list of "antibenefits" that is a mirror image to the list of benefits described above. Efforts are not focused, learning gaps are not recognized, motivation is not strengthened, and learning itself is unguided or absent. The most frequent cause for the "no feedback" feedback is probably the manager's fears that the feedback will be responded to negatively.
- "The worst feedback I ever got was the feedback I got third-hand, because my boss told everyone else but me." Feedback delivered "through the grapevine" leaves employees feeling confused and mistrustful. Such feedback also leaves the employee, and the manager, with none of the benefits described above.

The lack of feedback is probably the biggest problem we face here. The underlying dynamic involves the manager being either passive out of fear or passive-aggressive and afraid to confront the employee directly. Ironically, in our experience, such errors are even more likely to take place in the executive suite than on the shop floor (not that things are always great on the shop floor, either). Harry Levinson (1986), one of the pioneers of consulting psychology, suggested that managers find that the giving of feedback, particularly critical feedback, creates an unconscious sense of guilt on their part. Some managers fear that they will literally make others hurt or ill by criticizing them and, as a result, may withhold corrective feedback. Most of us fear the way others will react to our criticism and don't want to be hurtful. What makes the problem important for managers in particular is that they are in positions of authority. They know that their words have extra weight. Their assessments can affect their employees' compensation and careers. Managers can be vulnerable to such concerns, even though their employees may not see them in that light. But the problem can get worse.

If a manager feels disappointed in the performance of a subordinate and is fearful of the power of his or her anger, the manager tries to avoid thinking about it. The problem, however, doesn't go away. The manager's anger builds and, in what may be a rather unskilled performance, is released in a torrent, all at once. The formerly reserved and compassionate (or downright fearful) manager becomes the tyrant who delivers an explosion of pent-up feedback, threatens the individual's self-esteem, and focuses more on the person than on the actual task the employee was performing, or not performing. This may be accompanied by a trip to the human resources department and demands that "We've got to fire this person!" We were recently told of a situation in which a manager counseled an employee at breakfast for more than a year, trying to be helpful to him but never telling him what the problem was. Their relationship ended on a very angry note.

Is this an issue that emerges only when a manager is working with an employee who has a severe performance problem? The answer is no. In fact, the conditions for what Levinson (1986) describes as management by guilt may be even more compelling when a manager is coaching a good or great employee. That employee may have made significant contributions to the business unit. He or she may have good interpersonal skills. The manager may like the employee and indeed be friends with that person. Many employees, at all company levels, have told us that they didn't get helpful feedback even from managers who really seemed to like them. Fearful of having to provide critical feedback to the good employee, they provided none at all until forced to do so at performance appraisal time.

It is important to remember that, as we've stated, the good employee wants to learn and takes the task of learning seriously. "Top talent" is more likely to see feedback, even critical feedback, as helpful. The first step for any manager interested in developing his or her skills as a provider of feedback is to move beyond the belief that feedback, even when properly given, is injurious. So again, let's not give up on feedback. In fact, let's take a closer look at how it works. Let's change the setting to one in which feedback is taken as a given, an absolutely essential part of the learning process, studio arts education. Budding artists really can't develop in the absence of feedback. Box 9.1 describes a critique session in a class for emerging professional photographers.

BOX 9.1   Photo Class Critique

There are about 10 students sitting around at the end of a class on location portraiture. They've delivered images to the instructor, who is about to project each student's work through a computer and onto a large screen. He'll then review the students' work one at a time and provide them with feedback, in public. (Public performance feedback is usually discouraged in organizational settings. It's standard operating procedure in the arts.) The mood is somewhat anxious, but not overly so.

These students are used to the process. They've been through this many times before. Sometimes it's gone well and been a cause for celebration. Other times, it hasn't gone so well. After a while, it's no longer seen as personal. It's just business, as they say. Most important, one comes to realize that photographs, composition, technique, lighting, and so on are being critiqued. Usually, though not all the time, people are not.

Most students actually grow to like the process and anticipate the experience. For starters, someone is actually paying attention to their work. Good or bad, that means a lot in the arts (and in every other work activity, we would suggest). Beyond that, the students have come to realize that, in fact, these sessions help them develop as artists. But it's not a linear type of development.

The first student's work goes up on the screen. The instructor takes a look, and his initial reaction is positive. Then he notices something that bothers him. He utters the dreaded words, "I think that may be soft. Let's zoom in." Sure enough, the image looks fine, as most people would view it. If the photographer were trying to interest a magazine art director in the image, however, that art director would definitely zoom in to make sure that the part that is supposed to be sharply in focus is in fact sharply in focus.

The culprit here is obvious: camera shake. It's a basic mistake. Either the camera has to be held still or the photographer has to use some other type of intervention (tripods, fast shutter speeds, etc.) to make sure that the part of the image that is supposed to be sharp is sharp. It's a rookie mistake, though one that professionals make all the time. The difference is the professionals don't show the images they produce unless they are in fact appropriately sharp. They edit. The problem here isn't just camera shake; it's lack of care when choosing an image to display. There's no disputing that the image, which was interesting, shouldn't be up on the screen in that condition.

This is a coaching-friendly context. The instructor doesn't hammer away at the point. There's no need to make a big deal out of this. The student and her colleagues all know that this is a fundamental error. The feedback is very specific and without dispute (though not without some pain on the part of the student). The student knows this is an issue for her. She tends to view her images in their entirety and doesn't look for trouble in the details. She's working on it, and in fact, she can see progress, though clearly there's more work to be done. She resolves to look more closely at her images for camera shake from here on out.

The second student's images now appear on the screen. This student is more senior. One image is a silhouette of a person and, behind the silhouette, a very bright sky. The image is "backlit," as photographers say, causing the person's actual figure to appear darker than the background. Some would say that this is a violation of one of the rules of effective composition. The person, the subject, should be brighter than the rest of the image.

The instructor's reaction is immediately negative. "I don't like that; at least I don't think I do. . . . I don't know; let me look at it again." (We're not advocating that you start your feedback with "I don't like that" though this is an illustration of the fact that you don't have to be perfect. Overall, the coaching context was positive. That's what counts.)

The instructor pulls back from his feedback. He points out that this is a risky composition. He asks the student what she was trying to do with this image. (Feedback mingles with dialogue.) She says that she was trying to create something edgy and different and that this subject and the potential client were looking for something different. A lively debate breaks out among the students. Good image or not? This question is tougher to answer. Now the instructor isn't sure.

He raises several questions. How will this image be presented? What does the client want? Who is going to see the image? Many questions emerge that help the student, the instructor, and the class think through the pros and cons of this approach. There is no one right answer here. Yes, there are guidelines, but some of the most iconic images in print are loved precisely because they break the guidelines.

Here, we're dealing with a more sophisticated problem and notice that the nature of the feedback changes. Instead of the instructor nearly (though not completely) reinforcing a rule, ambiguity is embraced. Right answers evolve into a shared discussion of costs, benefits, and ultimately artistic and client preferences. The student leaves not so much with a clear understanding of what to do but with a set of questions to help her assess her own performance. Yes, feedback was provided by the instructor, but so was a willingness to think through the contingencies. Rules were made to be broken, but knowing when to break them and under what circumstances reflects a greater level of professional development.

Making Feedback Useful—A Summary

The point of this story is to draw attention to the reality that different feedback recipients, dealing with different kinds of challenges, have differing needs. Highly specific feedback can be enormously helpful when desired changes are clear. However, when the learner is dealing with more ambiguous challenges, there may be a range of appropriate responses available. Specific feedback—this works; that doesn't—may not help. In fact, it may discourage the kind of exploration, or brainstorming if you will, necessary to consider the full range of possibilities or create novel responses to the challenge. In order to help provoke the right kind of response, the individual providing the feedback has to position the feedback differently. Expertise is appropriate in the first example. Feedback firmly embedded in a dialogue is more appropriate in the second. Instead of saying, "This is the way we all have to do it," the feedback provider rather is saying, "That's my opinion, but there may be others; let's look at the issues here."

An understanding of how "expertise" is developed may be helpful here. Benner (2001) and Dreyfus and Dreyfus (1986) propose that expertise develops as part of passage through a series of stages in the learning process. In general, they suggest that individuals move from a reliance on abstract concepts, such as guidelines learned in the classroom, to a reliance on what has been learned from experience. One moves from thinking about a set of discrete details learned through memorization (at the most extreme), to an understanding of how the pieces fit together. This more holistic understanding of what constitutes effective performance continues to evolve over time, though its evolution is never finished. We become more adept at understanding new experiences by drawing in part on previous experience, but there's always something new to be taken into account. The learning never ceases. A simple way to think about these transitions is as follows (Benner, 2001; Dreyfus & Dreyfus, 1986; Hunt & Weintraub, 2007):

- The *novice* has no practice-based experience of the situation in which he is expected to perform. He may have been to the classroom and therefore can rely on abstract concepts learned there, but that's all.
- The *advanced beginner* is able to perform to a minimally acceptable level and is beginning to turn from abstract concepts to actual skills that have been developed through practice.
- The *competent practitioner* has experience and has begun to amass personal learning from the application of his efforts in practice. He develops a personal sense of what happens when he takes a particular action, at least in most cases.
- The *proficient practitioner* is able to see situations as wholes and understand the relationships among various problems, opportunities, and responses over the longer term.
- The *expert* no longer relies on abstract analysis but rather relies on what she might describe as intuition. She has amassed so much experience that she is able to respond almost immediately, at times without seeming to think. Notice, however, that she may have "forgotten" how she developed such expertise as a result, which can make coaching a bit of a challenge.

Also note that experts still encounter very novel situations. In fact, as one moves up the stages of expertise development described here, one is more likely to be asked to take on more ambiguous and novel challenges as a result. So expertise itself needs to continually evolve. Thus, the need for some type of coaching never ceases. CEOs, if they're smart, consult with boards, friends, and executive coaches. Great musicians take the occasional master class. Great athletes always have a coach nearby.

But the feedback provided to a novice is very different from the feedback provided to an expert. The novice may need answers (though not all the time, we would stress), and the expert is likely to need questions. Try to keep these ideas in mind as you consider the basics of providing feedback, as well as your own style.

The Basics of Providing Balanced Feedback

Before moving to a detailed description of the elements of the feedback process, we want to remind you of one useful tool, initially discussed in Chapter 2, that has to do with the actual content of feedback. Feedback can be directed at your observations about the coachee's intention or actions and/or at the impact of those actions.

- *Intent*—What was the coachee trying to do? For instance, the coachee may have intended to keep the meeting on track.
- *Action*—What did the coachee do? In order to keep the meeting on track, the coachee established a specific agenda and asked a team member to serve as timekeeper. The team member was to announce when the time for an agenda item was up, and the team was then to move on to the next item for discussion.
- *Impact*—What was the impact of the coachee's action? Unfortunately, some members of the team felt rushed by the time management actions taken and became less active during the meeting.

Hopefully, the value of distinguishing between the three is clear from this case. The coachee had the right idea and took what might have been considered a reasonable action, but the impact of his action was not exactly what he had hoped. Feedback that draws his attention to the disconnection between intent and impact can help the receiver of the feedback fine-tune his or her actions so as to take into account a greater range of potential impacts. There can be disconnects among any of the three areas under consideration: intent, action, and impact. Exploration of each in the coaching dialogue can be of enormous value. The reality is that we can do the right thing for the wrong reasons, for instance, and it's important to understand the difference. Now let's look at the process by which feedback is delivered.

In describing the basic components of the feedback process, we will report on what the coaching managers we have studied have told us works and doesn't work. We'll also try to fit the various components more directly into the model of coaching described throughout this book. In this section, we'll rely heavily on work by Buron and McDonald-Mann (1999).

Before giving feedback, we make the assumption that you and the employee have discussed what he or she is working on and that you have given the employee an opportunity to reflect on his or her own performance. We also assume that you were clear on what aspects of the employee's performance you were trying to observe and what was important in the situation. Finally, we assume that you have had a chance to get some good solid data about the performance of the employee, data that you trust.

We also assume that you have decided what your goal is in giving the feedback. Are you providing feedback to a novice or an expert?

In addition to learning, is your goal to help appraise or celebrate the employee's previous actions? Or is your goal to encourage the employee or provide helpful information as he or she looks forward to the next challenge? Either way, the basic structure of feedback is the same, and the suggestions for how to manage the process are similar. Having said that, the art of coaching, an art that one learns only with practice, is in knowing how to offer feedback in a way that conveys as much useful information as possible (see Box 9.2).

BOX 9.2   Feedback, the Basic Requirements

Feedback content should include the following:

- The situation in which your observations were made
- Your observations of the employee in action
- The impact of the employee's behavior or actions, particularly on you

Before offering feedback, be sure to do the following:

- Set the stage for your feedback discussion in a way that will encourage the maximum degree of openness, which is essential to learning. Make sure that the location, degree of confidentiality, and timing are appropriate to the individual and the situation.

Effective feedback has the following characteristics:

- Solicited by the employee
- Focused on what the employee is trying to accomplish or has told you that he or she wants to learn

- Given with a frequency appropriate to the employee, context, and challenge
- Given, whenever possible, right after an action and the employee's reflection on his or her action
- Given, whenever possible, with a helpful, not an angry, attitude
- Specific, using behavioral terminology or a comparable description terminology
- Focuses on the task, action, or behavior, not on the person
- Direct and usually begins with "I" statements
- Delivered without interpretation
- Checked by the coaching manager to make sure that the employee heard the message the manager wanted to deliver
- Followed by the question "What can you do with this feedback?" (or words to that effect)
- Followed by the suggestion of a follow-up meeting, particularly if the feedback to the coachee has been negative

Feedback represents a form of communication, or a message. What should the message include? Keep in mind the categories of intent, action, and impact. Feedback content usually includes the following: a description of the *situation* in which you observed the employee; a description of the *behavior* of, or *actions* taken by, the employee you observed; and finally a description of the *impact* of the behavior or actions of the employee on others or on a relevant business outcome. "Here is what I saw, and here is what I think was the impact of what I saw" is the basic structure of a feedback message. Note what is included and not included in the message. What *is* included is factual information, to the highest degree possible.

What is *not* included is an interpretation. You may have to climb the ladder of inference a bit when describing what you "think" is the impact of a particular action or behavior; but oftentimes, you'll know. You'll know because you can describe the impact of the employee's behavior on you. "I don't know what others might have thought about your approach to this, but I liked it. It really addressed my concerns." If you describe the impact from your vantage point, you're making very few inferences. After all, an individual's manager is a key stakeholder in the actions of that individual. The impact on you, as manager, does count, and the impact you experience from the actions of an employee may be similar to the impact experienced by others. You can therefore state, "This was the impact on me," with real authority.

On the basis of our own research and review of the writing to date on personal learning, we encourage you to always consider the importance of the employee's goals while delivering feedback. If you *focus on what the employee is trying to accomplish or has told you he or she wants to learn*, you have been given license by the employee to provide feedback accordingly. Consider the alternative, as described by one of our former students and coaching manager trainees. The following is a true story:

> I just had an illuminating experience regarding feedback that I thought you might find interesting. I contacted a colleague about a job when I was applying for positions in the company he worked for. I sent him my résumé, and he said he would forward it along to any manager he knew of who might be hiring. Today, I got a two-page response from someone else who works at my old colleague's firm, a complete stranger, giving me "feedback" on my résumé. I was completely at a loss for words—not at all what I was expecting and least of all what I wanted to hear. It was interesting to notice my own response to this completely unsolicited and unwanted feedback. Although the author of the feedback letter made very good points, and I am very impressed that he took the time, I could feel my anger rising as I kept reading the e-mail. The anger started with the second sentence that read, "I have a few concerns with the way that your résumé is crafted." I was particularly upset at this point because several professional career counselors had worked with me over an extended period of time to write the résumé. Because of the nature of the feedback, it is very unlikely that I will implement any of the points. A major lesson learned from this—don't give unsolicited feedback!

(We point out that the author of the above story also learned nothing from this particular manager about jobs in his business unit, which was the author's original goal.) This may seem like a rather small matter, but we believe that it is not. The author of the above quote was a classic victim of the "butting in" syndrome. Every relationship has boundaries, and we violate those boundaries at our peril. If you have taken the time, as a coaching manager, to establish good communications with your employee and have gone to the trouble of finding out what the employee wants your help with and then you veer off course on the basis of your own agenda rather than the employee's, this will often be experienced as a violation of trust.

Granted, you may at times have to speak for the organization. That is OK if you clearly signal your intent with a statement such as "I know this is a bit away from your own agenda, but I have to speak for the company now and give you some feedback on a different topic." On a less formal level, the simple question "Do you mind if I give you some feedback on that?" can also help you seek the learner's permission for changing the boundaries of the relationship. However, it is important when using the latter question to note the power differential between you and your employee. It may be very hard for an employee, particularly someone of lower status (younger, newer, or less experienced), to say no to such a question, even if he or she really wants to do so. We recommend using such a question only when you're comfortable that the power and status differential between yourself and the employee is quite small and the level of trust is high.

Set the stage for your feedback discussion in a way that will encourage the maximum degree of openness, which is essential to learning. How and where you set the stage can vary quite a bit. In some situations, the scheduled individual setting is most appropriate. You may have been asked to go out and gather a significant amount of performance data for the employee, or the issues may be quite sensitive. Structure (a scheduled meeting) and confidentiality (away from everyone else) may help the employee focus on what is being said rather than on the reactions of others. In yet other instances, the stage may have been set by your working understanding with the employee. Perhaps the employee expects to meet with you in the hall, right after the big meeting. Particularly once you and your employees are used to the give-and-take of feedback, you may find yourself providing more of it in informal settings. Finally, in a mature team characterized by high levels of feedback, it would seem inappropriate to move the discussion to a private setting, offline. The point we are making with regard to setting the stage is to be sensitive to the employee's needs. When in doubt, ask. If you're not satisfied with the answer, the old rule "Praise in public, criticize in private" should serve as your guide. We encourage you to always set the stage in such a way that the self-esteem of your employee will be minimally threatened. (We do realize that in the arts and in some other contexts, public critiques may be appropriate, as stated above. In addition, when teams are trying to improve their performance, it may be more appropriate to provide an opportunity for feedback giving and receiving in the group setting.)

Setting the stage also involves a consideration of timing. Feedback, particularly if it is based on substantial data collected by the coaching manager, perhaps involving others, may be eagerly sought but anxiously anticipated by the employee. Substantial feedback takes time to absorb. If you are going to engage in a major feedback intervention, make sure you and the employee have sufficient time to thoroughly discuss the issues raised by the feedback.

If feedback is being given to enhance an employee's learning and the employee is trying to build effectiveness in addressing a challenging goal, then feedback from multiple observations will be useful. Your intent should be to give the employee enough data to build a "video" of his or her performance over time. This suggests that it is best to *give feedback frequently* and focus frequent feedback on what the employee is trying to do differently.

Likewise, feedback that is given *right after an action and the individual's reflection on that action* is more likely to result in learning. The events are fresh in everyone's mind. Feedback that is timely is thus important as well. It may be necessary for you to take a few minutes to figure out what you want to say, but don't delay too long.

Although sometimes, with more senior-level coachees, the coaching manager may find that a bit of ambiguity in the feedback process can be helpful, you should be ready to provide feedback that is specific and focused on the task, action, or behavior. By specific, we mean descriptive. We return to our oft-used metaphor of the mirror. It is important to gather data that accurately reflect the employee's performance. Feedback involves delivering those data in a way that is helpful. The mirror says very little about why things are the way they are. Rather, it simply describes how things are. Use data from the left column of your observation sheet (see Chapter 8) to describe actual behavior. Note, however, that while the feedback should be specific, for the sake of clarity, as discussed above, when providing feedback to those with more expertise, you will likely need to move out of a one-way communication of your specific observations to a coaching dialogue regarding their meaning. Finally, keep in mind, as cited above, the value of positive feedback. Positive feedback should not be provided just to encourage the recipient. Positive feedback can aid learning and development.

We've already described the importance for the coaching manager of *having a helpful attitude* while delivering feedback. If the coaching manager runs into the problem described (above) by Harry Levinson (1986), that of being angry, we recommend tabling the discussion until cooler heads prevail. You probably can't do a good job of carefully delivering a focused message when you are angry. The reality is the tone of your voice, the affective coloring of your presentation (your mood), and your body language will give away your feelings. If you are a typical adult, people can tell. Just ask your friends. If the employee feels that you are angry, he or she will respond to the feeling, not the content of the message.

For the receiver of feedback to be able to make use of the data provided by the coaching manager, the information must be presented *clearly and simply*. The language and style of the presentation should be appropriate to the audience. Avoid nondescriptive or technical terms unless you are sure that the receiver of the feedback can work with those terms and can understand what the terms actually mean.

The best feedback is also usually quite *direct*. Directness usually requires the use of "I" statements. "This is what I saw." Some of us have experienced, and probably all of us have heard about, feedback statements that begin,

"We don't think . . ." The reality is that unless the employee knows who you are talking about when you use the word "we," such a feedback statement may have very little credibility. "We" statements can also make the employee feel "ganged-up on" or attacked. If the coaching manager has to provide feedback on behalf of several individuals, it is much more effective to be specific about who said what.

Avoid interpretations drawn from the second, or above, levels of the ladder of inference. For reasons previously discussed, such interpretations are likely to generate defensiveness—and, worse yet, are likely to be wrong. Interpretation occurs during the coaching dialogue through the use of questions. Our favorite example of inference masquerading as feedback is "You have a bad attitude." Such a statement is actually devoid of data and represents a pure interpretation. A descriptive statement that would support such an interpretation might be something like "You told the last three customers who walked in the door that you hated working here." Note that such a descriptive statement is in some ways even more hard-hitting than the interpretation. Data almost always carry more weight than the inappropriate use of inference.

After delivering feedback of importance, the coaching manager *asks the employee what he or she heard.* Such a question can seem awkward, but it is very important to make sure that the right message was given in the feedback process. If you are coaching on the fly or coaching under stressful conditions, the effectiveness of your ability to communicate and of the employee's ability to comprehend may be limited. It is important not to leave the employee with the wrong impression and the emotional fallout that may come from the wrong impression. An anxious employee can interpret a simple statement such as "I thought you had a hard time with that" in many erroneous ways. Though not what the coaching manager intended, the employee might walk away from such feedback feeling defeated and unwilling to try again.

Finally, *ask the employee what he or she can or will do with the feedback.* Ideally, feedback leads to additional reflection and then action. Having delivered the feedback, or after delivering each point of the feedback, the coaching manager should stop, make sure that he or she was understood, and ask for the employee's thoughts about how the feedback can help. Remember that the coaching process begins with a coaching dialogue. It is important to keep the dialogue going by providing plenty of opportunity for the employee to reflect on the feedback you have provided. A little silence during these periods is OK. It is far better to offer some feedback, ask for the employee's reactions, and then wait, rather than hurry on to the next point. Indeed, if the feedback has any real substance to it, it is natural for the employee to need a few minutes to digest what has been said. Make sure you, the coaching manager, don't do all the talking!

After the feedback is given, the coachee may move ahead with future reflection and action. If the feedback is particularly negative or problematic, however, *it may be wise to schedule another meeting to follow up soon after the meeting at which the feedback was given.* Even under the best of circumstances, critical feedback can be difficult for some employees to manage. Very critical feedback will be difficult for many. Follow-up meetings show concern for the coachee and symbolize the coaching manager's commitment to the coachee's ongoing learning.

Before closing this section on the basics for providing balanced feedback, we should discuss in more depth what the word *balanced* is intended to convey. It is not intended to convey the age-old practice of providing a "feedback sandwich." The feedback sandwich begins with good feedback, moves to critical feedback, and then closes with good feedback. Although it is overtly constructed out of concern for the coachee's self-esteem, the need for a "sandwich approach" suggests that the feedback is a surprise and may in part be interpreted as a punishment. The sandwich approach also requires the feedback to offer something positive as well as something critical, which may not be appropriate.

If the employee is seeking feedback on something that he or she has chosen to work on, the coaching manager's feedback may be much more focused. Consider the following comment offered to a team leader who had requested that her manager give her some feedback on how she could help her team make better decisions: "When you said, 'We should come to closure now,' several people in the meeting just stopped talking." The coaching manager is offering these observations in response to the employee's request. Such feedback still needs to be given with the employee's self-esteem in mind, but there is little information to "sandwich" and little need to do so. The employee and coaching manager are focusing on specific, mutually agreed-on developmental goals.

By *balanced*, we mean thoughtful, accurate, and respectful. We said in this chapter that coaching requires practice. It is a discipline, really. Working from a good observational position or on the basis of data provided by others, the coaching manager packages that information and provides it to the employee. The employee is truly interested in the perspective offered by the data and, as a result, feels as though he or she has been helped. The employee's learning—not his or her self-esteem—is at issue.

The Emotional Impact of Feedback

Although there are very useful rules of thumb for constructing and delivering feedback, we've come to understand that there is more to the discipline of providing balanced feedback than mastering the mechanics of packaging the data. Learning, as we all know, requires some risk taking, some courage, tolerance for some real defeats and pain, and ultimately a great deal of persistence. Learning, especially learning that takes us outside our comfort zone, is a very personal affair whether we like it or not. It is probably for that reason that employees sometimes (we hope not too often) hear a carefully crafted task-focused piece of feedback and turn it into a statement about their worth as individuals, even though the coaching manager intends just the opposite.

Feedback, when viewed from a perspective beyond the immediacy of a single manager/employee interaction, includes a rich array of emotional signals that can shape how the coachee experiences and ultimately processes the feedback. Confusion about, or failure to attend to, the management of emotionally laden messages that accompany feedback is perhaps one of the greatest sources of "feedback blowback," the negative reaction to feedback that many managers and employees fear.

One of our coaching managers told us a story about a major developmental experience from early in his career. While he was employed by a small but well-thought-of consulting firm, he had somehow managed to get an assignment consulting with what was, at that time, one of the most dynamic and glamorous show business organizations in the world. He spent 6 months working with the senior management of the organization, doing what sounded like a spectacular job. He hobnobbed with the rich, famous, and powerful. He learned an enormous amount about himself and his profession. It was a learning experience that shaped his career. When he returned to his consulting company's home office, no one wanted to hear about it. He was told to write up his personal report and file his expense account. In his performance evaluation several weeks later, he was rated very favorably by his manager, receiving a rating of 4 instead of the usual 3. However, his manager focused only on contribution to the bottom line, not on the young consultant's experience of the work and the learning that had taken place. Having been given that rather uncommon (for this firm) rating, he received a nice bonus for his efforts. His manager felt as though he had been generous with his feedback and helpful to the young man. The young consultant felt unwanted and began to prepare his résumé. It wasn't that he didn't like the rating or didn't want the bonus. Rather, he felt there was something missing in the manager's feedback.

The manager provided relatively specific feedback about the consultant's performance in relation to the organization's goals by focusing on the financial contributions that resulted from his efforts. He then rewarded the consultant's performance accordingly. We hope that by this time, the reader will note that part of the problem in this example was the manager's failure to attend to the employee's goals as well as the organization's. In addition, the manager did not consider the emotional meaning of the kind of feedback he was offering—and not offering—for that particular employee in that particular context. We suggest that coaching managers can enhance their own effectiveness by taking into account the emotional messages implicit in their feedback and by trying to match the message to the needs of the situation. That may sound complex, but a simple matrix covers most of the situations most managers will encounter (see Table 9.1).

Feedback describes what just happened. It reflects back to an individual a picture of his or her actions, behaviors, or decisions. However, feedback

Table 9.1   Managing the Emotional Content of Feedback

	Examples of Coaching Actions or Statements	
	Past Orientation	Future Orientation
Emotionally Symbolic Statements or Actions	Celebration	Encouragement
	• "Good job" • Superlative statements: "How in the world did you pull that off?" • A formal celebration • Discussing what this means for the employee's career or at least the next step • Helping the employee deal with defeat	• "I think you can handle that" • "What additional supports do you need?" • "Try it again"
Cognitively Oriented Communication	Performance Appraisal	Personal Development
	• "This is how that situation looked to me" • "These are the final results and how they relate to your work"	• "Here is the gap that I saw" • "It looked to me like you might try doing that differently"

can be given with a variety of intents in mind on the part of the person who gives it. The intent of the feedback may be to help the employee gain a perspective on what just happened—or to help the employee move forward into the future. A manager may say to an employee, "That was an effective presentation and demonstrated your command of the details," to indicate that it was completed in a satisfactory way and why. On the other hand, such a statement may indicate that the employee should be aware of what a great job he or she did this time—while planning the next presentation, which will take place tomorrow. The context when added to the comment provides an indication as to how the employee should interpret the feedback. In the latter case, the feedback is given with the intent of building the employee's confidence in preparation for the next performance. Feedback is a response to past actions, but it can also be preparation for the future.

The point to remember here is that the emotional message accompanying the cognitive one has a great impact on what the coachee will hear. As discussed in our quick visit to the photo class critique, photography students want to learn from the feedback, but they also need the emotional awareness that someone is paying attention to their work. The fact that someone else has taken the time to look at their work, even if the outcome is a critical review, is encouraging.

The story of our friend the consultant illustrates the importance for coaching managers to be aware that the emotional and cognitive components of feedback are quite different. Some people are used to getting an A. For them, a report card with "straight A's" is perhaps not such a big deal. For others, top grades are a struggle. This young consultant, perhaps unsure of himself, had achieved an important outcome and learned a great deal along the way. This knowledge would soon be lost to the firm, assuming that the young consultant followed through on the impulse to leave. Note that all the while, the manager felt that he was coaching the employee, giving him useful feedback about what it takes to be successful at the company: revenue generation.

What form might such a celebration have taken in this case? Celebrations could have ranged from simple interest on the part of the manager to asking the consultant to stage a lunchtime seminar in which he would describe what he'd learned to other consultants engaged in similar kinds of activities. The failure to do either represented what the employee seemed to infer as a very clear message: "We don't care about you as a person." Granted, the employee may have been unfairly climbing the ladder of inference. Such is the nature of symbolic rather than direct communication, however. Symbolic communications invite interpretation.

Similarly, future-oriented feedback has an emotional component as well. Feedback that says "I think you can do this" is much more potent in this regard than "This is the gap between your current performance and where you need to be." The latter needs to be said, but the coaching manager should consider what kind of emotional message should accompany the cognitive one. Does the coaching manager want to offer encouragement? If he or she does not, the employee may experience the feedback as discouraging, no matter how factually it is offered.

We hope that several lessons emerge from this discussion. First of all, missing or incomplete spoken feedback does not mean that the employee gets no feedback at all. Inaction on the part of the manager is also feedback. The employee will fill in the gaps. The employee will particularly wonder, "Did I do a good job?" or "Does the manager think I can really handle this?" Ultimately, like it or not, the employee will be thinking about questions such as "Does he like me?" "Am I cared about?" and "Is this a good manager to be working for?"

Second, whatever else the manager does that is closely related in time to the feedback event may be watched by the employee and incorporated with the feedback itself. Our favorite is something we call the "good feedback that punishes." An employee has a very successful engagement with a difficult customer, for example. The manager is ecstatic about the employee's success. He then promptly assigns her every difficult customer he has had the misfortune to deal with. Ask yourself: Does this kind of feedback communicate a genuine interest in the employee? Of course not. If the coaching manager thinks someone has done a great job under difficult circumstances, he or she should first communicate that fact and then express a real interest in the employee's development by negotiating the next assignment. In this case, the manager should ask the employee if she wants to be thrown back in with the tough customers again or try a different kind of assignment.

Maximizing the Value of That Imperfect Instrument, Feedback

It is interesting to review the scientific literature on feedback and find that, even when delivered effectively, it is not a panacea. Our hopes for the power of feedback have grown over the past several decades, encouraged by the research and writing on systems theory and cybernetics. Cybernetic theory holds that systems, including the individual in interaction with his or her environment, can be self-correcting if they are effective at accessing and working with the right kind of information. Typically, this is information from both inside and outside the system. The tremendous emphasis we place on gaining input from the customer is one manifestation of this belief. If we can just figure out what the customer wants and make sure we deliver (by getting feedback from the customer), our organizations will be on track. This is, of course, true only to an extent.

As any CEO or marketing manager will tell you, "Easier said than done." Which customers do you need to get information from? How do you know the feedback is accurate? How do you get customers to take the time to give useful feedback? Most customers don't really want to give you any information; they want to take their product or service, assuming that it works properly, and go home.

A new brand of systems thinkers (Senge, 1990) draws our attention to an additional aspect of feedback in this regard. The gap in time between feedback and action tends, even in fairly tightly coupled systems, to result in a delay in our ability to interpret the impact of any particular piece of feedback. During that delay, the conditions in the system may change. Imagine that you're standing in a shower trying to get the water to just the right temperature. You stick your hand under the shower and find that it is a little too cold (that is feedback), so you turn the hot water up a bit. It is still too cold, so you turn the hot water up some more. Now it is almost just right, so you turn the hot water up one more time, just a bit. Suddenly, it is way too hot! Suppose an employee has been working on building her skills as a team leader and receives coaching help and balanced feedback from her manager in the process. She may try a number of different tactics, for instance, to improve the effectiveness of team meetings. Unfortunately, it may be months before she or the manager finds out whether or not those tactics actually worked.

Feedback, then, even when effectively delivered, is an imperfect source of information about our work. Despite its imperfections as a learning tool, however, it is still quite important. *We believe that feedback is likely to be most useful when it is offered as part of a systematic approach to coaching.* By a *systematic approach,* we mean following the steps of creating a coaching-friendly context, looking for coaching moments, creating a coaching dialogue, knowing what to look for and how to observe, providing balanced feedback, collaboratively interpreting the causes for any gap between actual and desired performance, and setting some meaningful goals for change.

When the coaching manager takes a systematic approach to coaching, the goals of the coaching are fairly clear, the manager's role as a helper is fully established, and the employee's role as a learner who takes responsibility for his or her own growth and development are also fully established. This can be seen in a working relationship between a coach and an athletic team. Coaches and athletes are fully engaged in working together toward a common goal. Athletes know that, given the nature of their competition, they have to improve to achieve that goal. It is a given that feedback is focused toward that goal, and it is offered to individuals who want it (presumably everybody on the team). In such a coaching-friendly context, the coach isn't the only one providing feedback. Team members also give feedback to one another. Consider how this takes the pressure off any one particular feedback intervention. Feedback from multiple sources, directed at one particular issue or problem, might have to be given on a number of different occasions to be useful.

Let's say the coach sees that a particular play isn't working. It may not be clear right away what is wrong or what needs to change. Team members struggle to figure out what the feedback is telling them. The problem may not even be clear to the coach. The team may have to discuss, or dialogue, among themselves and with the coach to understand what the feedback is actually telling them. Perhaps it has to do with the way one player is executing the plan or how several players are working together. *Feedback at its best is additional knowledge that will be explored and understood in order to determine what it really means.* Feedback should not be the last word on the subject. It is merely the next step.

Your Development as a Provider of Feedback

Learning to give useful feedback takes some courage, a bit of basic analysis of the learning needs of the other party, and some practice. Helpful feedback needs to be clear, and the ability to speak clearly about what one has seen is a skill that must be developed. Further, as we discussed in the previous chapter, the ability to speak clearly rests on the shoulders of the ability to *see* clearly. The best providers of feedback possess some of the skills of a good anthropologist. They are curious, keep their eyes open, can report on what they see with a degree of objectivity (though even anthropologists will tell you that objectivity can be tough to maintain), and can communicate their observations in a fashion that others find helpful.

Because developing effectiveness as a provider of feedback also involves learning on the part of the coaching manager, it is probably necessary to get feedback on your feedback! Such a two-way learning process, in which the coaching manager gives feedback to an employee and gets feedback on his or her effectiveness in doing so, is greatly facilitated by a good relationship between the employee and manager—in other words, a coaching-friendly context. But as we have warned repeatedly, don't let this rather in-depth exploration of feedback scare you. We want you to know how feedback works, at its best. But you don't have to be perfect at providing feedback to be helpful.

What Does It All Mean?

10

Collaboratively Interpreting Learning Needs

In this chapter, you will learn the following:

- How to use the coaching dialogue as a method for helping you and your employees understand the key learning challenges and root causes related to the coachees' learning goals

Case 10.1: What's Going On With Jack?

Jack was appointed sales manager late last year, and you've been keeping an eye on how he's doing, or at least you think you have been. You want him to be successful and don't want to just let him hang out there on a limb waiting to see who might saw it off. Jack is an independent sort, though, and although he says he wants your coaching, he really wants to focus on results. You've encouraged him to also think about process, but he feels he can handle staffing, keeping people motivated, setting the vision, and the other demands of leadership.

This isn't one of those situations in which the best salesperson was promoted to sales management but has no management skills. You hired Jack into his sales position with the idea that, on the basis of his work history before coming

(Continued)

(Continued)

to your firm, he'd quickly be able to assume managerial responsibilities. He had positions as sales team leader, supervisor, and sales trainer in his last two companies. In preemployment interviews, you asked him pointed questions about issues he'd dealt with as a supervisor, and his answers to every question made Jack sound like a knowledgeable individual who understood both sales and management. You brought him in to sell for 6 months while he learned the products and then moved him into the sales manager position, with responsibility for two sales supervisors. Each of those supervisors has 10 field sales representatives reporting to him. Jack was asked to set a new vision for the group and work along with the supervisors to execute it.

Jack knows you are a coaching manager and wanted to work for you for that reason. You talked with him about your leadership style and expectations and made it clear that he must take charge of his learning but that you would be there to coach him. When he responded, "Coach me on results, come in and check in with the staff and customers at the end of each quarter, give me some good feedback, and help me keep improving," you felt very comfortable. The two of you agreed that you should keep an eye on sales, employee product knowledge, and employee morale as key indicators of how Jack was doing. You told him he needed to make the numbers, keep his people motivated and on target, and keep himself satisfied and growing. All seemed well, particularly given the scope of Jack's job and the 6 months you gave him to get to know the product and the rest of the team.

Unfortunately, Jack didn't make it through the first quarter before you started to get some disturbing e-mails and phone calls, first from the sales representatives you know quite well and then from one of the supervisors. Each message told essentially the same story: "You have to do something with Jack. He's getting in the way by asking us to generate a lot more paperwork on each sale. He is demanding all the information he can get. After each sale, he wants us to complete an extensive survey having to do with customer type, customer need, financial arrangements, product configuration, literally anything you could imagine. We've tried to accommodate him, and we've also told him that this extra paperwork isn't helping the customer or the company. We don't even know what problem he's trying to solve." Jack had been insistent. In fact, he'd been downright angry when people had suggested to him that there might be another way to handle his need for all that information that wouldn't create so much additional red tape.

You had worked hard to create an environment in which feedback could pass from sales rep to sales rep, from sales rep to supervisor, and on up the chain. You want people to coach one another. You also expect open communications in your organization around any new initiative.

You feel suddenly like kicking yourself. How could you have missed something so important about Jack's leadership style? Yes, he does a lot of the things you want him to do, but you now realize he is doing some other things that really run counter to the work group culture you tried to create. Your mind races to what you are sure is the right diagnosis: Jack is a new, nervous manager, and evidently, his confidence is low. He's having trouble building a partnership with the supervisors, whom he didn't choose himself. You believe that the impact of all this is that he's becoming something of a control freak. He wants every piece of information he can get his hands on. He'll never make it as a manager this way, you think. He's got to trust his supervisors and his reps, listen to them, and learn from them.

You feel some guilt about all this. Did you set him up to fail? You feel certain of what you should do. You have to call him into the office and start giving him more pep talks, start telling him to relax. You feel suddenly more comfortable. You have a plan.

Ah, the view from the upper rungs of the ladder of inference is fine, isn't it? Especially when relying only on one-way communications such as angry e-mails. After all, what manager doesn't recognize what appears to be Jack's problem? The new manager, even a nice one, becomes something of a control freak during the transition. Sometimes it just goes away by itself, when the "lightbulb" goes on in the new manager's mind. At other times, the manager has to get hit in the head by the proverbial baseball bat.

The trouble is you don't know at this point what is going on. You have a well-educated guess. You and Jack have agreed on what you should help him keep an eye on. However, you don't have Jack's self-assessment, his interpretation of what has been happening and why.

Our coaching managers have told us that one of the biggest hurdles they face is that of avoiding the rush to judgment. We've already discussed this as it relates to observation, but obviously it's an even more important consideration when trying to figure out what key issues are in play for an individual coachee. In this case, the rush to judgment, which is based on inferences made while gathering performance data, leads to an interpretation stemming from the coaching manager's past experience, not from a dialogue with the coachee. Unfortunately, an action plan, perhaps an informal one, may then be developed that targets issues or problems completely unrelated to the gap between actual and desired performance.

Let's consider some other possibilities for Jack's behavior. (We are not excusing his behavior but are not condemning it, either. We want to understand it.)

Jack may indeed be nervous, but he may also be angry. He may be trying to get hold of what he sees as excessive sales expenses. He may be trying to track customer data for feedback to marketing. He may be fearful that one of his reps is accounting for business inappropriately, to inflate his or her commission. Someone else in the company may be leaning on him to conduct the survey. This may have been the way other firms with which he has worked always did business. He may come from a cultural background in which employees are expected to obey business leaders and leaders are not expected to have to explain their actions to followers. Granted, one theme in all of this is his lack of communications with his boss, but beyond that, we find many possible causes for this gap between his current performance and his desired performance. And if his rationale, his *intent,* borrowing from the previous chapter, is actually aimed at dealing with a serious problem, your interpretation of his behavior and your feelings about it may be quite different from what you're experiencing right now.

The phrase *performance gap,* meaning a gap between actual and desired performance, has a negative connotation, unfortunately. It must be emphasized that such a gap more often exists for very good reasons. The phrase *performance gap* equates in our view with the phrase *learning curve.* If you're going to undertake a challenge that will require the building of new competencies, you should expect a performance gap or learning curve. If you don't experience such a disconnect between your current and your desired performance when being challenged in new ways, you must be lucky. Ironically, that luck may not bring you luck in the future. If you accidentally come up with the right answer the first time, you very likely will not be able to come up with the right answer the second time. You don't know how you got there.

Jack may have set up a stretch situation for himself, one that demands even more of his leadership style than he has experienced previously. He may be doing better this time than he had done in previous attempts. Remember that the data you have at this point are "snapshots" when viewed from the perspective of his career overall. You need more information about what this means, and so does Jack. You need to know why—or do you?

Do You Need to Know Why?

You may be saying to yourself, "I don't need to know why Jack is doing this. The fact is he needs to communicate about this issue with the supervisors and the reps. I'd just tell him he has to do it." We understand your approach and your feelings. The question here is "Does knowing why add any value to Jack's situation and to his learning?" Certainly, if compliance, not learning, is your only concern, you might just tell Jack to explain what he is doing to his supervisors and have them explain it to the sales reps; if you thought Jack's behavior was damaging the integrity of the group or the customers, that would be an appropriate action to take. However, your goal here is to help Jack learn. You'd like him to become a better communicator, if that is in fact the problem.

Make note that this is when you have to display emotional intelligence yourself. If you've just received a significant amount of feedback from others that the person you put in charge is causing trouble, you may feel guilty and angry. You may want to jump into action. Remember Woody Hayes, the football coach, and try to stay on the sidelines, at least for a bit. Summon up a helpful coaching attitude and focus on the learning process if that is indeed your goal.

Do you need to know why? Another example suggests an approach by which coaching managers can answer this question on a case-by-case basis. Let's say that you are speaking to a large group of people without a microphone. Someone gives you feedback by saying, "Please speak up." It doesn't really matter in this one instance whether or not you were speaking too softly because you underestimated the size of the crowd, overestimated the acoustics of the room, overestimated the strength of your voice, are shy, or don't know what you're talking about. The reason in this instance isn't terribly important. You can fix the main problem right away by speaking up. This is a small issue and not central to your overall plan for self-development. You speak up, people seem more comfortable, and your talk proceeds with greater impact.

What if this happens on a regular basis? What if you always speak too softly while addressing a group despite the fact that you are routinely asked to speak up? It then becomes important to get to the root of the problem. Feedback directed only at the offending behavior doesn't lead to change.

Before leaving this example, let's assume that you knew in advance that the CEO of your company—or even the president of the United States—was going to be in the crowd you were addressing. Let's further assume that in addition to speaking too softly, your overhead slides were in bad condition, and you were not terribly well prepared. This is an important situation in which there is a significant gap between your performance and the desired or expected performance. If your boss could control her temper after such a performance, she might find it possible to actually help you understand not only what you did wrong. (We're sure she would inform you about that!) She would ideally try to help the two of you figure out why this performance failure occurred. The implications could be significant. Perhaps you are terribly frightened of speaking in front of senior managers because you have had very little exposure to them. Perhaps you know nothing about public speaking and didn't understand how to prepare. Perhaps there is a significant cultural gap between how you believe you should behave and how the manager believes you should behave.

We suggest the following rule of thumb: *If there is a recurring gap between desired and actual performance and/or if there is a gap between desired and actual performance when the performance is an important one, it is important to understand the key issues that are related to the gap, the root cause(s).*

Does Jack's problem qualify under this rule? Although you don't know whether this is a recurring one, we would say that this is an important performance gap. His role is an important one. He is early in his tenure in that role. Many people are being affected by his behavior. Perhaps most important, he's very talented. Both you and Jack should expect your efforts to yield more than mere compliance on his part.

The Coaching Dialogue

Once the coaching manager and the coachee have determined that it is appropriate to search for the root cause or causes for any performance gap, a continuation of the coaching dialogue can help both of you look for those causes. You know what happened. You now want to understand *why*. The coaching dialogue encourages the coachee to reflect on the feedback the coaching manager has presented. Provide the feedback, ask the employee for his or her thoughts, and wait. See what the employee has to say.

A return to the coaching dialogue is important for several reasons. First, if you tell Jack the "right" answer, it is your answer. It may not be his. Perhaps you tell him that you can empathize with what is it like to take over a new group. He hasn't been thinking about that; he has just been thinking about trying to get a handle on sales expenses. This disconnect between your comment and his mind-set is significant. However, let's say for the sake of argument that when you make the comment indicating you understand how hard it is to take over a new group, Jack says, "I never thought of that. I guess you're right." Is Jack then focusing on the issue that he wants to focus on, or is he focusing on the one you want him to focus on? Giving Jack time to reflect on the feedback you have received encourages him to take full ownership of whatever diagnosis and implications emerge from the dialogue as it moves forward. It encourages him to keep learning more about how to think for himself.

Asking Jack to reflect on the feedback is also more likely to encourage him to consider the range of alternative causes or issues and come up with the right one(s) on which to focus. If his own analysis of the situation dominates, assuming you have created a coaching-friendly context in which he can speak openly, it is more likely to be accurate.

The coaching manager can aid in this process, if the coachee is having trouble, by using the basic coaching questions: "What were you trying to do?" "What is the impact of what you did?" "What do you need to do differently to have the impact you're hoping for?" Such questions serve to keep Jack focused on the basic principles of experiential learning: action, reflection to assess the impact of the action, and experimentation with new approaches or different actions. Along the way, the coaching manager can encourage the coachee to consider alternatives other than the obvious.

Root Causes

Behavior associated with most human action is what psychologists call *multidetermined*. If you decide to go to the store for a cup of coffee, the decision that resulted in that action may have been influenced by a variety of factors. You wanted some coffee. The store was close by. Your spouse wanted to go with you. The car was all warmed up and ready to go. You like the coffee at that particular store, and so on. The same is true for actions at work. Actions are driven by the thoughts and feelings of the individual, what is happening on his or her team, and what is happening in his or her organization. An accurate understanding of the cause of any particular action, and therefore of any particular performance gap, may have to take into account a number of different factors.

For this reason, it is difficult to offer an exhaustive list of factors that the coaching manager and coachee should consider while trying to understand the root cause(s) for any performance gap. Furthermore, because the context of your exploration is action in business and not, say, anthropology, it isn't necessary to use words from a textbook to articulate your diagnosis. Ideally, you use words and phrases that make sense to you as a coaching manager and to your employee.

Nevertheless, we do feel that it is useful for managers to have some sense of the factors that typically show up when trying to understand a performance gap. In addition, two factors that we'll discuss in this section are important to keep an eye on because they are so common: cultural diversity and organizational change.

It is a mistake to focus on the individual employee to the exclusion of all other possible factors as you and the employee try to understand the causes of a performance gap. The gap may also reflect a variety of interpersonal, team, or organizational-level issues. We will start with the individual-level factors and then move to those beyond the individual level of analysis. Again, we remind you that a performance gap can occur for good reasons as people stretch themselves. The diagnosis shouldn't be seen as a criticism. An overview of our nonexhaustive list of root causes can be found in Box 10.1. For our purposes here, we're going to focus on the first group of issues, those having to do with the individual.

BOX 10.1   **A Nonexhaustive Listing of Learning Needs and Root Causes for Performance Gaps**

Individual-level factors—related to the tasks within a role or the role itself:

- Lack of knowledge or awareness regarding self, others, or contexts
- Lack of skills
- Lack of motivation
- Culture and cultural diversity–related factors

Organizational factors:

- Team issues
- Contextual issues
- Leadership support
- Poor distribution of talent, attitudes, and resources
- Organizational changes that make desired performance difficult to define
- Organizational factors that increase the likelihood of unintended consequences

---

Individual Factors

Individual performance requires the mobilization of *knowledge* and *skills*. Many if not most individual-level root causes for a performance gap occur because one or both of these factors are undeveloped. We return to our discussion of Jack to illustrate. Let's assume that the root cause in this situation has to do with Jack's inability to communicate to his supervisors his need for the information. Jack may not have *awareness* of the importance of effective communications. He may not have a conceptual understanding that people are much more receptive to change if the reason for the change is explained in advance. Jack may still be very skilled at communicating. Perhaps he can give a great speech. Being able to do something, or having the *skill,* doesn't mean you know when to use that skill.

Alternatively, Jack may know that it is important to communicate but may be very ineffective as a writer or presenter. This skill, the ability to execute a desired behavior or action effectively, is absent or underdeveloped. Opportunities for practice, feedback, role models, mentors, conceptual discussions, formal classroom training, and reading can all help address knowledge- and skill-related performance gaps.

A range of other individual-level factors can also create performance gaps. One question that Jack must face is whether or not he actually wants to face the hassles associated with having to communicate every decision to his followers. He may have the ability to communicate, and he may know how to communicate, but if he is unhappy with the need to communicate, he is unlikely to be successful in doing so. He may not be *motivated* for the task at hand. Motivation, as we discussed in Chapter 3, is terribly important, particularly for people in challenging jobs. "You have to want it bad," as the saying goes.

Note that individuals may be motivated to tackle most of the tasks associated with a particular role but may still find that certain aspects of that role are distasteful. If Jack is naturally introverted and more comfortable with analysis than with action, he may not appreciate how much effort he will have to put into selling his ideas to others. The coaching manager and Jack might use several possible tactics to address such a problem. First, Jack might have to "go against the grain" and work on developing a skill that he will find distasteful to use. Unfortunately, he may dislike having to exercise such a skill even if he becomes quite effective at doing so. Some leadership development practitioners insist that when people are in stretch assignments, they will probably need to work on skills they normally don't want to use (Lombardo & Eichinger, 2001). After all, it is possible to become quite effective at laying people off, but who enjoys doing so?

There is now a significant debate under way regarding whether the "key" to development is to leverage one's strengths or to fix one's weaknesses. We're going to go into that in some detail in our discussion of planned career development, in Chapter 12. Suffice it to say for our purposes, both deploying one's strengths effectively and fixing weaknesses that get in the way are relevant to understanding performance gaps and learning needs.

The real question behind this debate probably has as much to do with motivation as with any other single factor. What does the coachee want? Managers will have a bigger impact on productivity by being sensitive to the importance of harnessing what can be described as "enduring life interests" (Butler & Waldroop, 1999). Once the manager and the employee understand the employee's interests, they can work together to shape or "sculpt" jobs that can capitalize on those interests. However, even a job that is well suited to a particular individual's motivation is very likely to also test that individual's ability to overcome the impact of his or her own personal limitations from time to time. That's really what learning is all about. On balance, if the employee likes the role but dislikes certain necessary tasks, it is probably in his or her best interest to learn to develop those needed skills, no matter how anxiety-provoking or distasteful. Dale Carnegie and Toastmasters International are two examples of organizations that have quite successfully helped numerous individuals confront one of the most common workplace fears, that of speaking in public.

Nevertheless, it may also make sense to consider remaking the job through job sculpting when appropriate. Jack might be able to address the need to communicate more effectively with his employees by having one of his supervisors, someone much more outgoing perhaps, take on that responsibility. There are two issues to consider in this regard. First, is there anyone else in the organization with the time and ability to help make up for Jack's deficit? Jack should also consider, however, whether or not he is creating a more permanent deficit in his own competency profile by not addressing the problem now. If Jack's long-term plans don't involve roles that require a great deal of communicating (granted, this is hard to imagine), he may decide that there is no compelling reason to build those skills now.

Employees are often very reluctant to talk about whether or not they actually want to be in a prized role. Admitting that one doesn't want to be in such a role can be perceived as a career-limiting move (or, as we say, "CLM"). One may fear that such a discussion will leave the manager with the conclusion that the employee wants out and isn't fully committed to the work. The coaching manager then has a real problem. Is it appropriate or even ethical to leave someone in a role in which he may ultimately fail, in spite of his apparent fit for the role, hurting himself and the company in the process, because he may not want to be in the role? It may take a number of discussions and a truly helpful attitude on the part of the coaching manager for an open dialogue to develop around this issue. Nevertheless, our coaches have told us that if they have created a very coaching-friendly context, the question "Are you sure this is the right job for you?" can be discussed. This is particularly the case if the employee trusts that the manager will try to help him or her through what may be an important career transition.

Cultural Factors

In a diverse world, the coaching manager will frequently have to consider whether or not cultural factors may influence the gap between actual and desired performance. Cultural assumptions, often implicit and undiscussed, can have a significant impact on how people behave by shaping the way individuals view a task and the options for responding to a task. Concepts such as leadership, goal setting, time management, negotiations, teamwork, influence, assertiveness, respect, and decision making, to name just a few, are defined either explicitly or implicitly in very different ways in different cultures.

It is difficult and often inappropriate to stereotype the behavioral patterns and perceptual outlook of people in any given culture. Nevertheless, some regularities do appear to be worth noting. Geerte Hofstede (1993), in a classic series of studies completed for IBM in the 1980s, found profound differences across cultures, even among employees from the same company, along the following dimensions that are relevant to this discussion: hierarchy or power orientation, comfort with ambiguity, time orientation, and the importance of context.

Hierarchy or power orientation refers to what in the United States might be described as "respect for and obedience to authority." Strong adherence to hierarchy leads individuals to pay careful attention to the statements of their leaders and to adhere to the rules they perceive to be appropriate in any particular situation. In hierarchical cultures, authority is less likely to be challenged. In highly innovative U.S. companies, for example, individuals with a very strong sense of respect for hierarchy might be seen as conservative and unwilling to think "outside the box." They might also be less comfortable engaging in conflict or "getting to the point" if they fear their actions could be seen as a challenge to those in authority. As a coaching manager, you might see someone who is quiet in a meeting as being timid, by virtue of his or her personality. Perhaps the quiet individual even believes that it would be rude to speak up. Although you as a coaching manager encourage the employee to do so, that person is nevertheless unfamiliar with being assertive, or "appropriately" assertive for the situation. Assertiveness is one behavior that can be very difficult to mimic or fake.

Comfort with ambiguity reflects an individual's tolerance for uncertainty. In some cultures, such as the United States, uncertainty tends to be valued. In other cultures, ambiguity or an absence of rules, procedures, or plans can create a significant level of discomfort. Those who seek certainty might look for written directives and be less likely to wade into an unstructured problem without careful study. Note that the very model of coaching discussed in this book requires a fairly high tolerance for ambiguity, because it puts a great deal of the responsibility for learning on the employee and less on the manager or the organization.

The influence of context involves the degree to which protocol and tradition dictate how communication should proceed. In high-context cultures, greater emphasis is placed on protocol, and communication tends to move from the general to the specific. In low-context cultures, communication tends to be more to the point, an approach that can come across to individuals from high-context cultures as rude. An employee from a low-context culture may appear to be quite aggressive to an employee from a high-context culture. For instance, in a recent executive education program in which managers from both the United States and the United Kingdom participated, participants from the United Kingdom described their U.S. colleagues as being "overly direct." The directness of the managers from the United States created significant discomfort, particularly for lower-level U.K. employees. An employee from a high-context culture who is on the receiving end of very direct feedback early in a meeting with his or her boss may feel quite attacked, whereas in a low-context culture, the employee might feel appreciative that the boss is getting to the point.

These examples merely begin to describe the tremendous diversity of personal styles and decision-making processes that emerge from cultural variation. Cultural variation can even be found among employees from the same country. In the United States, "Southerners" and "Northerners" are thought to have very different approaches from the perspective of values and time management (though these differences may be eroding in the face of demographic mobility). In addition to learned differences between groups that have to do with cultural diversity, one can add differences that are based on race, age, and gender. The challenge for the coaching manager is to avoid seeing a particular action or behavior as being determined by individual factors when it may also be determined by the employee's cultural or group identification.

How can you tell? If the coaching manager thinks that culture may play a significant role in how an employee is approaching a particular task, it is usually possible to raise that issue as part of the coaching dialogue. We have found that a simple question such as "How might people deal with this in your country or culture of origin?" is often well received by the coachee, who is usually more than happy to talk about the differences in approaches between the cultures. Most businesspeople now know that cultural, racial, and gender diversity can affect communications, marketing, product development, leadership, team effectiveness, decision making, and other business processes. If the coaching manager is tactful in positioning the question and gives the employee time to reflect, most employees will respond by trying to consider the role that cultural diversity is playing in how they view and respond to particular situations. (We can't guarantee this, unfortunately. The impact of culture is felt on an implicit or unspoken level, and as such, some people may not notice it or may doubt its power.)

The important point is this: It is critical to treat people as individuals and try to understand the role that cultural assumptions or membership in any identity group (gender, race, or country of origin) may be playing in the employee's performance and learning needs. Perhaps in no other aspect of coaching is it so important for the coaching manager to always keep wearing a learning hat (Schmuckler, 2001).

What do you do if the employee does state that culturally based attitudes may be affecting his or her performance? It is important to keep in mind that with regard to the impact of culture on any part of the learning or performance process, a judgmental stance won't help. After all, if someone is behaving in a fashion that is consistent with good practice in his or her culture of origin, to evaluate that practice punitively would seem confusing at best and very offensive at worst. The reality is that it is difficult for people to unlearn one way of acting, particularly when it brought them success, and then learn another way of being that seems "foreign" to them.

An open discussion of the impact of culture on performance allows the employee to decide what course of action he or she should take. We're not saying that the employee struggling with a culturally defined approach to work that may result in a performance gap is automatically entitled to define the organization's performance standards or processes. The coaching manager will probably need to maintain consistent performance standards at the same time. As in all situations, coachees need to consider what they can or should do to respond to those standards. For instance, a team leader from a culture quite different from the culture in which she is now working has to confront the fact that she can't impose her cultural style on the team without creating a variety of negative consequences. Ideally, the team members work together to understand one another's different communications or leadership styles. While working outside your own cultural context, you ultimately have to decide whether or not you want to try to adjust or to help others adjust to you.

Team and Organizational Factors

We end this discussion of possible root causes by stressing that individual action and behavior don't take place in a vacuum. In teams and organizations, *talent, attitudes,* and *resources* are not always rationally distributed to support the work that needs to be done. Giving someone lots of responsibility but no authority, for instance, obviously creates the potential for a gap between actual and desired performance on the part of those involved.

The coaching dialogue creates an opportunity for the coaching manager to gain insight as to what is going wrong or right on a team and intervene as a coach or as a manager. Unfortunately, too often employees have learned to expect that their managers will blame them when something goes wrong, even if the root causes were outside their control. We have stressed the importance of taking a helpful attitude as you coach, particularly toward those employees in the "good" to "great" categories. These people want to be successful. If these employees say they haven't got the resources to do the job, perhaps they are right. We encourage the coaching manager to listen to such feedback and not immediately conclude that it is an excuse. Yes, you may ultimately decide that you should encourage the individual or team to push on despite the fact that conditions are not perfect, but failure to acknowledge problems at the team or organizational level can seriously undermine trust.

Unless you are in combat and have to ask people to do the impossible, it is appropriate for workers to expect that they will be given a rough approximation of what is needed to do the job they have been asked to do, even in an age that requires "more with less" from so many workers. If you recall, the second element of the Gallup 12 elements (Chapter 6) linking employee engagement and productivity was "I have the materials and equipment I need to do my work right" (Buckingham & Coffman, 1999). In addition to considering whether or not an individual or team has the right talent for the job, you may need to keep in mind other resources as well, such as financial, material, time, and managerial resources.

Managerial resources include the time and interest of whatever level of management is ultimately responsible for holding the individual or team accountable. A team may require additional help from you, in addition to your coaching efforts. In particular, it may require more time.

Finally, it is also wise to consider the degree of *organizational change* that is taking place in the context of the employees you are coaching. The importance of this factor should be obvious. In times of change, which are increasingly the norm rather than the exception, it may be difficult or impossible to adequately define performance gaps. Under conditions of great uncertainty, employees may not know whether or not they performed a task adequately using the appropriate process. Indeed, their manager may not know, either. The employee, team, manager, and perhaps organization are all experimenting. They are learning together through enlightened (we hope) trial and error.

Consider the implications, for example, if Jack's group was selling a specific set of products in a multiproduct company. Product knowledge is everything in such a scheme. Now his firm decides to focus on selling multiple products to each customer through one sales account and one salesperson. Jack has to help his supervisors and sales representatives learn an entirely new approach to relating to their customers. The relationships they build with customers must be deeper and stronger through a longer period of time. Jack may try to match sales representatives with various customers on the basis of their previous experience and on the overlap of their experience with the customer's industry. Is this the right way to go? In discussing such a change with his coaching manager, Jack talks of his uncertainty regarding how to involve his customers in such decisions. He's been asking them what they want. The coaching manager may not know, with certainty, the right answers to such questions.

Jack tries out his plan for customer involvement, and it creates havoc among the sales force. Their anger drifts to the manager's level and constitutes the feedback that the manager must now give to Jack. Does this mean that Jack was insensitive to the needs of his sales reps? This was an experiment that he undertook with his manager's understanding. Everyone is being stretched. It makes sense, then, to (a) provide him with the feedback that his reps are starting to rebel and (b) help him think through what he was trying to accomplish and what he needs to do differently as he moves forward. The reality is that *change brings on unintended consequences*. For instance, people involved in leading a change effort may not, for good reasons, be aware of the importance or power of one particular component of the organizational system, such as the very powerful individual contributor who keeps to himself—except for the fact that he is an old friend of the CEO. Under these circumstances, the coaching process and a shared effort to understand the gap between actual and desired performance can generate important learning for the individual employee, as well as for the team or organization as a whole.

We stress, though, that when a coachee is trying to get a job done with inadequate resources, we're not implying that the employee should assume a "victim"-oriented stance. Working in a less-than-ideal context creates lots of opportunities for learning. Coaching can be directed at the influence skills required to get more resources, for instance. Coaching can be directed at realigning a project plan so that a team can achieve the best possible outcomes under the circumstances. Organizational constraints should be acknowledged by the coaching manager but then can become "grist for the mill."

The Importance of "Getting It Right" When Interpreting Performance

There are times in life when it may be better to do nothing than to do something poorly. This lesson was brought home to us through a story told by an employee working with a very effective coaching manager. This young engineer was evidently known for his ability to solve enormously complex problems and explain those problems in lay terms to businesspeople. He was about to give the most important presentation of his young life in front of his own CEO and the leaders of several important customers.

When the time came, he stood up and froze. He was completely unable to put his thoughts into words or make sense of his own overheads. The CEO was clearly not pleased but said little. In an effort to end the pain, the young engineer's manager stood up and took over. The manager was very upset after the meeting but held her temper in check. The engineer was shocked by his own failure to perform (that can happen) and fearful. Clearly they needed to talk. The manager, who basically trusted the engineer, asked him what was going on. The engineer was at a loss. Finally, the manager asked, "Is something wrong? Is anything bothering you?" The engineer, who was loath to talk about his personal life at work, confided that he'd just put his mother in a nursing home. Perhaps he didn't realize, he said, just how much that had shaken his concentration. The manager expressed confidence in his ability to handle situations like this in the future. Although he was quite anxious in light of this incident, his manager assigned him to do another presentation several weeks later. Once again, his anxiety did detract from his performance, but not nearly so badly. He got through it and covered the necessary material. His manager noted the improvement and predicted a slow but sure recovery. Over time, that is exactly what happened.

If the manager had criticized the employee after the original incident, she would have been doing so on the basis of an inference that the cause of the problem was perhaps his lack of preparation or even a lack of ability to work with senior managers. Working from such an inference would have undermined her ability to accurately understand the source of the problem. In criticizing the employee, she would also have undermined what little confidence he had left. She would not have helped him develop an awareness of the impact of his personal life on his performance and the need to address work and life stress proactively. (Had she known that he was going through such a major family transition, she never would have asked him to present in such a high-stakes context in the first place.) Ultimately, she might have lost a great engineer.

Most of us can tolerate criticism when it is directed at a real fault, but to be criticized for not being prepared when in fact we are struggling with an overwhelming level of stress can generate long-term resentment. We encourage you to notice how often you rush to interpret the actions of others before finding out the true cause of their actions. To put it another way, *try to precede every conclusion with an open-ended question.* The subtitle of this chapter, after all, is "Collaboratively Interpreting Learning Needs." Perhaps in no other aspect of developmental coaching is the notion of collaboration more important.

Goal Setting and Follow-Up

11

Making Change Happen

In this chapter, you will learn about the following:

- A reasonable approach to development planning
- How to reasonably integrate goal setting and follow-up in your activities as a coaching manager without burdening yourself with additional paperwork
- How people change through coaching and how follow-up can help people through the stages of change

Interviews with coaching managers tell us that follow-up is perhaps one of the most underrated tasks of developmental coaching. Effective coaching managers follow up, sometimes formally, but often informally. Whenever possible, they know who is working on which projects on an ongoing basis. They are aware of who is learning a new Web design technology, who is designing a brochure for the first time, who is leading a project team through a crisis, or who is trying to position himself or herself for a significant promotion. They keep an eye on how these people are doing. They look for *coachable moments*. Perhaps most important, they help keep people focused on what they need to learn.

The importance of follow-up stems from two basic realities of personal development. Learning, especially learning that stretches an employee, can be quite difficult. Most coachees need ongoing support, if for no other reason than to make sure that they are getting the kinds of assignments that will help them keep learning. Just as important, it seems that if the manager does not follow up in some fashion, he or she is sending a message to the employee that discounts the importance of the employee's learning efforts. Ideally, of course, the manager follows up because, in most instances, the learning in which the employee is engaged is important to the business goals of the work group. Learning at its best is important to the success of the group as well as the success of the individual employee.

Follow-up, interestingly, begins with some sort of goal setting. In the absence of some type of goal, or marker, it will be hard to assess progress for the coaching manager or the coachee. Again, while we encourage people to write their goals down, in practice, we've found that coachees and coaching managers frequently utilize a more informal, verbal process. The key point here is that the most *compelling* goals have been talked about by the coachee and the manager and are relatively well understood on a day-to-day basis.

The idea of having to engage in goal setting and follow-up when it comes to employee development does raise questions in the minds of some managers. Some managers immediately think that goal setting and follow-up mean filling out more forms from human resources (which is not true). Some have mixed feelings about whether or not they should be involved in trying to "plan" someone else's development. Development seems optional to them, and they may fear that they will come across as micromanaging their employees.

It is important to understand that follow-up safeguards the coaching manager's return on investment. If you spend time coaching, you want it to have an impact. In this chapter, we examine the process of goal setting and follow-up and offer a few simple guidelines that can help coaching managers successfully encourage the process in a way that is neither bureaucratic nor time-consuming. As with all aspects of developmental coaching at its best, the employee takes as much responsibility for goal setting and follow-up as possible.

Planned Development

We're going to talk about career development in greater depth in the next chapter. Let's, though, look at development planning as a coaching tool. Most organizations now formally link development planning to performance appraisal (even if inadvertently). The development planning form is usually attached to the performance appraisal form, as the last page. There is nothing inherently wrong with linking development and performance management, in theory. However, as we have said, the two have very different purposes, and their purposes can sometimes conflict. Employees may choose development targets solely because they believe "that is what the boss wants." As you'll see, an employee's development goals should relate to the needs of the business in most cases but should also relate in a meaningful way to the needs of the employee.

Nevertheless, implicit in the act of linking development planning and performance appraisal is the assumption that the tools of performance appraisal, such as stating clear goals and holding people accountable for goal attainment, can be used to promote employee development. Indeed, there is some evidence that holding employees accountable for defined developmental goals is more likely to ensure that they will follow up and that change will take place (Antonioni, 1996). Is this all we need to know about goal setting and follow-up? Consider the following examples.

Patrick looked around in his organization and saw who was getting ahead (which is what he wanted to do). He noted that there were several skills that seemed to characterize those people, among which was the ability to give effective presentations. He set this as a developmental goal for himself and devoted considerable energy to enhancing his presentation skills. He asked his manager for opportunities to present more often and to get feedback from his manager or someone else in the group when he did present. His manager agreed that improving his presentation skills could really help Patrick's career and was happy to support this developmental goal. After all, if Patrick could become really skilled at presenting, he could take on some of the load for the department. (This is an example of a synergistic learning project, meeting the needs of both the employee and the business unit, as previously discussed.)

None of this was ever documented. (We do suspect that Patrick probably put it in his formal development plan, but after the fact. Recording the goal, for Patrick, was not central to the learning project in which he was engaged.) The initial coaching dialogue with his boss, almost totally driven by Patrick, took place over lunch. Probably the most important pieces of work his manager had to do in this case were to (a) establish a coaching-friendly context in his department that would make such conversations possible, (b) look for appropriate opportunities for Patrick to make presentations, and (c) make sure that when Patrick did present, he or one of his colleagues was there to offer him a chance to reflect on his performance and receive appropriate feedback, until Patrick seemed ready to work on his own.

Is this a "too good to be true" story? The reality is that often, in an environment that encourages development, employees will pinpoint goals that are both important to themselves as individuals and helpful to the business unit at the same time. They focus on such goals with a great deal of commitment. Granted, this requires a clear vision of what one needs to learn and persistence in working toward the learning goals.

Too often, however, this is not what happens.

Consider another example. John is an up-and-coming consulting engineer in a large utility company. His boss considers himself to be a pretty good coaching manager to his employees. John is very talented, especially from a technical standpoint. However, he has a pattern of overcommitment of which he and his boss are both aware. In his enthusiasm and desire to get ahead, he takes on too many projects. He jumps in, starts something big, and excites his internal customers, but before too long, he has spotted another opportunity and jumps to that one. The first customer is left without sufficient support, and work on that customer's project flounders while John devotes himself to a second project. Customer number one then complains to John's boss.

Over the course of 6 months, John's boss gave him repeated feedback about the problem. He told John that if he developed a reputation for not following through with customers, internal or external, his career at the firm could be adversely impacted. John seemed to see this and did acknowledge that he needed to work on maintaining a focus in his efforts. John's boss laid down a very specific goal as part of John's written development plan: Over the next year, John was to focus on his three major projects and that was all. John's boss hoped that John would experience the benefits of focusing: being able to generate higher-quality solutions while experiencing less on-the-job stress. John agreed with the goal and the explicit limit set by his manager.

Six months later, John's boss was back in human resources complaining about him. John had gotten involved in two more major projects, had stretched himself way too thin, had some more angry internal customers, and was very stressed and angry himself as a result. The human resources manager asked John's boss why he hadn't stepped in and held John accountable for following the plan they had previously laid out. John's boss replied, "Well, to tell you the truth, those other two projects are really important to the company, and if John can make a bit of progress on either or both of them, that would be a help to me."

This story has two morals. First, a formal goal-setting process alone does not ensure that the goals will be accomplished. Neither John nor his boss kept to the plan to limit John's project load. Second, we should not underestimate how difficult it can be to break habitual routines. Trying to limit himself and to focus more may make sense to John on an intellectual level. However, when people try to make significant changes in their work or their lives, they often run into serious resistance. The resistance may come from the individual, but it can also come from his or her environment. A reasonable approach to setting goals and following up has to take the process of change into account.

Setting Goals

The power of goal setting as a means of improving performance has been well understood for several decades (Locke & Latham, 1990). Simply put, a clear statement of mutually agreed-on and clearly specified goals is more likely to result in the attainment of those goals than a less precise or more implicit goal-setting process. At the performance appraisal and business unit levels, the goal-setting process has been institutionalized in many firms as "management by objectives" (MBO) programs. The employee commits to a particular result, with his or her manager, and is held accountable for that result. When executed effectively, the process tends to ensure that the goals of each particular unit in the organizational hierarchy are aligned and relatively up-to-date. Research on goal setting offers more guidance as to what constitutes effective goals and an effective process for setting goals. The guidelines described in this chapter for effective goal setting and follow-up are summarized in Box 11.1.

BOX 11.1   Characteristics of Effective Goals and Goal Setting

The most effective learning goals are described as follows:

1. *Specific and measurable.* Manager and employee should be able to observe the impact of learning. The goal should be stated as a defined outcome: "Here is what I'll do differently."

2. *Time-bound.* Time boundaries that include specific completion dates help employees measure their progress.

3. *Challenging.* Challenging goals are motivating, though they are also naturally difficult.

4. *Few in number.* A relatively small number of developmental goals allows employees to focus.

5. *Developed in a participatory fashion.* Participation encourages ownership and commitment toward the goal.

6. *Aligned with the goals of the business.* Alignment supports all phases of the learning process (unfreezing, change, and refreezing) and supports maximum commitment to the goal.

The coaching dialogue question "What are you going to do differently?" is one way of asking an employee to commit to a particular action or goal. In the previous case, John, in response to the coaching dialogue that followed his feedback, might have said, "I'm only going to work on the three major projects this year; that's it." Such a goal statement meets several of the criteria of an effective goal (Whetten & Cameron, 1998). Effective goals are *specific*. They are unambiguous and measurable. John's commitment to focus on only three projects is unambiguous. There is also a time frame attached to the goal. Measurable goals are *time-bound*. Time boundaries are essential if one is to be able to measure whether or not the goal has been accomplished. Time boundaries also create an opportunity for employees to measure progress incrementally as they work toward goal completion.

Effective goals are also *appropriately challenging*. Challenge creates motivation. However, what constitutes "appropriate" will likely vary from person to person. In John's case, we can infer from the fact that John has had trouble staying focused in the past that sticking with just three projects for a 12-month period might be challenging. Even with a specific and appropriately challenging goal, however, this plan didn't work. John reverted to his previous style in a few months. Perhaps the potential rewards (tangible and intangible) inherent in the pursuit of this particular goal were not motivating enough for him.

In Patrick's case, he made it clear that he wanted to become an effective presenter, although how "good" an effective presenter is can be somewhat difficult to measure, as it is open to some individual judgment. Regardless, feedback from those to whom he has presented, his own manager and other colleagues, could give him a pretty good idea of how well he was doing. (The same feedback could also help him change his technique and improve his performance along the way.) Thus, the goal was, to a degree, measurable. Finally, given its importance to Patrick's career, it was appropriately challenging. He showed a high level of motivation in taking on the task. In Patrick's case, identifying a goal and working toward it worked quite well.

The reader will probably note that, in both cases, the goals that were set did not describe how the learning would actually take place. The archetype of the poorly worded development goal goes something like this: "I will take a course on negotiations (or whatever is the subject of the learning goal)." Such a plan doesn't meet the criteria for an effective goal. Taking a course is an action that might lead to the desired outcome, presumably, in this case, developing effectiveness as a negotiator. But one can also take a course on a topic related to a development goal and not achieve any real change. Taking the course does not guarantee commitment. *Pursuit of the goal,* being a great presenter, drives the learning. Taking a course in presentation skills is irrelevant for our purposes if the coachee isn't going to do a great job actually presenting.

We suspect that managers resort to such "event"-based developmental goal statements when they aren't clear about what the individual is really trying to accomplish. A developmental goal implies an *outcome* or a result that is to be attained. Ideally, the coaching dialogue, observation, and feedback have helped the coachee and the manager create a fairly clear picture of the outcome to which the coachee aspires.

An outcome-oriented learning goal might be stated as follows: "I'm going to lead a team that will achieve (the desired) results and enjoy working together." Then we can take it one step further and ask what this individual will need to do in order to achieve this goal, based on what she knows about herself. "In order to do that, I'm going to have to learn to seek out the input of team members in all cases before making a strategic decision. I will not criticize input from team members in the process." So her business goal, leading a great team, drives some learning-oriented goals. (Remember the coaching value chain discussed in Chapter 3. We're still working with the same concept.)

One simple way to think about learning-oriented goals is through the use of questions: *What should you start doing? What should you stop doing? What should you keep doing?* Based on some initial feedback from his coaching manager, a full description of Patrick's goal was this: "I want to learn to become more effective in giving presentations that senior management will find useful. In order to achieve that goal, I'm going to need to work on making my case using clear and simple language. I need to stop using so much jargon. I need to start explaining my objectives early in the presentation. I need to stop putting too much information on my overhead slides. I need to keep using humor to make my point." This full statement offers a fairly clear picture of the outcome to which he aspires. The most effective learning goals *clearly define the outcome of the learning.* We stress that attaining goal clarity represents a goal in itself. Patrick was able to describe those specific behavioral goals after his coaching manager had given him a rather lengthy critique of his most recent presentation. He had to synthesize his manager's feedback before he could pinpoint the specific issues he needed to address. It took him and his manager several discussions to get beyond the larger goal of improving Patrick's presentation skills.

The obvious benefits of focusing one's effort suggest that it is unwise to work on more than a few developmental goals at a time. Although there is no preset number of goals that one should address, it is commonly thought that working on more than three goals at any one time may be overly optimistic.

In the years since we completed the first edition of this book, we've come to understand just how hard it can be to rein in one's exuberance (or sense of panic) when it comes to choosing the numbers of goals on which to focus. In our MBA course on managerial assessment and development, we ask our students to put together a formal development plan (we'll describe the format in the next chapter). Routinely, these bright and enthusiastic individuals choose too many goals in spite of our admonition (and threats) to limit the number to three. It may be that the good and great who are heavily represented in this class bring with them a tendency to take on too much. Please beware that tendency if you see it in yourself. Taking on too much can mean that you'll accomplish nothing. One good and meaningful goal accomplished is worth far more than even three goals half completed. In deciding how many developmental goals an individual can address at one time, it can be useful to consider the following questions (Lombardo & Eichinger, 2001):

- *How difficult will the goal be to address?* An enormously difficult goal, particularly a goal that has an emotional component, will require a great deal of effort. While working on such a goal, it may be difficult to work on anything else. In John's case, his tendency to overextend himself was deeply entrenched. Learning to say no and focus on a defined set of projects may be quite difficult. He may find it painfully boring to work through the details associated with executing a project plan and maintaining a team.

- *How much support will the coachee have?* In the cases of Patrick and John, they both had managers who were more than casually interested in their development. Note than in John's case, however, his manager's attention to John's developmental goal wavered.

- *How similar are the developmental needs to one another?* Patrick wanted to learn to give more effective presentations. His secondary goal, closely related, was to become more comfortable speaking to senior managers. As a way of working on both goals, it seems appropriate for him to move from presenting to colleagues to presenting to senior managers.

- *What is the coachee willing to do?* This is perhaps the most important question of them all. How much is the coachee willing to sacrifice to pursue the goal? Patrick was so committed to becoming a more effective presenter that although he knew he would be nervous, he didn't perceive that as a barrier. He was willing to put up with it. John, on the other hand, seemed unwilling to give up the emotional charge he experienced when digging into a brand-new set of challenges. When things started to become routine, he wanted to move along and try something new rather than finish what he had started.

Finally, the process by which goals are established is important to their outcome. *Participation by both parties,* the employee and the manager, in the setting of the goal(s) is thought to improve the likelihood that the employee will follow through and achieve goal completion (Whetten & Cameron, 1998). A participatory process of goal setting should allow the employee to bring a greater sense of ownership, and therefore personal commitment, to the process of attaining the goal. A participatory process is clearly consistent with the idea that learning has to be driven by the employee.

Patrick proactively pushed the goal of becoming a better presenter. His manager participated by reacting in a helpful way. It appears that, in John's case, the goal may have been to some extent imposed on him by his manager. John agreed in general that he needed to focus more, but limiting his efforts to just three projects was his manager's idea, not his. Although he did agree, he may not have taken full psychological ownership of the goal. (Of course, his manager may have needed to impose the goal to achieve compliance if John's tendency to overcommit had created too much damage to John or the business unit.)

How formal, then, should the goal-setting process be? We recommend that both coaching manager and coachee always write down a goal statement but know that our recommendation is likely to be ignored. So, when should you really make it formal and written? If the development goal is *very difficult or complex,* if it may take a *long time to accomplish,* or if the goal will require a great deal of focus, a written goal statement can be quite valuable. A written document can serve as a reminder over time of the decisions that were made by the coaching manager and coachee. A written document can serve as a vision for success if the complexity of the situation makes it easy to be overwhelmed by ambiguity. (The latter might occur for instance during times of significant organizational change.) Finally, a written document can serve as a bridge to a new manager should the coaching manager move on or the employee transfer to a new group. However, a written goal statement does not guarantee success, as we see in the case of John. To better understand the problem John is facing, it is useful to consider one additional aspect that often arises during the learning process in developmental coaching: the need to unlearn.

How People Change

It is one thing to learn a brand-new skill. The individual studying accounting for the first time typically has no previous conception of how all those numbers work. However, many of the learning challenges people face confront them with the need to change, not just to learn. By *change,* we don't mean a personality change, but we do mean a personal change. People often have to unlearn skills or concepts that have served them in the past but no longer work in their current situation and will not work in the future to which they aspire.

John's situation may be an example of the need to *unlearn*. He had actually developed a reputation as an extremely helpful individual contributor and consultant to other groups. He was always curious. He was very smart and was a fast learner. He could take in large amounts of information by scanning documents, synthesize that information, and then present it to others. This brought him to the attention of a vice president who began promoting him up the managerial career ladder. Note, however, that this very same "strength" could become a weakness if his work required him to focus on a particular problem in greater depth. John's old trick of scanning, instead of making him appear to be a quick study, made his analysis look superficial. To be successful, he has to let go of this "quick hit" style of working. What does this require?

Kurt Lewin and his followers were among the first to describe the change process that addresses John's learning goal (Schein, 1979). Lewin proposed that personal transformation of the type required of John involves three steps: unfreezing, change, and refreezing. Typically, people move through these phases in a somewhat linear fashion, although regression to the previous stage is not uncommon if the personal change is significant or if the environment does not support continued movement through the change process. It is worthwhile to briefly examine each step.

Unfreezing

Unfreezing requires developing a readiness for change. In the case of Patrick, he knows he needs to change and is ready to begin the work of doing so. (Admittedly, Patrick also has less to unlearn.) John, on the other hand, has an awareness of the need to change brought on largely by critical feedback delivered by his manager. This feedback has begun to unfreeze John; it works in one of several ways.

When John is confronted with the disappointment of his customers, he begins to see the impact of his behavior in a way that is not consistent with his self-concept. He normally sees himself as being helpful. How could he have made others angry because he wasn't helpful to them? He experiences a *disconfirmation* of his self-concept. He may also experience *guilt* or *anxiety* because of this disconfirmation. However, if he feels only that he has not been helpful, he may react by becoming intensely defensive. He also needs to feel that it is OK to try another way—that it is *safe to change*. His manager stated that he would provide that sense of safety by clearly siding with the change effort. He told John, "No matter what anyone else says, you're on these three projects, and that is it. If they have a problem with that, tell them to call me."

Unfortunately, as we noted, his manager's actions were not consistent with his statements. He saw that John was taking on extra work and did nothing to stop it. Indeed, it seems as though John's taking on the extra work was actually condoned by his manager despite his complaints. Perhaps unconsciously, he wants John to stay the way he was in the past because John's style, though problematic, was also useful. If this is the case, what John thought he experienced as disconfirming wasn't so disconfirming after all. Should John, then, take that apparently disconfirming feedback seriously? Perhaps not.

What if that had not been the case? What if John's manager had reacted at the first sign of John's overextending himself and talked with John about the problem? Such a clear statement might have been sufficient to keep John "unfrozen" and open to the possibility of learning a new way of doing things and of giving up his old habits. One of the most important questions that managers need to consider while working with an employee to set a difficult developmental goal is whether or not both parties really believe that the goal is essential. If either or both do not, then unfreezing is not likely to result.

Change

In the *change* stage, people are more open to learning. Indeed, they have come to accept that the learning is necessary and are ready to drive the learning themselves. They scan their world for helpful information. They may read about the topic at hand and seek out others who can help them. Patrick isn't debating the necessity of change. He's now interested in various approaches to improving his performance in front of groups.

During the learning process, the employee may need access to a variety of resources. Unfortunately, too often in business, managers make the assumption that the only learning resource that matters is the classroom. Classroom learning, reading, videos, and computer-based educational programs are all terribly important. The coaching manager should keep in mind, however, that in all likelihood, the most important learning resources are the opportunities that allow employees to develop their skills at work and the opportunity to hold a coaching dialogue. Patrick might find it useful, at first, to participate in a class on how to conduct effective presentations, for instance. Ultimately, however, he'll need his manager's help to get up in front of a group and make presentations in a serious business context. Feedback, ongoing dialogue, and follow-up are of course "free" (though there is a time cost).

John's approach to the problem, on the other hand, was quite different. Rather than reading about time management or operations or talking with others who had to make similar adjustments to their work styles, John was thinking more about how he could get around his developmental goal. He wasn't really in the "change phase" of learning very long before he began to slip back. His old, ingrained pattern returned. In point of fact, he just didn't want or wasn't ready to change. Unfortunately, with such an attitude, he was reluctant to reach out for help from his boss or others from whom he might have been able to get some encouragement. He became locked in a vicious cycle in which the lack of support he received interacted with his own behavioral tendencies and drove him further in the wrong direction.

Two implications may be drawn from this discussion. First, people won't really engage in the learning process until they are ready. They often become ready on their own. They may also recognize the need to change as a result of feedback from their environment. Second, while people are trying to engage in the learning process, especially the change phase, they need support. If people don't find the learning resources and the encouragement they need, they may slip back. They may also not signal to the coaching manager that they have slipped back.

Patrick was ready to learn about presentations. He needed two resources from his manager: opportunity and coaching. Given his status in the organization, he could not have arranged for either on his own. If his manager had not been responsive, Patrick's motivation to learn would have been frustrated. One would guess that ultimately he'd give up. It is interesting and saddening to consider how often this occurs in most organizations.

Refreezing

One of our training program participants told us an interesting story with regard to the challenge of *refreezing,* or making the connection between the new behavior, knowledge, or skill and the rest of his life. This gentleman had been an unrepentant workaholic. Until he started to suffer from health problems, he would routinely work 80 to 90 hours per week, even when there was no crisis to manage. His own manager told him that he needed to change; this wasn't the kind of behavior that would help the department in the long run. The manager suggested that he cut his working hours from 80 to no more than 50 each week. With the help of his wife and a counselor, he was able to do just that. Unfortunately, everybody at work became angry with him. He wasn't always at his desk when they needed him. He didn't return every e-mail within an hour. He actually delayed the completion date on one of his projects. As he assessed the situation, "These people had a good deal; they got two of me for the price of one." When he cut back his working hours, his manager did not hire a replacement. The result was that other members of the department became angry at his perceived lack of responsiveness. Over time, their anger gradually eroded his commitment to change. Within 6 months, he was working 80 hours each week again. However, his colleagues were no longer angry with him! In this case, the manager and the employee failed to anticipate that the employee's changes might affect others and to address this contingency.

If the change is not consistent with the rest of the employee's life as a whole, refreezing may not occur. Changes must also be consistent with the individual's personality, at least to an extent. Likewise, those in the employee's network of relationships must be able to cope with the employee's newly learned skill or new routine. They may need to change their behavior, too. Unless his organization changes, we see difficulties ahead for John in the refreezing area. At this point, others need him to be the way he was, not the way he says he wants to become. Patrick, on the other hand, can step into an important role. His ability to present will be very helpful to the organization. This analysis again suggests the importance for the coaching manager of thinking about the following question: If the employee succeeds in learning this new skill, will he or she be using that skill in a fashion that will be truly helpful to the business unit or company? If the answer is unclear or no, the change, the learning and use of the new skill, may not "take." In the worst-case scenario, the employee may cease to be competent at the particular skill in which he or she and the firm invested so much to develop.

Building Commitment for Learning and Change

Learning requires a commitment on the part of the employee, and it will often require a good deal of commitment on the part of the manager. This is particularly true when the learning goals are challenging. The goal-setting process and its follow-up can be used as a means of determining and reinforcing that commitment. The determinants of commitment to a set goal are well understood. They include several factors external to the individual, as well as several factors relevant to the individual himself or herself.

Most of the external factors that support commitment to a goal have to do with the manager's attitude (Locke, Latham, & Erez, 1988). Research shows that employees are more likely to be committed to goals arrived at through dialogue with a legitimate authority (the manager) who is supportive and trusted. The presence of support in the peer group is helpful as well. Finally, incentives, such as financial rewards or career movement, can (not surprisingly) encourage commitment.

Let us add one point that may be relevant for some managers. You may have accessed the services of an executive coach for one of your employees, as a means to support his or her development. The conditions under which that is appropriate have been addressed elsewhere (Hunt & Weintraub, 2007). However, we would stress that just because you have taken such a step doesn't mean you have discharged your responsibility as a coaching manager. Recent research (Hunt, 2004) demonstrates that those employees working with a coach are more likely to achieve their goals, and thus an ROI for the expense of the coaching, when their manager is actively and positively involved in the process. This is common sense, we would suggest. The manager is likely to be in a much better position to provide coaching dialogue, observation, and feedback support to an employee than is the professional coach. The latter, even if the coach is an internal coach from human resources or learning and development, is not as available in most cases. Simply put, the manager's role is more important in driving toward desirable outcomes.

From the vantage point of the employee, commitment to a goal, then, is enhanced when goal attainment leads to a desired reward (Locke et al., 1988). However, the coachee needs to expect that he or she can ultimately accomplish the goal. If that expectation is missing, rewards by themselves won't motivate commitment to the goal. People don't pursue a reward, no matter how valuable, unless they believe that their efforts will pay off (as anyone who has tried to lose weight can attest). Finally, goal commitment is enhanced if individuals pursuing the goal can recognize even incremental progress and give themselves self-administered rewards as acknowledgment of a job well done. If Patrick can recognize that his use of graphics software was better received in his last presentation than in previous efforts, he's more likely to try even harder next time.

As stated previously, commitment to a goal is also enhanced if the employee participated in establishing the particular goal (Locke et al., 1988; Whetten & Cameron, 1998). Most researchers note that it is possible to gain commitment to an imposed goal if the employee has the ability to participate in decision making about related discretionary goals. Interestingly, this creates an opportunity for employees to define learning goals in a participative fashion, even when dealing with an imposed business goal. If corporate wants to push a stretch, results-oriented goal of 15% growth, all managers and employees may have to go along. But in the process, they'll probably have to do quite a bit of learning. Commitment to the learning goal, then, may be strengthened if it is attached to the business goal.

Commitment to developmental goals will be enhanced when they are *aligned, more or less, with the needs and resources of the employee, work group or team, manager, and organization.* Patrick's goal showed this alignment, whereas in subtle ways John's goal did not. In considering how much commitment is possible to a learning goal, probably the most important question to ask is this: "If the learning prescribed by the goal takes place, will we be in a better position to meet our business goals?" If there is a high level of commitment to the goal because it is aligned with the task of the business unit or team in some fashion, it is very likely that follow-up will take place naturally, as everyone involved works toward that business goal.

An informal planning and follow-up process can work quite well under such circumstances. To the degree that fulfillment of the learning goal is essential to making progress toward a business goal, employees who need to unfreeze, or unlearn, in order to be open to new learning will find a great deal of support. They are much more likely to be confronted with good reasons for unfreezing during the natural course of their work. In the change phase, learning resources (coaching, classes, or opportunities to use skills) are more likely to be available to support learning because what is being learned is essential to the success of the business. In the refreezing phase, employees are more likely to find that their new skill or knowledge is valued by peers and managers alike.

Conclusions: Goal Setting and Follow-Up

Most coaching managers and employees engage in the real work of development on an informal, ongoing basis, particularly in a coaching-friendly context. We suspect that formal approaches to development planning have taken hold as a way to push reluctant or busy managers into doing some kind of developmental work with their employees. Unfortunately, this analysis also suggests that setting goals in the absence of other considerations (coaching and opportunities to learn and use new skills) may not be all that helpful.

Having said this, we still believe that it can be helpful for both employees and managers to give some serious thought regarding which approach is going to be most helpful in any given situation. Many employees find the structure of a written goal statement to be quite useful. Others know what they want and inhabit a fast-paced world in which they have no time for filling out forms. The lessons from this discussion are summarized as follows:

- Encourage employees to be responsible for setting realistic development goals and taking action on those goals. Test to see whether or not employees really own their goals and are willing make sacrifices to reach them.
- Consider also whether or not employees are really ready (unfrozen) to take on the tough goals. Assess whether or not they really believe that learning a new approach is essential to their current or future success.
- Encourage employees to focus on a small number of developmental goals. One goal can be overwhelming if it is a challenging one.
- Ask yourself and your employees the tough questions: Are your development goals aligned with what we really need to do in this organization or team? Will it help all of us if you develop that particular skill? If employees' learning will help the team accomplish its business goals, commitment is likely to be high, and the learning process is more likely to proceed successfully.
- Encourage employees to be clear about what they want to accomplish. Help them think about the outcomes of their learning efforts. This may take several discussions as employees and coaching managers pinpoint specifically what needs to happen. A useful question to ask might be "If you are successful in becoming a better negotiator, what would that mean a year from now? How would we see that in the business?"
- Be ready to support employees along the way. Access to learning resources, including the opportunity to practice, is a critical aspect of the learning process. Remember, employees may need some encouragement, particularly if the goal is a challenging one.

Coaching and Career Development

12

In this chapter, we discuss the following:

- The status of "career" development in the modern organization

- Important considerations for the coachee: career goals, learning goals, and political support

- Several cases that illustrate how developmental coaching can be utilized to help employees dealing with career development concerns

Is coaching for career development different from developmental coaching? In many ways, no. The purpose of developmental coaching is to help employees learn and develop new skills and knowledge. Helping employees develop new skills and knowledge is arguably the most important thing a manager can do to help them have a successful and rewarding career. This is really the flip side of our description of the coaching value chain. Value is created for the individual coachee, through learning skills that are presumably desirable to her organization and may be desirable in future roles.

Yet there are times when career development issues more explicitly take center stage in an employee's life and in his conversations with his manager. It could be at the completion of a project; during times of major organizational change, societal change, or crisis; or after a personal milestone, such as a birthday. Some employees think about their careers on a regular basis, particularly those who take a long-term view of their lives. We are amused by senior managers who say, "I don't want employees thinking about their careers or their next jobs. I want them thinking about today."

Our message to those senior managers is this: You can't control what people are thinking. Furthermore, thinking about one's future is a natural, healthy, and adaptive activity. You can try to suppress career-related talk at work. However, you do so at your own peril. If employees are not allowed, indeed encouraged, to talk about their futures from time to time, they will do so with someone else and may end up at a different company. Coaching for career development can be a key retention tool.

Many managers we've talked with over the past decade understand the importance of thinking through one's career direction and in fact do try to encourage their employees to do so as well. Nevertheless, if many managers have a difficult time coaching employees to learn how to do their current jobs better, anecdotal evidence suggests that even more of them have difficulty knowing how to approach employee career discussions. We empathize with them. Coaching managers may run into several important barriers. People sometimes don't know what they want. They may expect the manager or the organization to tell them what to do or give them special breaks. Many managers are loath to put themselves in the position of influencing their reports' career direction. They don't want to run the risk of being accused of "playing God."

The nature of the job search process doesn't offer much help in this context. In reality, it is difficult for employees to find out what kinds of opportunities are available in many companies—the job postings bulletin board doesn't mention them all. In most medium to large companies, and even in a number of small ones, opportunities for movement from one job to another emerge informally: A group needs to add someone else quickly; a function is expanding in another building; a task force is coming together to look at supply chain management. These emergent activities are all opportunities for career development if managers and employees know about them. This has important implications for our discussion below regarding what coaching managers and coachees can do to further their careers.

We stress that there is no easy way around most of these barriers, unless the division or organization has developed a full-scale career planning system whose function is to capture information about all career development activities and make that information available in a useable form to everyone in the firm. (And so many firms have been gravely hurt by recent economic developments; even those systems are in question with regard to their helpfulness.) Absent such systems, real career management efforts are likely to take serious time and effort. In difficult economic times, we suspect that the informal processes that do serve to support career development if they can be harnessed are more important than ever. If everyone can accept that premise and manage expectations accordingly, employees and coaching managers can do a lot to promote effective career development.

If the coaching manager has created a coaching-friendly context, employees are much more likely to raise career issues directly. How the coaching manager responds can have an important impact on the employee, the work group, and the coaching environment the manager has worked to create. Setting expectations and creating the right context for career development discussions can help place the responsibility for those discussions and the follow-up work where it belongs: with the employee. The role of the coach is to help, usually not to "do," and rarely to hand-hold. After an overview of career development, we'll describe a methodology for using developmental coaching to help employees productively address career issues. We'll then use case examples to illustrate several of the most common career issues facing coaching managers today and make some suggestions as to how the coaching manager might effectively intervene. You'll note that in this chapter the information we present to help you help your reports may be relevant to you as well.

An Overview of Career Development in the Modern Organization

We would like to begin by presenting the notion that while the word *career* has many meanings, one of the things that everyone should keep in mind is that a career represents a series of *negotiated outcomes*. By that, we mean that individuals have something to offer to organizations that have a need. That perspective becomes more important in the absence of what had been called "career ladders." Career ladders can be thought of as a predefined series of steps that an employee must take in order to advance. These steps might represent time in particular roles, or they might represent the attainment of a specific competency or certification. If you "jumped through the hoop" appropriately, you could expect a defined type of advancement.

Career ladders are, however, largely a thing of the past in most organizations. Organizational structures are flatter and much more fluid. Software giant SAS Institute, for example, has only four steps between an entry-level engineer and the CEO, for instance (O'Reilly & Pfeffer, 2000). Firms are also less stable due to downsizing and restructuring, making it difficult for them to effectively engage in long-term human resource planning. Some firms now have technical and managerial career paths, but in reality, too often the technical career ladders don't have many rungs. Even the stars of the new economy that did pay attention to career issues, such as Cisco Systems and Sun Microsystems, have experienced substantial staff reductions. These firms were firmly committed to retaining their knowledgeable employees as a competitive weapon. Their inability to do so underscores the fact that we cannot look to organizations alone for career direction. Indeed, most organizations no longer imply that they will take any responsibility for the career development of their employees. The best firms offer guidance, training, and, ideally, coaching but are in no position to take responsibility for the outcome.

Ultimately, then, for better or worse (some employees would probably have fared better under conditions of stable employment and traditional career paths), the employee is now in the driver's seat of his or her career. Most employees will have what career scholar D. Tim Hall (1996) describes as a "protean career." Employees will drive their careers, want or need to reinvent themselves from time to time as conditions change, and be engaged in continuous and lifelong learning (Hall, 1996). The employee's relationship with the organization will not be characterized by the kind of dependence found in the traditional structure and the old economy. Rather, employees and organizations will be interdependent. They need one another and can help one another.

When we could look to career ladders for guidance, we didn't notice that there was a negotiated exchange taking place. Most aspects of the exchange were prearranged by the company so as to meet the needs of both the company and the employees. By policy in some organizations, if you had demonstrated skill X, you were promoted to position Y when the next available position Y became open. You negotiated by pursuing company-prescribed skill development opportunities or gaining the required amount of experience. It was presumed that you'd welcome the opportunity to advance.

Now, in most cases, it's every person for her- or himself. Every person is different (to a degree), and every context is different. The company may not be able or willing to offer you an opportunity to advance no matter what abilities you lay before it. At the same time, the company may want an employee to advance but be told by the employee, "I can't. I need to spend more time with my family." The old lockstep pathway approach has been discredited by both the organization and the employee. This means that the development of career planning and negotiating skills is more important than it ever was. (There are exceptions to what we are describing here, largely in the consulting and professional services industry, and we'll pick up their story later in this chapter. For now, we'll focus on the large group of organizations and individuals who are trying to figure all this out.) So what does this mean for the typical employee? We'll look next at what it takes to manage a career under the current circumstances.

Knowing What You Want

Any expert in negotiations will tell you that you have to go into a negotiation with a pretty clear sense of what you want. This is particularly challenging when it comes to career management. In our experience, few aspects of modern life are less well understood than the notion of having a career goal. Too many people think that a career goal should pinpoint a single, specific target: "I will be happy if I have this job and no other." If most workers felt that way, workforce flexibility would be for all practical purposes nonexistent. A small percentage of people do have what psychologists describe as a "calling": for example, the youngster who knew from the age of 5 that she wanted to be a doctor and wouldn't be happy with any other career. If the calling is real, she will feel compelled to follow through and may indeed work happily in her chosen role for the rest of her life. Such individuals' target is very small. They have to hit it, or else they run the risk of being dissatisfied with one of the most important aspects of their lives, their work.

Most of us, thankfully, have a bigger "target area." We have broader interests. An employee might like working with people and also enjoy working with technology. This tells us something if we take such insights seriously (which we should), though it will likely be necessary to fine-tune things a bit. Let's say that an individual knows she is interested in technology. But does she like designing it or using it? The distinction is important. The individual who likes working with technology might like a role in management information systems. The individual who likes designing technology might like a role in a design-engineering group. These are two very different careers and work settings. The key point we are trying to make here is that there is likely to be more than one right job that will satisfy our career interests, but the options with regard to what we'll find satisfying are not limitless. We do have preferences, and they are meaningful. How do we discover those preferences?

Employees can often (though not always) get a handle on these questions with the help of a professional career coach and the use of a variety of assessment tools (standardized inventories that help an individual define interests, values, personal style, and skills, for instance). Although we recommend such an approach when appropriate and feasible, the reality is that most people either don't have access to such resources or, for a variety of reasons, won't make use of them. To address the need for more robust individual career planning systems, more organizations are offering such services through their employee assistance programs or through dedicated career counseling services. If those services are available, they can be very useful resources for the coaching manager and her reports. Reminding employees that such services are available empowers them and places responsibility on them for following through on defining their career directions.

However, a formal self-assessment process isn't the only way to gain insight into your career goals. Individuals can also make progress toward thinking about their goals if they take seriously the notion that what they want and like does in fact matter. That is not to say that we always get what we want. In difficult economic times, we're even less likely to get what we want, of course. The fact that we will face significant challenges should not, we suggest, be considered grounds for giving up the effort. Why? Simply put, if you have some awareness as to what you find satisfying in your work, you are more likely able to talk with others about how your job can be modified, at least a bit, to include the appropriate work that may be satisfying to you and still be of help to your organization, as was previously discussed. In addition, if you are doing something that you value, you're more likely to be successful. You're more likely to put in the extra time and effort required. (Note that motivation, time, and effort aren't the only prerequisites to success. It also requires competence, among other things, which we'll talk about further.)

Many of us, particularly early in our careers, don't consciously and explicitly stop to think about what kinds of tasks we like to do, what our values or life priorities are, and what we are good at. We may feel there is no point in taking such considerations into account because for economic reasons, we just have to take the first good job that comes along. Some people try to avoid such questions because they have been pushed into a particular role by social pressure, particularly from their families.

Although most people don't go through an explicit process of self-assessment, we do tend to self-assess implicitly. We learn about ourselves as we move through a series of jobs and other life roles. The engineering manager in a large firm jumps to a start-up and finds that the time he can allocate for his family diminishes considerably, far below a level with which he is comfortable. He also finds that he doesn't like the frenetic pace and frequent strategic reshufflings characteristic of the start-up life. He decides to return to the more stable and more focused environment of his previous firm. Ideally, he has learned something along the way about his priorities. He will now factor in the questions of family time and his own need to focus when he assesses the next opportunity. Trial and error then does play an important role in our learning, as long as we are able to continue the learning process. It is, however, all too easy to get stuck in the wrong role. Experimentation brings with it risks. Dialogue along with experimentation, however, can be quite a potent combination.

Like most teachers and consultants, we've heard more than our fair share from individuals who "hate their jobs." It has to be one of the most difficult and depressing aspects of our work. Ironically, some folks who do hate their jobs are able to demonstrate considerable success, up to a point and for a limited period of time. One has to wonder how much better these talented people could do if, say, half of each day they were doing work that they truly found meaningful.

One of us was debriefing feedback for an executive from her staff, as part of an executive development activity within her company. The feedback was rather brutal. Others saw the executive as dispassionate and uncaring. They felt she didn't communicate effectively and that she was not passionate about her team's agenda. She listened to the feedback and did not disagree. She began by saying that she knew she wasn't communicating with any sense of excitement. She wondered if she could really communicate effectively at all. She wondered if she just wasn't competent. She was asked if there were aspects of the work that in fact did provide her with some excitement, but unfortunately she said no. The follow-up question asked her if she was engaged in any non-work activities that were exciting. She immediately began to talk about a charitable effort she was involved in that targeted disadvantaged children. She cared a lot about this group because she had known quite a few kids growing up who struggled with similar problems. She wanted to help.

Her interest is laudable here, but what was even more striking was the change in demeanor during the coaching meeting. It appeared that she wasn't the same person. She sat up straight, she made eye contact, the volume of her speech increased, and she looked quite genuine. She spoke with real passion about her charitable work and seemed to be extremely competent at doing things that were quite similar to what she was supposed to be doing on the job but wasn't. She literally appeared to be a changed person from the depressed, disengaged executive of 10 minutes earlier.

Finally, she was asked if she noticed the change in her demeanor. She did notice it. She began to cry softly and said, "I know what this means." She was not incompetent. She was, however, in the wrong job, and she knew it. This of course is a problem for her as she was now going to have to confront some pretty tough choices. However, this is the right problem for her to confront.

We tell this dramatic story as it illustrates what can be a commonsense approach to the admittedly tough question "What do I want?" Simple questions about favorite courses in school, hobbies, favorite activities during the working day, favorite kinds of people and cultures, choice locales, and other experiences of personal preference offer us guidance. We need to talk about activities that we enjoy so that we can better define our target area or, one might say, our "shopping list" (literally, a list of 5 to 15 characteristics of jobs that serve as an expression of our interests; more about that below).

There are also self-help books that can help facilitate the articulation of career interests. The time-honored *What Color Is Your Parachute?* (Bolles, 2009) has served this purpose for years. Bolles's workbook-like approach helps individuals think through their interests (and other aspects of career planning and job search) in part through stimulating readers to think about questions related to those interests, taking a variety of informal inventories of reflections about those interests, and seeking the input of others whose observations may be of help. One of the outputs of this effort is again an ability to characterize the *kinds* of work, the tasks, that the individual is most likely to find satisfying.

We've also had good results using a tool called the *Career Anchors Self-Assessment* (Schein, 2006) with business-oriented students. Schein describes an anchor as an enduring collection of interests, values, and skills that evolves from experience. He provides a useful way to categorize those anchors into groups that include those who are drawn to the following:

- *Technical/functional:* those who are motivated to build greater competence and practice in a technical area
- *General management:* those who are drawn to careers in which they can use analytical and interpersonal skills to influence the direction of teams and organizations
- *Entrepreneurial creativity:* those who are drawn to the creation of new businesses, products, or services
- *Dedication to a cause:* those whose work is linked to an important set of beliefs and values, in the service of others
- *Autonomy/independence:* those who pursue work that will provide them with the maximum level of autonomy, the ability to "be their own boss" (Note that this is different from the entrepreneurial creativity anchor. The two certainly do go together, but the goals are distinct.)
- *Challenge:* those who pursue the most challenging assignments and work opportunities
- *Security and stability:* those who pursue work in order to create a stable environment for themselves and their families and communities
- *Lifestyle:* those who pursue work that can help them balance the demands of both work and nonwork roles

Students are able to see trends in the bundle of interests they bring with them. These trends again help define the kinds of activities that the individual is likely to find satisfying. The subsequent student-to-student dialogue helps them articulate a set of short- and long-term career goals. Psychoanalysis is not required here. Mature individuals talking about their interests within a framework that helps them organize those interests into a more coherent picture can accomplish a great deal. Indeed, many students are surprised by the experience. They report that they hadn't tried to articulate their interests before. Just the effort, the knowledge that their interests are relevant, represents a step forward. It is helpful for students to see, as well, that their classmates in business school are motivated by a variety of interests, not just financial concerns.

Note that these efforts do not tell the individual which *job* he or she should pursue. That's a common problem among job hunters. They look at the job title. That's the wrong approach. The title "vice president," for instance, means widely varying things in different organizations, even organizations within the same industry. The question is "What does the vice president actually do?" If we can list those activities and compare them with the activities that we find satisfying, we can look for overlaps. As we've already indicated, the overlaps won't be complete. We can't tell you how much of an overlap between what you find satisfying and what the job has to offer is sufficient. (We've had some spirited debates break out in our business classes over just this question.)

There are of course pragmatic considerations that define one's shopping list as well. Location, financial compensation, hours, and other factors are important. There is also the question of preparation and competency that we'll discuss below. We are advocating, however, that the individual's interests do in fact count.

We suggest that those coaching managers who are comfortable trying to help their employees think through career concerns consider using such an approach to help their reports create a dialogue about their interests. It is true that there are several challenges to doing so. Career interests can be very sensitive. Employees may be concerned that they are giving the impression of being less than fully committed if they express an interest in occupations substantially different from their current occupation. In the years since the first edition of this book was released we have also had a number of conversations with managers who expressed the concern that they might appear to be intruding on the privacy of the employee or getting into an area of concern that they were not prepared to handle.

Both of these concerns, from the employee and the coaching manager, are valid. We don't have a "one size fits all" response here. We've met many managers and employees who are comfortable with this territory and many who are not. But all parties to this negotiated outcome need to realize that in the absence of some ability to articulate their needs, it is most difficult for this discussion to move further.

Over the past several years we've had a chance to study this negotiation process intensively from the perspective of the employee, through our Fast Track MBA Program at Babson College. These advanced students are asked to prepare a detailed development plan early in their participation in the program. In the plan, they describe their career goals and the competencies on which they wish to work, as well as offering suggestions for how their development could be of service to their organizations. They are encouraged to then hold a dialogue with their managers, and in fact most do just that. One of the most interesting findings is that this dialogue can precipitate a kind of breakthrough for some students in their relationship with their own managers. Their managers, some of whom are not particularly good at coaching, are surprised by the level of preparation and the articulated goals of the students. They are then more able to respond to the students' tentative plans in a collaborative and frequently positive fashion. The student, the manager's report in this case, is driving the conversation. She or he shows up prepared and at least somewhat goal directed. Our hypothesis is that too often career coaching by well-intentioned managers is actually stymied by reports who don't know what they want. The employee and the manager, both uncomfortable with the entire topic, move too quickly through the conversation or bypass it altogether.

We hope that the reader learns one very important point from this discussion. The manager can't own the employee's career development challenge. The relationship between employee and company has evolved from a dependent one to an interdependent one, in large measure because of the need for firms to adapt to rapidly changing business conditions. We don't anticipate that the rapid pace of change will slow down anytime soon. The manager can help, but in a mutual and interdependent relationship, employees must take substantial responsibility as well. This relates not only to how they define their career goals but also to the kinds of competency development that they need in order to achieve those goals. Let's take a closer look at that area next, but before doing so, readers who have not tried to articulate their own career goals might have a look at Exercise 12.1.

Exercise 12.1   What's on Your Shopping List?

Consider the following questions and add a few of your own if you'd like. We're asking you to think through your own interests and then, from that activity, create your own shopping list. Describe the characteristics of a job that you would find most satisfying. Don't think in terms of job titles; think in terms of work activities. What would you be doing?

Dialogue Questions:

1. What were your favorite courses in high school and/or college?

2. What activities have you enjoyed most in past jobs? What activities have you disliked the most in past jobs?

3. What activities do you like the most in your current job? What activities do you like the least in your current job?

4. What kinds of nonwork activities do you find most enjoyable? What kinds of nonwork activities do you find least enjoyable?

5. What personal beliefs or values would you like to express in your work?

6. What feedback have you had from others about the kind of work you should do and shouldn't do?

Now, try to list 5 to 15 characteristics of what for you would be the most satisfying jobs. Don't worry, yet, about whether or not you are qualified. Competency development comes next. Too often, we discount our own interests because of externally imposed constraints. Those constraints do matter, we agree. If you find that you are drawn to the creative arts, for instance, and yet you have had no training in those arts, you'll have work to do to build a career there. However, an awareness of your creative interests may in the short term inform the kind of assignment you ask for even in your current role. Perhaps something that provided an outlet for that creativity might be somewhat more satisfying than your current list of duties. Career development drinven by your interests may not result in a major change for pragmatic reasons. However, incremental change may be possible.

Choosing Learning Goals

Having some sense of one's career goals is inherently important to one's ability to choose learning-oriented goals, to organize one's efforts to build competence in a particular area. Again, we draw your attention to the oft-made point here that competence creates value both for the organization and for the individual employee.

In most organizations the decisions the employee makes about which learning goals to pursue are made by the individual and his or her manager. Some assistance may be provided by the organization or professional standards where applicable. Again, the exceptions are those organizations that have developed competency-based career ladders. Let's look first at those firms that do in fact provide some guidance.

Firms that articulate competency-based career ladders are most likely to describe what it takes to move up and, at the same time, signal a clear message to valued employees that, if they gain certain competencies, they will more likely be able to advance. (Note that these firms are making a commitment, either implicitly or explicitly, to hire from within when possible.)

Competency-based career ladders also help employees set their expectations appropriately. Competency models were discussed at length in Chapter 3. An example of a competency-based career ladder is presented in Table 12.1.

Table 12.1 Competency-Based Career Ladder in a Consulting Firm	
Position	**Examples of Required Competency**
First level: Team leader: Leads small teams within a project. An entry-level management position.	Planning for team deliverables Estimating resource requirements Managing a budget Keeping team members focused on the task Good with details
Second level: Project manager: Plans the project and manages team leaders toward project execution.	Managing client relationships Project management skills Effective at influencing stakeholders
Third level: Program manager: Manages a number of project teams that are using a particular methodology or focusing on a particular industry. A firm-wide leadership role.	Managing industry relationships Effective at setting a leadership vision Able to communicate effectively with global staff

In the scheme laid out in Table 12.1, the coaching manager can help promote career development, at least for most employees, by making sure that employees get a chance to build skills at each level that will make them ready for the next. (We say "most" employees because some may not want to move up a career ladder and some may be judged as unable to move up because of their inability to perform successfully at a foundational level.) It is not surprising that the firms using competency-based career ladders tend to be the ones that most value the knowledge of their workers and compete by virtue of their ability to provide high-quality service. Retaining the best employees is critically important to these firms, and taking an aggressive interest in their career development is a very powerful way to do so.

If the learning goals are somewhat clearly defined by the competency model, coaching manager and employee should be able to utilize the model, as we've discussed previously, to help guide their work. However, there is still a great deal of room left for interpretation, as the reader will note.

Further, we also must contend with the fact that most of us don't operate within the bounds of such a well-defined set of competencies.

As discussed in Chapter 3, it is possible to break down the overall competencies required for a particular job into three large categories: the technical functional requirements of the job, the interpersonal requirements of the job, and the cognitive requirements of the job. In general, the technical functional requirements can be considered the ticket to entry and maintenance in a position. The cognitive and interpersonal requirements may be the subject of greater debate. The coaching manager is ideally, however, as discussed in Chapter 3, well positioned to help the individual sort out those competencies that are most valued by the organization and those that are not. (See Box 3.1 for help on this topic.)

The individual coachee needs to partner in the process by having a good sense of his or her strengths and weaknesses. Feedback from coaching sessions, performance reviews, and other forms of data are key tools in support of this self-assessment. The oft-derided performance appraisal, when well done, is a powerful tool for supporting an individual's self-knowledge, even if the performance appraisal has no linkage with compensation or promotion. (Those who would like to do away with the performance appraisal seem to forget that it can be a very important career development tool, even when its linkage with career development may not be explicit.)

Even with a thorough self-assessment, however, there will still be decisions to be made. We already discussed some of the tactical questions regarding the setting of goals in the previous chapter. One of the most important sets of strategic decisions has to do with whether or not the coachee chooses to work on those skills that might be considered strengths or those that might be considered weaknesses. This is currently the subject of a serious debate on the learning and development literature as we've mentioned previously. We take a very pragmatic orientation toward this issue, but let's look at it in more detail.

The strengths-oriented movement had its origins in the work of authors such as Buckingham and Clifton (2001). Those authors, working with data from the Gallup Organization, propose that managers are most likely to see the best performance as well as positively impact the development of their people when they provide them with opportunities to utilize existing strengths. The notion here is that by deploying those strengths, which are likely to be quite satisfying to the individual, the individual also gets an opportunity to further refine his or her natural talents. If the child is great at playing Mozart, let her play Mozart. Indeed, provide her with all the support available if the child hopes to be a concert pianist some day. There is significant logic to this argument. Indeed, how can one expect to be "great" at a particular task if one's performance does not rest at least in part on naturally emerging talent? Yes, those talents may need to be refined, but it's much easier to promote development when the development effort rests on the shoulders of those talents.

Here's the problem. Most job descriptions are more complex than "play Mozart." Actually, we suggest that even a great musician's implicit job description is far more complicated as well. Success in the arts depends on a great many complex factors, including the artist's ability to create a network of supportive individuals in adulthood. We'll come back to that point below. But the reality for most business and organizational jobs is even clearer. Technical functional abilities by themselves, which are often a requirement for entry into a job, are not sufficient for advancement. The talents that brought us to the job may not be sufficient to help us keep the job or grow beyond the job.

A number of authors have drawn our attention to this problem. Eichinger (2007) suggests that most of us present five or so relative strengths (strengths in comparison with other areas of action in which we are not as skilled) but raises the question as to whether or not those five strengths are likely to be adequate to position an individual for growth (and for organizational success) in a competitive context. You may be good at certain aspects of the managerial role, but do you have the most critically needed skills for that role? Eichinger's work suggests that there are eight highly critical competencies that are infrequently displayed by managers, including creativity, dealing with ambiguity, building effective teams, and innovation management. In other words, what we're talented at doing may not be critically important to what our organizations need.

Further, research on derailment, those factors that have a significant negative impact on an individual's career, suggests that relationship problems are most important in this regard, not technical functional skill deficits (obviously this may vary from role to role) (Kaiser, 2009). Relationship management is not a universal talent, as you may have noticed. Yet, it may be one of the most common impediments to career growth.

This research, and there is a great deal more that points in the same direction, suggests to us that it is critically important to take a pragmatic approach to the choice of learning goals if you wish to advance within a particular field. Yes, you have to identify and utilize your "natural" talents, at least to an extent. But in order to effectively utilize those talents the individual may need to work on skills that are quite removed from those given talents so that those abilities that may be considered "weaknesses" may at least be brought up to a competency level that will keep him out of trouble. As we mentioned above, the great musician who alienates promoters in the highly competitive and changing music business may find herself losing engagements, even though her musical talent is enormous. There may be others who are just as good but who are easier to work with.

Knowledge of the real requirements of a role, then, is key to deciding the goals on which one should work. We'll talk about the relationship implications of this fact in the next section. Again, we assume that the coaching manager can frequently provide just such knowledge if the employee is interested in advancing within a knowledge area related to her current work. In addition to a learning goal's relevance for career advancement, it's also useful to consider the degree to which a particular learning goal might take the individual outside of his or her comfort zone, as discussed in the previous chapter.

Here we must return to the notion that the best learning goals are those chosen by the learner. The coaching manager can inform his or her reports of what appear to be the most critically important competences to set as targets for development. Only the individual can decide whether or not she is truly committed to choosing what can be very difficult goals. The coaching manager and the coachee need to be watchful that the coachee doesn't make *apparent* commitments that follow the prevailing wisdom (Kaplan, 2008). Commitment has to be preceded by serious self-assessment and reflection on the part of the coachee when choosing a tough albeit necessary-for-advancement learning goal. Peer pressure, parental pressure, and spousal pressure notwithstanding, working to become better at something like innovation management or public speaking can be enormously daunting if that work does not rest upon natural talent. The advice we give to our coachees and students is this: Consider carefully whether or not this learning goal fits in with your career goals. Is it important enough for you that you are willing to face significant anxiety and the possibility of failure, in the service of your larger goal? Is it important enough that you will sacrifice time with family and friends in its pursuit? (That last question can be particularly tough.) If so, then let's move ahead.

Who You Know Does Count: Networks, Supporters, and Blockers

So what does it take to develop in your career? It takes information, commitment, and an opportunity to practice. It takes coaching. Hopefully, the coaching manager is there to help (with everything but the coachee's commitment). Alas, it takes more. Again, we stress, a career is in part a negotiated outcome. The individual needs access to information, needs a variety of forms of support, and may need to deal with those who actively or passively may block his or her efforts. If this starts to sound like organizational politics, then we're making our point. Serious development work takes place in a political context.

It has long been clear that successful leaders rely on their networks to get things done. Leaders, if they are successful, are change agents. They make things happen. We would suggest that it's helpful to view career development in the same way. Career development is an exercise in change management. If significant development takes place, things will not be as they were before. Some individuals may even be negatively impacted by an employee's development. If you promote someone, for instance, those left behind may have to change their own workflow and set of responsibilities. Change needs support. It comes at a price. Change then entails the management of risk.

Let's start with building support for change. The employee's network is a key tool in this regard. The network brings him information perhaps beyond that available from his manager. The network may inform the individual about opportunities. It may also bring him friends who are willing to help. The network can provide feedback as to where he stands and as to his perceived competencies (Ibarra & Hunter, 2007). The network can alert him to potential trouble.

Now we state the obvious. Some people are good at building a network and have taken the time to do so. Some people are good at building a network but haven't taken the time. Finally, some are not so good at building a network perhaps because they are terribly uncomfortable at the thought and value private time more than any other. In our experience, one of the most important roles that a coaching manager can play if he or she is trying to help an individual with career development is to help him with this thorny problem. There are two basic interventions that the manager can try.

First, the manager can signal that building a network is valuable. Networks are important for more than just career development reasons. Indeed, they can help solve operational and strategic problems as well (Ibarra & Hunter, 2007). There is every reason to encourage employees to proactively and/or informally take the time to build relationships with those inside and outside the organization who may be able to help the employee do his or her job better. In the process, relationships will be made that can also support career development. This will help those individuals who have the ability to network but haven't taken the time.

Those who are not particularly good at networking may benefit from more formal approaches. Assignments to task forces and committees are just two examples. Putting individuals into contact with others to perform a task can facilitate the process of relationship building even for those who are uncomfortable with social interaction. Work assignments provide people with something to talk about: the task at hand. Networking out in the open requires that an individual identify someone with whom to network, create an opening, engage in small talk (frequently), and so forth. Formal assignments that create connections between people level the playing field, a bit, between those who are extroverted and those who are not. However, coaching may be helpful as an additional support, as we saw in the opening case in Chapter 2. A detailed description of the nature of effective networking is beyond the scope of this book. However, we suggest that a few basic points be kept in mind:

- *Networking is best done on an ongoing basis.* Networking done at the last minute, when an employee faces forced redeployment for instance, is most difficult. All employees should be encouraged to identify and get to know others with mutual interests as a part of their jobs. Social networking technologies, when appropriate, can help.
- *To network is to participate in a community.* Remind coachees that networking works because it involves *mutual* aid. Networking is nothing more than people with common interests sharing those interests and on occasion helping one another.
- *Individuals seeking to build a network should, as such, self-assess.* "What do I have to offer others?" Too often, an individual without a strong sense of confidence will say, "Not much." It's important to get beyond that. If you have little to offer, expect little in return. The coachee may have something quite intangible to offer, such as concern or empathy. Intangibles matter.
- *Like a community, a network is best nurtured.* It will take some time to keep one's network alive. We've talked with so many students and employees over the years who felt that they were goofing off by talking with someone not directly involved in their immediate work (yes, students in fact have told us this as well, believe it or not). We disagree. Building relationships isn't goofing off. It is strategic work.

This discussion of networking directs our attention to its role in support of development. Networking provides access to information and support. However, the concept of networking also allows us to consider the fact that there may be individuals who believe it is in their interest to block another person's development or a particular development activity. This can take place for a variety of reasons, some of which we've already mentioned. Development changes the way people work at times and, as such, requires adjustment on the part of others. Development also takes place within a context of scarce resources. There may be competition for particular developmental assignments. Development can raise questions about status, respect, promotion, and compensation. Finally, family members and friends may have to sacrifice in the service of development as well. The latter can be particularly painful.

We increasingly encourage our MBA students engaged in development planning to consider seriously the question of who might be negatively impacted by their development or who might perceive that they are being negatively impacted. In other words, we're suggesting that it's useful to move beyond the concept of networking to consider how an individual's development will influence or be influenced by the range of stakeholders within which the developmental plan will take place. Who needs to be taken into consideration, why, and how? This type of thinking is consistent with the notion of action planning for change. In Box 12.1, we utilize a framework developed by colleague Anne Donnellon (2000) that links action planning and career development from a stakeholder perspective.

BOX 12.1   Career Development and Action Planning

Action planning is too often characterized by a lack of planning. We take an action, and we see what happens. Sometimes it works, and sometimes it doesn't. There are, however, significant risks to such an approach that we hope to mitigate by taking a more intentional approach. Let's say a coachee has proposed a rather significant step in her development, a temporary transfer to another group that is taking on a major new product development initiative. You believe that she's got the right competencies and that this would be a good move for her. You agree to provide her with support, but you see trouble ahead. She's got to be the one to manage that trouble. You can help, but you are acutely aware that managing trouble like this can be developmental in and of itself. The action planning framework (Donnellon, 2000) suggests the following steps.

1. *Analyze the situation.* Identify the goal and the problems. (Prioritize the problems. Some are not that important. Some may be deal breakers.) Identify any underlying causes. Consider stakeholders, their interests, and their power.

The goal is as stated above. Your coachee has got your support. There are some logistical and restaffing issues. The two of you have specified these. There are some significant stakeholders involved, however. The manager of the product development group is a friend of yours and your coachee's. Your coachee has nurtured a relationship with him over the years. He knows what she can do, and he's happy to have her on board. That's key. However, the division vice president may be a real problem. He's wanted to put someone from another division in that slot. These slots are pretty rare. So there is a competitive issue here. In addition, he did pass along some negative feedback about your coachee after a recent staff retreat. He didn't like her presentation at the retreat. You didn't pay much attention to that because the reality is he doesn't like many presentations under any circumstances. Now you realize that may have been a mistake. Your vice president isn't a bad guy. He's just really cautious. He may have questions about your coachee's ability to do that job.

2. *Get started with action planning.* Consider your goals. How will you define success? Consider alternative ways of pursuing those goals. Identify multiple solutions if you can, and identify the strengths and risks associated with each. Identify an optimal solution if possible.

You and your coachee have reviewed the analysis above and realize that the goal may need to be modified a bit. Yes, the goal is for her to effect this temporary assignment, but it also has to be for this to take place in a context that will help build her visibility and support. It will do no good if she does a good job there but the vice president is still skeptical. The logistical problems within your own group regarding communications and staffing are pretty clear. The two of you list the action steps and decide who is going to do what. You do not anticipate any resistance. Indeed, your own team is aware of this activity and supportive. The more daunting question has to do with the vice president. You ask your coachee to outline some options, including the following:

- She can go to him and respond to the negative feedback that she's now heard regarding the presentation at the retreat.
- She can go to him and ignore the negative feedback but keep him abreast of the plan.
- She can look for opportunities to talk with him in a less challenging context so that he can get to know more about her work.
- She can ask you, her manager, to talk with him, to smooth the way.

You then discuss the strengths and weaknesses of each approach. The latter has the most risks. Typically the vice president does not respect people who don't talk with him directly. Your coachee supports this. That was her least preferred option. You talk about how you've worked with the vice president in the past. He is open-minded. However, he likes to be informed of important decisions and their rationale. We don't know for sure that he's going to be a barrier to this plan, but he could be if he's not well informed. Your coachee decides that the optimal solution is to get onto his schedule, tell him about the plan and its rationale, and seek his guidance and feedback.

3. *Continue action planning.* Prepare a set of steps for the action plan in an iterative fashion. Consider "if–then" possibilities, possible reactions, and what might be done to manage those reactions. Create contingency plans as appropriate.

(Continued)

(Continued)

Coaching manager and coachee rehearse the conversation with the vice president. The coachee will start with a rationale but will also acknowledge that she and the vice president haven't worked together before. She'll be ready to give him a brief overview of her career and how she came to this point if he'd like. If he brings up the retreat presentation, she'll ask for feedback and use it as an opportunity to consider what she might have done differently. She will try not to be defensive. The rehearsal helps. If he brings up another possible candidate for the product development assignment, she'll respond positively and clearly signal that she welcomes some positive competition. He's a big believer in the value of internal competition. She'll then ask for next steps in the decision-making process.

In this case, the plan was carried out and proceeded somewhat as anticipated. The vice president was very impressed at the coherence of the plan even though he had some concerns about the coachee's readiness. He was probably not going to be a huge supporter of the plan, but he wasn't going to be a blocker. The transfer took place.

Some of you may be thinking that that was a tremendous amount of analysis and work in order to effect a simple and temporary transfer. However, others of you are thinking, "No, it's actually harder than that!" We agree with both perspectives. It is a lot of work. And it can be worse. However, the failure to think through key steps in development is one of the reasons that development efforts are so often thwarted. Significant development activities have impacts, and those impacts require management if they are to be successful.

Using Developmental Coaching to Address Career Concerns and Promote Career Development

In the previous sections, we've tried to outline some of the very real challenges managers and employees face when trying to intentionally manage career development. These challenges, though, obviously represent significant learning opportunities. The effort to define one's goals, choose learning targets, and manage the political context of one's development tracks directly with the work of leadership. When you help your employees manage their careers (to the extent you can), you help them learn something about how to lead themselves and perhaps others. Before moving to some more specific case examples we want to offer the following tactical guidance for those who want to encourage employees to think about both performance improvement and longer-term development.

- In the coaching dialogue, *from time to time, encourage employees to reflect on what they find satisfying or meaningful about their work.* Ask them how they feel about what they are doing, where they are, and where they want to be. Doing so proactively communicates your interest in the long-term welfare of employees as well as helping them articulate verbally their interests. This doesn't have to be done often, but we do encourage you not to focus your efforts solely on the issues of effectiveness or learning. This step helps employees self-assess what they want out of their careers. When this takes place in a relaxed atmosphere, employees may begin to consider aspects of themselves that are critical to their future job satisfaction but that they may not routinely think about. Of course, it is important not to react negatively to employees' reflections. Listening with a helpful attitude is probably the most important career intervention the coaching manager can offer.

- *Provide balanced feedback whenever possible in your reaction to employees' reflections.* Your feedback may include your thoughts about employees' strengths and weaknesses in relation to their career interests, or it may include information about opportunities, or the lack of opportunities, that relate to employees' interests. Direct your feedback specifically at areas or issues requested by the employee. Don't offer unsolicited critical feedback or unsolicited support. In a coaching-friendly context, some employees will use the coaching dialogue as an opportunity to "think out loud" about their careers. For example, when one of your employees suddenly says, "I think I want to go to medical school," don't immediately assume that he is looking for your help in getting there. Appropriate dialogue questions that can help you determine where to focus your feedback include the following: "What would you like from me?" "How would you like me to help?" or "What kind of feedback would be useful to you on this?" Our point is that you may well be your coachee's most important source of information.

- *Whenever possible, encourage employees to build relationships with others who work in areas associated with their career interests.* Facilitate such networking opportunities if you can. As stated above, employees may not recognize the importance of doing so or may consider networking to be a form of political manipulation. Employees who are reserved or less socially confident may also find networking to be particularly challenging. You can be supportive, but it is not appropriate to take responsibility for this challenge. The employee has to drive the career, regardless of his or her personal style. You might encourage an employee who feels significant social discomfort at the concept of networking to consult with the company's human resource group or employee assistance program. A number of well-established training programs can be helpful to employees struggling with this challenge.

- *If possible, use "job-sculpting" tactics to reshape the employee's job in line with his or her career interests* (Butler & Waldroop, 1999). However, we do caution not to make up a job just to meet an individual's needs. The job probably won't last, and it may not be doable. It is important that coaching managers know what they can and can't do while considering how to define job roles. Do not succumb to any efforts to push you beyond what makes sense for the business.

- *We've stated here that listening may be the most important intervention the coaching manager can offer.* Listening to someone talk about his or her career seems easy on the surface, but this is not always the case. The coaching manager may have a strong reaction when someone says, "What I've learned is that I don't like doing this!" or when the best employee in the group says, "I have to leave to spend more time with my family." We hope such career insights won't be the most common ones encountered by the coaching manager. However, given changing employee values and the fact that employees don't always pursue career opportunities wisely, the coaching manager should be prepared. In our experience, it is difficult to predict where a career discussion will lead unless you have very thorough knowledge of a particular individual.

- After listening, it is important not to jump into helping. *Encourage the coachee to define a goal or a need and a next step.* You may then be able to provide useful feedback on the basis of your understanding of what the business unit or organization can offer. You may be aware of other people who could help the employee. Respect your own limitations and those of your firm and do so without guilt. In the next section, we'll see how these five components of the developmental coaching model work in practice while dealing with career-related issues.

Coaching for Career Development

Every employee has his or her own career story. There are too many possibilities for us to offer specific advice for every contingency. We have chosen here to discuss three of the more common career concerns that managers face today. These examples are all true, though they are disguised. The real-life case examples that we present here all illustrate common principles: the importance of the coaching dialogue, a careful and helpful response to the employee, an awareness of what you can and can't do, the use of job sculpting whenever possible, and the value of linking people up with other resources that can help.

Case 12.1: The Good Employee Who Has Become Bored With Her Job

Joyce had been working in customer service for more than 3 years. She was amazingly effective at her job. She had good interpersonal skills. She seemed unflappable no matter how angry the person on the other end of the line was. Joyce clearly liked helping people, had great product knowledge, and was able to bring most calls to a speedy and successful conclusion. Last year, she was awarded the CEO's coveted Employee Recognition Award for her service to the company and its customers. Her manager was very proud of her. Nevertheless, Joyce's manager knew it couldn't last forever. It was obvious that Joyce was quite intelligent and sophisticated. In recent discussions with her manager, she revealed that she was getting very tired of doing the same thing, day in and day out. No matter how successful she was, she found herself losing enthusiasm.

Her manager wasn't at all surprised and empathized with her. Normally, her manager would begin to think about how to move her up to the next step, perhaps into a supervisory role. Unfortunately, the firm had an ironclad policy regarding the educational background expected of supervisors. This was a barrier that the manager did not think Joyce could surmount, regardless of any stakeholder analysis they might consider. Supervisors had to be college graduates. Joyce had finished only high school. He mentioned this to her at one point in the discussion, and she explained that she also had major family commitments and was in no position to begin college at night, even though she'd love to. She felt that when she wasn't at work, she had to attend to her family.

Joyce's problem is a common one, known to managers in many organizations. Certain jobs tend to be quite distinct from the normal network of jobs in a corporation. Telemarketers and customer service personnel are often chosen for their interpersonal skills and natural intelligence. Their pay is relatively low. They are taught firm-specific or product-specific knowledge, along with customer service or sales tactics, and are put to work. If the firm has done a good job of hiring, these employees will be successful for a period of time; then they may become bored. They may look around for alternatives but find few natural paths outside their current role. Often, they start to express frustration with their low pay, though this doesn't seem to be the primary problem most of them report. In all likelihood, the job has lost its challenge.

The problem of lack of challenge can occur for any employee who has been in a role for an extended period of time and has successfully conquered its demands. In Joyce's case, the loss of challenge is compounded by the normal personal concerns of midlife (Hall, 1986). Midlife and midcareer bring with them an awareness of the limitations of one's life. There seems to be little time left to start over and to build a new career self. Responsibilities for the family are often overpowering and leave little time for personal ambition. Aging and health concerns emerge for the first time.

The desire to do something challenging, perhaps even special, can intensify. Most people still have powerful needs for growth and psychological success (Hall, 1986). If the coaching manager has created a coaching-friendly context, she'll know that Joyce's feelings about her work have changed. She can't change Joyce's reality, but she can encourage Joyce to think about what kinds of challenges she might want to undertake. It is not unusual to find that employees, particularly if they have spent a lifetime battling to maintain a basic economic living standard, have never had someone whom they respect express an interest in their careers. The opportunity to reflect and consider what growth might mean can represent an important breakthrough in and of itself. The coaching dialogue between coaching manager and employee, which rests on empathic listening, can be extremely important to a successful outcome.

The coaching manager can give Joyce feedback regarding her strengths and encourage her to consider how she can use those strengths in other ways. She may need additional information about alternatives to develop a picture of what is possible. There may be activities within the firm—for example, task forces, United Way drives, and new product launches—in which Joyce can use her skills without bumping up against the (essentially bureaucratic and perhaps unnecessary) requirement that she have a college diploma. Workshops and courses held at the company may help her fill specific gaps in her education and qualify her for lateral roles that could reinvigorate her sense of challenge. The act of searching for more information and beginning the process of establishing an informal network of contacts may give Joyce a sense that progress is possible. Meanwhile, her manager may be able to help her redefine her role in the organization without running into the organizational policy that threatens to keep her stuck in her current role. (We have seen coaching managers go to the CEO and get a policy waver on occasion, though such an intervention will not always be possible, or wise.)

Why do anything at all? There are really two answers. The first is a human one. Once the coaching manager has integrated helping into his or her management style, helping becomes the natural thing to do. Second, and of far more pragmatic interest, Joyce has been a top talent for the firm and can probably do much more. She is an asset. However, the "asset" will lose value for the company if it is not managed properly. Helping her restart the engine of challenge is the right thing to do for all stakeholders in the business, customers, other employees, and owners. Finally, this situation is probably being watched. Will you as a manager try to be helpful to someone seen as a leader or not? There are significant morale concerns in play.

Case 12.2: The Employee Who Wants to Move Up (Too Fast!)

Mary is one of the best team leaders in her division. She has a real command of the tactical, day-to-day demands of her job. In her 2 years with the firm, she has consistently performed at or above the level of other "best performers" in the company. Her manager has recently heard rumors that she may be thinking about leaving. Mary likes the company but fears that it will take forever for her to move up the ranks to program manager, a more strategic position responsible for building longer-term customer relationships. Her manager knows from previous discussions that Mary aspires to a leadership position and wants to have a big impact. However, he also knows that she has a lot to learn about the challenges of sustaining long-term client relationships through difficult times. She is technologically savvy and good with people but doesn't have a deeper feel for the economic forces that can affect a customer relationship. Unfortunately, it seems as though her previous manager did little or no coaching. Mary was given an assignment, executed the plan, and was sent on to the next assignment. She did a good job, but, from her point of view, her work wasn't viewed in a larger context. Her previous manager also didn't help her by sharing a definition of success, the competencies required for advancement to the next level.

Her manager wants her to stay with the firm and would like to see her advance, but he also needs to help her understand what she needs to learn and the value of the experience she is getting as she moves up in the ranks.

What should the coaching manager do in such a situation? Should he be the bearer of bad news and confront her on her "incompetence"? Is Mary's desire to move up before she is ready a manifestation of arrogance or just a natural expression of her ambition and self-confidence? Sometimes arrogance can be a problem. Very smart people don't necessarily have a great deal of self-awareness just because they happen to be smart. Is it your role to tell her that, in essence, she needs to lower her expectations?

We suggest a number of alternatives to consider before jumping in with a great deal of unsolicited critical feedback. First, the coaching dialogue needs to be handled sensitively. If Mary feels that her manager is not interested in her growth and ultimate promotion, she will likely go elsewhere when the opportunity presents itself. The coaching manager can encourage her to reflect on her readiness by carefully reviewing with her the requirements for promotion.

Let's assume that the career ladder in Mary's firm is comparable to that described in Table 12.1. Movement to the project manager level requires her to have a greater understanding of customer relationships, as well as the ability to build influential relationships within her own firm. Some firms also have a "years in role" requirement that the coaching manager may not be able to influence, but the key barriers to Mary's promotion are a lack of skill in two relatively specific areas. If she can understand those requirements and reflect on her knowledge in relationship to them, she may begin to build a clearer picture of what she needs to accomplish to move ahead. The interchange with the coaching manager now changes. It moves from one in which there is the potential for an adversarial relationship—Mary says she wants something, and the manager says no—to one in which Mary articulates her needs and the coaching manager tries to help by considering how he can provide her with opportunities to learn the required skills. Mary can focus her on-the-job development efforts on goals that will take her in the desired direction. In our experience, most employees, even those who are most ambitious, can show patience if they have a "line of sight" between what they are doing now and their ultimate goals.

The problem, then, is a lack of understanding of the real requirements for promotion. In some cases, this may also reflect a failure on the part of the business to define those requirements. (See Chapter 3 for advice on how to develop an informal description of the skills required for a particular role if your company offers no such guidance.) If that is the case, the coaching manager will need to take up the task of spelling out those requirements clearly and thoughtfully so that the employee can identify the learning gap.

If the firm doesn't spend some time trying to define the requirements for jobs, particularly new ones, and communicating those requirements to people in the firm, the promotion process will appear to be political. Under such circumstances, minority candidates and women in particular are likely to assume that the process is unfair, and they may well be right. The coaching manager, assuming he or she has some integrity, can do two things under these circumstances. First, the coaching manager can try to influence the firm to develop a more rational approach to defining jobs. Second, the coaching manager can help employees develop the right relationships so that they have a chance of moving up in the firm when opportunities arise.

Case 12.3: The Employee With Work and Family Concerns

Ash is one of the best consulting engineers in the senior product support group. He has the talent and drive to move to the very top of the firm in 5 years. Since the birth of his second child, however, he's been increasingly concerned about the long working hours required to keep up with the rapid pace of technological change in his product area. Over the course of his career, furthermore, he has been "taught" to keep such concerns to himself so as not to appear less than 100% committed to the company. His new manager has encouraged the people on the team to be open about their concerns and needs. Unfortunately, Ash's previous experience has made it more difficult for him to take up such an offer. His productivity has declined, and his own team has begun to express concerns about his effectiveness. His manager, frustrated at Ash's lack of openness, prepares critical feedback for a constructive confrontation meeting with Ash. Once Ash hears the feedback, he begins to reflect on the fact that the demands of his growing family are worrying him. He feels he is failing on both fronts.

Ash's problem is common but often exists "below the surface" (Vincola, 2001). Many employees have trouble balancing the demands of work and family. Furthermore, many develop the belief, through experience in other organizations, that to talk about their difficulties, especially at the senior level, can ruin one's career. Such a belief can make it extremely difficult for the coaching manager to start a coaching dialogue. The lack of a coaching dialogue can lead to disaster. In one study of how managers and employees deal with work and family conflict, in every case in which the employee brought up the problem with his or her manager, the manager was able to engage in some type of problem solving with the employee and find a solution that made it possible for the employee to remain in the firm. However, in every case in which the employee did not bring the problem up to his or her manager, a performance problem resulted (Hunt, 1994).

The implications of this perspective should be clear. The big problem with work and family conflict issues is the failure of employees and managers to have a conversation to address the problem. Here we see once again how difficult it can be for employees to articulate what they want and need. We suggest that managers be attentive to this challenge, as discussed above. Once such a dialogue takes place, work and family concerns may cease to look like career issues. Granted, the manager will not be able to offer concrete options, such as flexible work schedules or telecommuting, in every case. Most good performers don't want a work/life balance problem to force a career change. They are motivated to work with the coaching manager and will often negotiate in good faith until a compromise solution can be met. If the employee is good, it is in the interest of the manager to bargain in good faith as well. Consider that 80% of the effort of a great performer may still yield an economic output that is several times greater than that of a mediocre or poor performer.

Work and family career issues don't usually last forever. Luckily, time is on everyone's side. Children grow up, crises pass, and the demands on employees are not always uniformly overwhelming. The coaching manager with a long-term focus can usually compromise, at least around the issue of time, for a period.

Ash's manager encourages him to talk with several different people. His firm, like many firms, has a work/life resource program that can provide Ash with information and referral to a variety of additional services. In addition, he encourages Ash to have coffee with several other senior managers who meet regularly to discuss work/life balance issues. These executives are thinking through strategic options that the firm might consider most helpful in retaining good employees, such as Ash, who are having difficulty with work/life balance. The executives are interested because they have been through similar struggles themselves.

Conclusions: Developmental Coaching and Career Development

Addressing career concerns is the logical outgrowth of developmental coaching. Employees want to learn for a variety of reasons, one of which is to help them prepare for their next roles, whatever they might be. Linking career development, however, does face some significant strategic challenges as discussed. While the challenges need to be taken seriously, tactical solutions can be useful: Encourage employees to reflect on their career interests and goals, and respond by offering balanced feedback, job sculpting, or contacts with others, which can help employees move toward their career target areas. Offer these resources when they are aligned with the needs of the business. Finally, be prepared to let go. You are in the people development business, and at the end of the term comes graduation.

Developmental Coaching and Performance Problems

13

In this chapter, we describe the following:

- The difficulties of applying developmental coaching to performance problems

- Some of the root causes of performance problems and persistent gaps in performance

- Guidelines for helping the employee with a performance problem improve his or her performance

In the years since we originally wrote *The Coaching Manager,* we've had probably more questions on this topic than any other. We've also had more case examples thrown at us in seminars of individual employees whose performance was poor, sometimes bordering on unethical or illegal. We understand the problem. These are the kinds of issues that keep managers up at night. They dominate time, and sap strength. The problem from our perspective remains, though, that there is a significant level of confusion between performance management and developmental coaching. We stress again that developmental coaching is most helpful with the vast majority of employees who want to do a good job and want to grow on the job. While the concepts of developmental coaching are useful to keep in mind when managing serious performance problems, you're likely to need other tools as well. In fact, those other tools may be more important than what we have to offer here. On the flip side, though, there are times when a good employee may develop a serious performance problem that will require the use of both the tools of performance management and the tools of developmental coaching. That caveat having been offered, we'll try to explore the key issues here.

As we've already stated, an initial gap between actual and desired performance is not usually a problem. While people are learning a new skill or trying to use a skill in a new way or context, their performance, naturally, will not be expert. At some point, however, with practice and learning, the gap should close to an acceptable degree, or disappear completely. It may take time. Learning a complex symphony may take years. Learning a new programming technique may take a day. The employee may move on to the next challenge, and once again, a gap between actual and desired performance may appear. This is the nature of the relationship between learning and performance. Such a pattern does not reflect a performance problem when viewed from the perspective of developmental coaching in a coaching-friendly context. This being said, what does constitute a performance problem? (It may be falsely identified as a performance problem if the manager expects no learning curve. That is not a reasonable expectation unless the hiring and selection process has been managed in a fashion to deliver a fully competent individual into a specific role.)

How's a manager to tell the difference between a performance problem and a learning curve? We propose several commonsense answers. At the simplest level, the hallmark of a performance problem is an *ongoing gap* between actual and desired performance, a gap that is not closing and may be worsening. Even the worst performers will be successful on occasion, but for those with performance problems, the gap is there much more often than not. Perhaps most people can close a deal sometimes, but organizations need salespeople who can close deals consistently. If someone in a sales role can't sell consistently after he or she has had an opportunity to learn the job, with appropriate support (selling something that customers might want, we should add), a performance problem exists. Additionally, performance can also deteriorate. On occasion, a gap may reappear. A performance gap may be observable in an activity that the employee seemed to have mastered. For example, someone who used to be able to sell may no longer do so routinely, even though few other conditions have changed.

We have put forth the proposition that developmental coaching is most effective with good to great performers who want to learn. Don't people with performance problems want to learn? One would imagine so; after all, it is in their interest to do so. However, the answer to this question is, unfortunately, sometimes yes and sometimes no. Sometimes the person with the performance problem wants the problem to go away, wants to deny the problem exists, or just wants to survive until the end of the day.

The problem has to do in part with the person and his or her context. As we'll discuss below, many performance problems are influenced by factors over which the manager and even the employee may have little or no control. Performance problems can be driven by personal problems, personality, team dysfunction, and even organizational change. Performance problems often have to do with the simple fact that we are who we are, and we may be in roles that require us to be someone we are not. We cannot change our personalities or the personalities of others. Psychoanalysts tell us that we can come to understand ourselves better and perhaps channel our energies more effectively (no small accomplishment), but in terms of interests, intelligence, and personality-driven behavior, we can't change all that much.

In Chapter 11, we described the three-stage learning model: unfreezing, change, and refreezing (Schein, 1979). The model is extremely useful but has its limitations. Not every problem can be unfrozen. People will try, however. The process of trying to help the individual with a performance problem has some unintended consequences of its own.

If the job of an individual whose performance is persistently problematic is to be salvaged, he or she will likely be on the receiving end of highly critical feedback from his or her manager, or others. Even in the most difficult of situations, there may be no other way to communicate to the employee that a serious performance gap exists and must be addressed. After a time, it can be difficult for any employee, no matter how mature, not to feel attacked. Worse, the employee may come to see herself as a personal failure. If the person is sensitive and/or the problem is serious, that feeling of being attacked will lead the employee to become very defensive. Such defensiveness can be overt or covert. People want to keep their problems hidden if they can, out of pride and self-preservation. As problems worsen, both the employee and the manager may feel threatened. The context for developmental coaching, which demands that the manager be nonjudgmental, can become poisoned. Both manager and employee can become very angry. A manager or other team members may not trust the person with the performance problem.

As already mentioned, developmental coaching is only one tool at the disposal of the coaching manager. Other tools include performance appraisal and a variety of direct and indirect rewards and sanctions. In addition, in most organizations, the coaching manager can call on additional resources outside his or her business unit for help. Human resource managers, training and development managers, outplacement firms, and occupational health and employee assistance program (EAP) counselors may all have roles to play in helping the coaching manager work with a performance problem. We recommend that the coaching manager consider a diverse set of approaches for dealing with performance problems. In this chapter, we provide more background on some of the most common performance problems and in doing so develop a set of recommendations that may help.

Before moving ahead, however, it is probably worth raising a question we've explored before, regarding other matters: Why bother? Most coaching managers we have met would probably be aghast that we ask such a question because they see it as their job to try coaching whenever a problem exists. This outlook fits their values, and it is important for them to be true to those values. Trying to help the performer with a problem can allow the manager to sleep better, a not unimportant outcome. And of course, their efforts may work, despite the cautionary tone of this chapter. We have seen people successfully address chronic performance gaps on a number of occasions. Finally, if the manager has established a coaching-friendly context, other people in his or her organization will expect performance problems to be addressed. One of the expectations that people hold in a coaching-rich environment is that people will help each other out if at all possible. It is the coaching manager's job to continuously model such a helpful attitude. It will pay off in the long run, if not in every case. So for a number of very good reasons, most coaching managers tell us that they will try coaching even if they aren't sure it will work. For these reasons, it is worth considering some of the root causes of serious performance problems.

Causes of Performance Problems

The causes of poor performance are numerous. We present here an overview of the most common. This overview is meant to illustrate several important points. First, it is important to note how much performance-related behaviors are multidetermined. There are likely to be several causes for any particular behavior outcome.

The "system" in which a performance problem emerges can be viewed as including the individual and his or her relationships with all aspects of his or her life, including the self, work roles and relationships, and nonwork roles and relationships. They each have a part to play, and they influence one another. The net result for the manager is that a performance problem may be beyond his or her coaching influence. The problem may involve aspects of the individual's "system" that the manager is unable to reach. Therefore, intervention strategies that affect multiple roles or aspects of the employee's life (bringing in human resources, health services, or employee assistance, for instance) may be usefully considered. From the perspective of most coaching managers, this is a hard-learned lesson. Businesspeople with a "can-do" attitude like to be able to solve problems. The key point here is that the coaching manager should actively seek the help of others when dealing with a significant performance problem.

Poor Managers and Poorly Communicated Expectations

The Gallup study argues convincingly that one of the most important determinants of an individual's effectiveness is the quality of his or her immediate supervisor (Buckingham & Coffman, 1999). Consistent with the Gallup findings, which we discussed previously, our experience leads us to believe that the first two core elements are key:

1. The employee needs to know what is expected of him or her at work.

2. The employee needs to have the material and equipment required to do his or her work properly.

Poor managers are often poor communicators. The following quote comes from a senior-level individual contributor who had been referred to us by his manager. This individual had been labeled as having a performance problem. "You'd be working along, thinking everything was fine for a month or so, and then she [the manager] would call you into her office, after refusing to meet with you for weeks. She would start telling you everything you had done wrong in the past month, mostly mistakes that you didn't even know were mistakes. She would change her mind about what she wanted, or would just lie."

We were fortunate in being able to get both sides of this story. This senior-level employee was in fact not performing up to the company's expectations for his particular role. Unfortunately, he didn't understand what was expected of him until his work came to be seen as a problem. The reader may empathize but wonder what this case has to do with coaching. We found out when we interviewed the manager. She was angry with this particular employee and wanted to know what she could do to coach him to more adequate performance. This was the right question for her to ask. However, she went on to explain that she didn't feel she needed to tell this employee what he was supposed to be doing. He was senior enough and old enough and ought to be able to figure that out for himself.

In this case, we decided that coaching was needed—for the manager. What her employees needed was the foundation for coaching: clear direction. Even though the members of the team were quite senior, they still needed to get a tangible vision of where she wanted them to go. They needed her to be more available so that they could talk with her to address the inevitable ambiguities that emerge when people are trying to do something important or innovative. The moral of this story is that one of the first things the manager should consider when dealing with a performance problem is whether or not he or she has contributed to the problem by failing to execute some of the basic tasks of management. The coaching manager must make sure that he or she has clearly set expectations as a first step in examining what appears to be a performance problem.

The Wrong Person in the Wrong Job

We've mentioned throughout this book that developmental coaching requires that employees and their organizations have at least some overlapping goals and expectations. Furthermore, an employee in any role needs to have a foundation of strength for that role if he or she is to learn and grow to become a superior performer. Developmental coaching cannot turn a great engineer into a great engineering manager unless the candidate also has a foundation of interpersonal skills, an ability to work with a variety of people, and an ability to plan and organize the work of a team. Some people, including some great engineers (or salespeople, creative marketers, or counselors, etc.), may not have that foundation.

Unfortunately, sometimes companies knowingly put the wrong person in the wrong role. This can occur for a variety of reasons, including a labor shortage or a well-respected employee's wish to move into a different role for which he or she is not suited. Companies may give such an individual a "try" out of a misguided sense of loyalty, a payback for many years of superior service.

One of us recently consulted with an extraordinarily creative optical engineer who had become quite depressed. She had somehow come to believe that the only way she'd ever get the status she wanted was to go into management. Her company reluctantly went along with her request. She then found herself doing performance reviews, managing a budget, and dealing with interpersonal conflicts. She began to fail at all this and became increasingly upset with herself for doing so. The reality is that she had a severe performance problem in the manager's role. It didn't take much encouragement for her to go back to her manager and renegotiate her role, returning to individual contributor status. She was relieved, as was her family and the company. There was an immediate improvement in her mood, and in a short period of time, she developed a new product design that resulted in several patents. All the developmental coaching in the world would not have helped this individual turn her situation around as long as she stayed in a management role. In fact, it might have made things worse.

In our view, the key to addressing this problem is *prevention*. Organizations and managers need to keep in mind the power of identifying the right talent and fitting that talent with the right roles and the costs of failing to do so. Many organizations now hire more for personal or cultural fit than for technical skill in some roles. Although this practice sometimes makes a great deal of sense, it requires that companies and employees carefully consider employees' technical potential for new roles to which they might be assigned once they work in the firm. The "stretch" assignment should be acknowledged as such. Prior to taking such a stretch, the employee and company should carefully consider whether or not the potential is there for the employee to learn and be successful in the new role. Just being a team player does not mean that one can be a super salesperson or an effective manager.

The Right Person in the Wrong Situation

Alternative work arrangements and global assignments can also inadvertently disrupt the ability to perform of an otherwise highly competent individual. Changes in work arrangements can disrupt key support systems that sustain an employee's performance. Diagnosis requires careful attention to context.

Employers are increasingly being asked to allow employees to work from home for instance. There are numerous potential advantages to the appropriate utilization of such arrangements. Employees' ability to manage work and family role balance challenges may be strengthened. Commute times and gasoline utilization can be minimized. Office space costs may be lowered.

But at the same time, such alternative work arrangements can be challenging. Employees utilizing such work arrangements need to be capable of doing so. They will likely be working with less supervision. They will need to communicate with peers and customers, internal and external, in different and often more proactive ways. The core activities and tasks associated with their jobs may be the same. Everything else may have to change. And finally, performance problems may at first be unobserved by management. Things can get worse before the usual alarms are raised.

The same challenges of course are associated with international assignments though the employee working globally may face a range of additional challenges. In addition to exercising greater independence under conditions of lessened support, these employees have to deal with cultural transitions and in some cases time away from the family. Family issues precipitated by international assignments can also be of concern.

Obviously, we're against neither alternative work arrangements nor global assignments. In fact, we think that both offer important developmental opportunities for the right individuals and organizations. We are, however, advocating that careful attention be paid to creating the conditions that support successful job performance by those working in novel contexts. In particular, careful attention should be paid to defining those competencies required for successful performance under alternative working conditions. Those competencies are likely to be different from those required for success under traditional working arrangements. Careful attention to the required competencies then also suggests that selection and development processes be geared toward building those competencies. Employees who have successfully navigated through international assignments can be of enormous help to organizations hoping to learn about the competencies and support systems necessary for success. Consider every such assignment an experiment. Carefully assess the results so that you as a coaching manager can continue to learn about what works for your employees.

Personal Problems

The fact that personal problems can interfere with performance comes as no surprise to most managers who have been on the job for any length of time. Divorce, alcohol or drug abuse, mental health problems, problems with children, medical illnesses, and other personal issues can all affect an individual's ability to perform. What does come as a surprise to most managers is just how prevalent these problems are. Using depression alone (a medical illness affecting mood and cognitive functioning) as an example indicates the scope of the problem. A study funded by the Washington Business Group on Health demonstrated the potential impact of depression on behavior in the workplace (Vaccaro, 1991). Each year, 10 million people will experience the symptoms of affective illness, the medical name for depression. One-year prevalence rates for major depression at Westinghouse were 17% for women and 9% for men. This survey was taken in a managerial/professional workforce. If we consider, in addition, the impact of other comparable personal problems, such as alcohol addiction, drug abuse, and other serious stress-related problems, it is easy to see just how important this factor is.

Unfortunately, people often have difficulty talking about emotional problems at work because of the powerful stigma attached to them. In addition, some problems, such as alcoholism, drug abuse, and domestic violence, are denied by those with the problem. They don't see it in themselves, and they don't make the connection between their problems or actions and their poor performance. This greatly delays their taking positive action and seeking help. Denial and delay mean that personal problems that don't have a great deal to do with work can affect the workplace. The substratum of the problem could be a medical illness or personal dysfunction of which the coaching manager may not be aware.

In addition, the coaching manager must be very careful about intruding into an employee's personal life, particularly if such intrusions are uninvited. The manager also needs to keep in mind that he or she is not a clinical diagnostician. In the United States, managers must also keep in mind the confidentiality protections afforded to employees by the Health Insurance Portability and Accountability Act of 1996 (HIPAA; see http://www.hhs.gov/ocr/privacy/ for more information). HIPAA privacy statutes, while designed to protect patient privacy, also impact what managers and others inside an organization can say or document regarding the medical status of an employee. Many organizations have HIPAA officers who can provide consultation around these policy considerations. Simply put, though, managers should not share information about the medical status of an employee, known or inferred, with others.

While awkward, such policies actually make sense. Unless you're a trained health care professional, talking about an employee's medical condition can lead you down the wrong path. What looks like a psychiatric problem may in fact have more to do with an employee's drinking or drinking by the employee's spouse. The employee who smells as though he or she has been drinking may actually have a medical illness. If managers try to intervene in such problems, they run the risk of provoking a legal response, such as a lawsuit, on the grounds of defamation of character, or worse. Because performance problems driven by personal problems are so common, we present an example in Case 13.1. The case is fairly representative of what a performance problem driven by a personal problem is like for the manager and the employee. Note that, at the end of the day, the most helpful thing the manager can do is focus on performance. When you focus on performance, you can have a positive impact and avoid intruding on difficult legal and ethical grounds.

Case 13.1(a): What the Manager Sees

Barbara is a 29-year-old sales representative for a large high-tech medical products firm. Her duties require her to introduce expensive medical equipment to hospitals and biotech companies. She has been working at the company for the past 2 years, having been hired right after completing her undergraduate degree. For the first year, her performance was outstanding. Six months ago, she began to work for her current manager after a reorganization. Her manager meets with her monthly and stays in touch by phone every few days.

Almost immediately, her manager began to hear complaints from customers who reported that Barbara had made technically confusing and even unfriendly sales calls. One customer complained that she had become angry when he balked at signing up for the latest release of the company's software. Another reported that she was late for their meeting and seemed disorganized. She had been slow to complete her expense reports, and her sales reports didn't seem very well put together, either. Finally, at the last sales meeting, she expressed a great deal of anger at the most recent reorganization. Her angry comments became louder and more vociferous after a few drinks.

At this point, the nature of the problem wasn't clear. Some sort of performance decline was clearly in evidence, but her manager had heard nothing about this from her. The manager speculated that the problem might have to do with the reorganization, her reaction to his management style, or something going wrong in her personal life. He decided to talk with her and bring up the customer feedback. Consider how you might start such a dialogue. That interchange yielded the following information.

Case 13.1(b): What the Manager Hears

In the manager's conversation with Barbara, Barbara reported that she was somewhat mystified at the customer complaints. She blamed the customers, seeing them as particularly difficult. She also expressed the feeling that others in the organization were trying to force her out because she didn't like the recent changes at the company. Then she told the manager that she has been under a great deal of stress because of her daughter's ongoing bout with a serious medical illness. She stated that she was a single parent (which her manager knew) and got no help from anyone else. Finally, she said she was angry at her manager for raising these problems with her and wondered whether he wasn't one of those who wanted to move her out of the company. The meeting terminated on a very sour note.

Though Barbara seemed profoundly defensive, it is difficult not to feel sympathetic to her plight. After all, many of us have experienced medical problems at one time or another. To make matters worse, the medical problem in this case involved her child. The dilemma for the manager was significant. He needed Barbara to get her performance back up, a need that she didn't recognize at that point. At the same time, he wanted to help her deal with her personal problems and didn't want himself or the company to be seen as uncaring.

If the manager is in a firm with an EAP, an employee counseling service, an occupational health nurse, or a physician, he could encourage her to get help. In most companies, he could call for consultation on how to help Barbara himself. He might also encourage her to talk with their human resource representative or see what other support the company might offer, such as family medical leave (unpaid federally mandated leave available in the United States to employees with a medical or family problem). Ultimately, though, he still needed her to perform. The manager could try being supportive up to a point, but if customer complaints kept streaming in, he would need to do something.

This case illustrates the importance for the manager of being clear as to what the employee with such a problem needs. In this case, is Barbara going to be open to learning? Would the manager and the employee be better off if the manager simply pressed her to comply with certain basic performance standards? Barbara appeared to be in no mood for learning at this point. She was probably consumed by the demands of day-to-day survival. However, given the problems she was having with her customers, her manager needed her to comply. The manager might have been able to achieve compliance by clarifying expectations, providing direct and even critical feedback, and using performance management tactics up to and including taking some type of disciplinary job action against her in the worst case. At the same time, if he could offer support, Barbara might be able to salvage her current job and her career. The manager did clarify with Barbara that the performance issues had to be addressed, regardless of her perception of the situation. However, he also suggested that she contact the company EAP, which she agreed to do.

Case 13.1(c): What the Manager Never Knew

Barbara contacted the EAP in part to pacify her manager. In part, however, she also knew that she wasn't doing well. She initially asked the EAP counselor for help in dealing with the stress that she found so overwhelming, but in their conversations she revealed something else just as serious. She had experienced a recurrence of cocaine addiction, a problem she thought she had solved years ago.

(Continued)

(Continued)

In her worry over her daughter, she turned back to drugs to make herself feel better, and soon she had the additional problem of her addiction. Because she had successfully participated in treatment in the past, she was able, albeit reluctantly, to see the problem more clearly and was able to discontinue cocaine use. With additional support and treatment, she was then in a much better position to deal with her daughter's illness and continue her job. Once the cocaine addiction was being treated and she ceased drug use, her job performance quickly improved.

The reader may feel a bit tricked by the presence of this underlying, quite serious personal problem on top of the very real problems she was willing to talk about with her manager. Unfortunately, such "tricks" occur frequently in life, and they can wreak havoc with the coaching manager's efforts to help an employee.

The moral of this story is twofold. First of all, when someone admits to a personal problem, don't try to deal with it yourself. Get help from your own manager, human resources, or health and employee assistance services. Second, if you try coaching when you believe that a personal problem may be interfering with performance, pay careful attention to whether or not you are able to see progress. If you aren't, the coaching may not be working. In Barbara's case, developmental coaching might have delayed the manager's "tough love" stance and, in the process, delayed her seeking help.

Character

Character is the manifestation of an enduring set of behavioral tendencies: the way individuals habitually interact with the outside world, how they defend themselves, and how they treat others. If problematic performance is driven by a personal problem, the manager is more likely to see volatility in the employee's performance or a pattern of performance decline. If the problem is driven by the individual's character, the employee's behavior will be more consistent.

Harry Levinson (1978) was among the first to draw our attention to one of the most difficult characterological presentations in the workplace, the "abrasive personality." The abrasive personality may be thought of as the "porcupine" of the business world. The dynamics that lead to the development of an abrasive personal style are varied, but the process begins in childhood.

The symptoms include a tendency toward being condescendingly critical, needing to be in complete control, dominating meetings, being quick to attack, being quick to debate, being preoccupied with status and power, taking credit for oneself when success is due to the work of others, and appearing cold and distant or intimidating. The abrasive personality is also likely to be an "overestimator" whose behavior tends toward arrogance, as we discussed in Chapter 6.

The coaching challenge is probably clear to the reader. This constellation of behaviors could wreck the career of even the most talented employees, particularly if their work calls for them to interact with or lead others. The underlying need such individuals are expressing through their habitual behavior is the need to see themselves as perfect.

If individuals assume that they are perfect or, more likely, have a need to see themselves as perfect, it is very hard for them to open up with their managers and define learning goals about anything, let alone how they come across to others. The process of coaching is blocked by the employees' personalities, just as their personal styles block other effective interpersonal processes.

Levinson (1978) suggested that the only hope a manager has of coaching such an individual is to approach him or her frequently, with a helpful attitude. The abrasive character's style can easily provoke anger in others. The coaching manager should try not to fall into such a trap. The manager's expression of anger will lead to the employee's angry reaction to the manager's anger, leading to a vicious circle in which very little learning takes place.

The coaching manager must then repeatedly hold out the coaching mirror, using balanced feedback to reflect back to the employee the observed behavior and its impact on the manager and others. Inaccurate or overly general feedback will be discounted as reflecting some sort of bias on the manager's part. Ultimately, such employees have to begin to see that their behavior is negatively affecting their own goals or running counter to their self-concepts. Coaching managers are in the difficult position of trying to affect behavior using rewards and punishments (Waldroop & Butler, 1996).

To even consider changing, the abrasive personality may have to endure such negative feedback that it is ultimately punishing. No one could tolerate it if there wasn't the promise of something better at the end of the ordeal. The promise of something better is the opportunity for the individual with a significant character flaw to have the impact he or she wants to have. Once the employee realizes this, he or she can take more ownership for the coaching work to follow.

Dan was a brilliant product manager but was routinely disrespectful of the people who reported to him. If he didn't like their work, which happened frequently, he would lash out at them in public. He picked on one individual in particular, who ultimately complained to the company's CEO. The CEO was sympathetic but slow to act because of Dan's potential contribution to the firm. Finally, Dan berated a customer who didn't seem to understand the marketing plan Dan was pushing. The customer's CEO complained to Dan's boss, and the company decided to take action.

Dan was told by his CEO that such outbursts were not going to be tolerated. He could easily be promoted if he controlled himself over the next year, but he would be fired if he did not. He was offered the help of an executive coach and/or a therapist if he so chose. Confronted by a bad job market for executives at his level and the need to support his family, Dan decided that he'd better respond to his CEO's feedback. He began to show some ability to exercise control over his outbursts in his dealings with others. Complaints to the CEO ceased and Dan kept his job, but he was not promoted. He often stated that he was keeping his feelings to himself merely to "stay out of trouble with the boss." He never took ownership of the need to learn how to influence others without incurring hostility. Ultimately, it was clear to all that, although he was complying with their directive, he could not be trusted in a higher-level and more independent role.

As already indicated, character and character flaws are relatively stable and consistent patterns of behavior. This suggests that Dan has probably been treating people badly for years and made it into a position of some responsibility regardless. How did that happen? It happened in all likelihood because he was "making his numbers." Many organizations and senior managers are capable of casting a blind eye to misbehavior that is capable of ultimately destroying an individual's career. They are making money and don't want to disrupt the employee's efforts. Such short-term thinking can lead to tragic consequences. If Dan had been confronted on his misbehavior earlier in his career, he might have been able to address the issue in a much easier and more developmental fashion. At this point, he had to be threatened, and it should be noted that in many cases even such threats don't work.

Could developmental coaching help employees like Dan? On occasion yes, but as with other interventions, we suggest that coaching managers monitor and evaluate their impact thoughtfully. Most coaching managers would like to believe that people like Dan can learn a new way, but they may merely show compliance. Psychotherapy might have helped Dan better understand his need to be perfect, but that is beyond the scope of the manager's portfolio.

We should also add that this is tough, time-consuming work. Many coaching managers have told us that they never like to give up on an employee, but sometimes there is no other way. On occasion, setting a limit on an employee, even a limit that ends up in the employee's departure from the company, can be helpful. We know of very effective managers and individual contributors who freely admit that if their previous managers hadn't had the courage to fire them, they may never have confronted the problems that were destroying their effectiveness.

Team Problems

Serious performance problems can also be rooted in team problems. This is particularly true when there is a relatively high degree of interdependence between team members. If two people need one another to complete their individual tasks, both have to perform. Assessing the impact of team functioning on individual functioning becomes more important as organizations seek to enhance innovation and improve communications by purposefully bringing people together to work. Of note, the people being brought together may be from different occupations, each with his own distinct approach to his work, or from different cultures, each with his own set of cultural assumptions.

It is extremely difficult to assess individual performance problems under such conditions. Unfortunately, it can also be the case that individual performers with problems, such as the abrasive personality mentioned in the previous section of this chapter, can cause team problems.

Coaching, then, may need to involve a two-pronged approach. The coaching manager may need to spend some time coaching the various individuals on the team while intervening at the team level to address team-level problems. It could be that the team has not adequately sorted out individual roles, has trouble as a team dealing with conflict, doesn't have an appropriate mechanism for members to communicate with one another, or does not have adequate resources to do its job. Any of these team-level problems, and others too numerous to mention, can cascade down to affect individual performance. In this case, then, it may not be accurate to say that developmental coaching won't work. It may be more appropriate to suggest that developmental coaching may need to be supplemented by other activities.

Organizational Change

Finally, organizational change can also create performance problems that won't necessarily succumb to developmental coaching. When organizations change, the rules change. We recently talked with a brilliant and innovative operations person who had a spectacularly successful career in a manufacturing organization because he was able to introduce new ways for the company to make its products. His world-class innovations helped the firm take a leadership position in product quality and time to market. Even though his approaches required considerable investment on the part of his company, the payoff made his work economically viable. Then, due to changes in the company's market, the company's strategy changed. The business began to focus on cost cutting and the standardization of operations. Our innovative engineer continued to push for more innovation and increasingly found himself alienated from a senior management group that had once been big fans. He was subsequently terminated.

Organizational change had created a person-to-role misfit that had not previously existed. Note that the job description and title did not change. We could argue about whether or not the company was wise in taking this new tack in its strategy, but the point is, cost cutting was the direction it chose. The engineering manager could not find it in his heart to embrace the new strategy. Ultimately, his lack of commitment to the new vision was obvious. His presence began to do more harm than good from the business perspective, leading to the decision to terminate. He is now doing very well in another company, in which he can exercise his creativity in a fashion that is valued. To be helpful to this individual, developmental coaching would be more oriented toward helping him define his career goals and assisting him in meeting those goals, even if it were to mean leaving the company.

Addressing Performance Problems: Some Coaching Guidelines

The coaching managers we've talked with don't tend to give up easily, as we stated earlier. Perhaps that is as it should be. Their success rests on their having a helpful attitude, and they need to follow that impulse wherever it takes them. However, they have also told us that they have their limits, which is a sound insight to keep in mind. We hope that the following guidelines will help the reader intervene in serious performance problems as effectively as possible:

• Make sure that the employee with the apparent performance problem clearly understands what is expected of him or her. Ask yourself whether or not you have adequately communicated such expectations, and make no assumptions about what the other person "ought to know."

• View coaching interventions as experiments. Set up milestones to help you and the coachee assess progress, or the lack thereof. Honestly assess progress. If progress is not forthcoming, consider the possibility that coaching may not be working.

- Seek input from others who may have knowledge of the employee and the performance problem. Don't go it alone. You want to be sure that bias and various perceptual distortions aren't clouding your assessment. (Remember that perceptual biases can work both positively and negatively.) A side benefit of consulting with others is that your own learning can be enhanced.

- It may be necessary to alter the balance between self-assessment and feedback. In the developmental coaching model presented in this book, reflection and self-assessment by the coachee are critical to encouraging employee learning and ownership of the issue at hand. Unfortunately, an individual with a performance problem may need more feedback to promote "unfreezing" than an individual who is more oriented toward learning. Feedback may also be useful if the only option is to insist on compliance, even in the absence of learning. However, take special care to make your feedback balanced, accurate, and respectful. Your own attitude while delivering the feedback is important. If you are trying to coach, even under difficult circumstances, a helpful attitude is a must.

- Encourage the employee to consult other resources. Even though employees may associate the company EAP with the stigma attached to emotional problems, most EAPs offer a range of help, including career counseling, family counseling, and referral to external resources. Typically, they are also confidential. With additional support in a confidential setting, the employee may be able to let go of some of his or her defensiveness and engage in a more productive self-assessment. We offer one caveat, however. Senior executives are sometimes reluctant to take advantage of an in-company EAP for a variety of good and not-so-good reasons. If that is the case, the senior human resources manager can often locate other resources, external to the company, with which the executive might feel more comfortable working.

- Follow-up is absolutely essential. Your only hope is that unfreezing can take place. As discussed previously, when unfreezing is necessary, the employee may need frequent feedback and frequent assessments of the impact of his or her actions. It is essential that employees at all levels be held accountable for their actions. Otherwise, unfreezing or other approaches to resolving performance problems are unlikely to occur.

- Make sure that your coaching efforts are aligned with other organizational factors, such as job design, compensation, and team functioning. As we showed in Chapter 11, sometimes follow-up is not successful because other factors in the organization are working against the coaching effort. When dealing with a performance problem, it is probably more important than in any other kind of coaching activity that the entire system surrounding employee and manager be aligned.

Using Coaching to Leverage the Investment in the Classroom

14

In this chapter, we describe the following:

- The challenge of transferring learning from the classroom to the workplace
- A set of guidelines that coaching managers can follow to help facilitate the transfer of learning

The authors have spent considerable time and energy creating educational experiences for practicing managers, frequently in a classroom format. We've also talked with numerous individual contributors and managers about workplace-based educational efforts, as well as with human resource development professionals responsible for improving the performance of employees and businesses. There is considerable hope for and yet some frustration with classroom education as a vehicle for promoting developing business talent. The legends Bill Gates, Steve Jobs, and Ed Land (none of whom graduated from college), among others, remind us that the classroom alone is not the ticket to greatness that it was once thought to be. Does it still have a place? Biased though we are, we insist that it does but that the interaction between the classroom and the workplace often breaks down and has to be repaired.

Developmental coaching by managers offers a powerful vehicle for greatly leveraging the benefits of classroom educational experiences while at the same time ameliorating the frustrations, at least to some degree. We encourage any manager whose employees participate in either onsite or offsite classroom learning, even on an infrequent basis, to pay special attention to the advice offered in this chapter.

The Nature of the Problem

Enormous sums are spent by businesses throughout the world on classroom training each year. In 2004, the American Society for Training and Development reported that the outlays in the United States for such activities as a percentage of payroll had increased from 2.2% to 2.52% from 2002 to 2004 (Sugrue & Kim, 2004). While recent economic turbulence has no doubt negatively impacted the growth of learning and development activities, we can only anticipate that in a knowledge-based economy they will continue to represent an important organizational investment in years to come. Naturally, the nature of the classroom activities provided is likely to change. We are seeing significant increases in the use of online Web-mediated classroom and development tools for instance. For our purposes, the point remains the same. Discrete educational activities are taking place in significant numbers. This represents a significant opportunity for those interested in deploying developmental coaching to leverage the impact of such investments.

At the same time, on a day-to-day basis, employees and managers report an uneven level of satisfaction with the impact of classroom training. One of the more common complaints issued by both is that even though a particular classroom experience was extremely well done, it may not have met the actual needs of the employee or the business. In that case, the content of the training hasn't been put to good use.

In Chapters 1 and 2, we described the basic model of experiential learning. Learning is thought to take place when an individual acts and then has a chance to both reflect and receive feedback on the action. Classroom education enhances the ability of the individual to learn from reflecting on his or her experience because it provides concepts against which actions can be judged. In the classroom, participants can learn a new approach to selling a particular product. They can then assess their previous performance against the model they learned in the classroom. They may then choose to use aspects of the sales model learned in the classroom to enhance their performance in the field.

What if the participant makes no direct connection between the classroom and practice in the field? Learning can be extinguished in a devastatingly short period of time if what has been learned in the classroom is neither used nor rewarded (Noe, 1999). Note that this is an example of the "refreezing" problem discussed previously. The learning doesn't fit that well with other aspects of the learner's situation.

The link between learning and action is particularly important for most adults. Adults learn differently from children (Knowles, Holton, & Swanson, 1998) and typically exhibit the following behavior:

- They need to know why they are learning something.

- They are more self-directed in their learning. Adults do much better when they take responsibility for the learning goal and the learning process.

- They bring more work-related experience into the learning effort (which means that they may need to unlearn, or be unfrozen, if they are to be open to learning).

- They enter into the learning experience with a problem-centered approach to learning. They learn to solve problems or meet challenges. Some individuals certainly love to learn for the sake of learning throughout their lives, but they are less common than those who learn to help themselves address specific questions or concerns.

It is for this reason that study after study has shown that the most important lessons executives learn are the ones they learn on the job (McCall, Lombardo, & Morrison, 1988). Executives retrospectively report that they learned the most from job assignments, particularly their first supervisory assignment and assignments that were difficult and challenging. They also report learning a great deal from other people (good bosses, bad bosses, or mentors) and from facing personal and business hardships. Some classroom experiences were quite helpful. However, the experiences recalled as helpful were seen as such because they addressed the problem or challenge the executive was facing at the time the course was taken. The classroom experience, in other words, provided the executives in this study with concepts they could use immediately.

Transfer of Learning

The challenge of putting learning into practice is described by human resource development professionals as the *transfer of learning* from the classroom to the workplace, which is the ultimate goal of any workplace-sponsored learning (Noe, 1999). This is what most employees want to see happen as well, particularly those who want to grow and succeed. Transfer of learning involves taking specific elements or concepts from the classroom and being able to use them at work. Employees learning C++ (a programming language) should be able to use the identical programming techniques developed as they solved practice problems in the classroom when they return to the workplace. The executive completing a leadership course should be able, at the next board meeting, to use the new ideas he or she developed about influencing others. Such a transfer of learning is facilitated by a number of factors. Obviously, it is facilitated by similarity of content between the classroom and the challenge the individual faces at work.

However, other factors can serve to facilitate or inhibit the transfer of learning as well (Rossett, 1997). A poorly designed or poorly executed classroom experience won't provide much learning to transfer. Mandatory training experiences that don't address the individual's goals or needs obviously violate the principle just described. Compensation systems, as well as other policies, procedures, or organizational-level cultural assumptions and norms, will also exercise powerful constraints on the possibilities for using new learning. Executives who participate in classroom training on leadership frequently hear about and come to believe in the value of teams. However, when they try to implement a team-based activity in their companies, they may run into significant obstacles, such as cultural norms and compensation systems that discourage the use of teams, the sharing of responsibility, and the rewarding of teams in addition to individual performance.

Finally, the attitude of the learner's manager and, to an extent, his or her peers can also play an important role in determining what learning is transferred from the classroom to the workplace. If the learning is seen as not being aligned with what the boss and the other employees value, the boss and the peers are likely to be indifferent or hostile to what has been learned.

The result is not merely a failed investment of time and money in the educational process, but significant employee cynicism as well (Rossett, 1997). The employee/learner ends up feeling cynical about the organization's waste of money and his or her manager's lack of interest in performance improvement. Ultimately, and even more sadly, the employee may feel cynical about training and development in general, believing that it is not helpful. Employees who are ordered to undergo training that takes time and teaches them content that runs counter to what it actually takes to get ahead in their organizations are likely to see the training experience as punishing rather than developmental because of the time lost from work, for which they will be held accountable.

The reader will note that the problem of lack of alignment among employee goals, organizational goals, and classroom training is quite comparable to what we described in Chapter 11, "Goal Setting and Follow-Up."

Learning takes work—and not just on the part of the learner. The learner's manager and peers are more likely to put in the time and effort necessary to make the investment in learning pay off when it is aligned with what they generally need to do to be successful.

Effective transfer of learning is probably most readily observed in technical skill-building programs. If a group of employees is going to be working on a new assembly line, their tasks will, for the most part, be delineated before they ever see the line in person. The detailed assignment for each station on the line is developed by manufacturing engineers. The tasks associated with each role are carefully described. Each task is then matched with a description of the skill needed to complete the task. (Soldering a particularly hard-to-reach wire requires knowledge of soldering as well as fine motor coordination and patience.) Employees know that they must learn the particular set of required skills to be successful in these new positions. Even though the training is mandatory, a context that can sometimes discourage transfer of learning, in this case, the value of the training is clear to employees.

Each employee will be trained in the classroom on each particular skill and then be expected to perform the same skill under nearly identical conditions, once the assembly line begins operation. Their manager needs them to use the skills they learned in the classroom and stands ready to support them with coaching once work on the assembly line has begun. Because it is an assembly process in which the workers must depend on each other in order to be successful, they help each other learn through peer coaching or emotional support. Finally, they are rewarded financially and with recognition if they successfully perform the newly learned skills.

It should be noted that such alignment is somewhat easier to achieve because of the relative certainty and stability of this type of operation. It is clear what has to be done. There is little room for discretion on the part of employees or their manager regarding the performance that is ultimately required for success. This is not always the case. Frequently, the correct way to undertake a particular task or role is less clearly defined. This is particularly true in rapidly changing contexts such as those faced by managers, business professionals, and technology professionals.

In the knowledge economy, there is debate about everything from how to write a strategic plan to how to negotiate. A company may order everyone to attend training in cross-cultural sensitivity, for instance, without having clearly articulated a desired outcome beyond that of mutual respect. Just as frequently, employees may be encouraged to take a course that, although relevant to their developmental goals, lacks any real assessment as to whether what is to be learned will fit in with the workplace when the employees return. The net result is that employees can end up enrolling in classroom learning programs without either manager or employee having a real sense of what will be learned or whether or not the learning fits in with the needs of the workplace. This problem is compounded when employees are ordered to undertake "40 hours of training" each year without sufficient guidance and without considering whether or not what will be learned is aligned with the needs of the business, manager, peers, and employees.

Cases 14.1 and 14.2 illustrate the challenge of building alignment that can support the transfer of learning from the classroom to the workplace. Case 14.3 offers a specific illustration of how developmental coaching was used after a classroom program had been completed.

Case 14.1: The Wrong Executive Education Experience at the Wrong Time

Jack came from a rough-and-tumble family business in a rough-and-tumble industry. He was told that he must attend an executive education course in leadership as part of the preparation for moving up to the chief operations officer role in his firm. He ultimately attended the program recommended by his firm's bankers. One of them had attended the same program previously and found it to be quite useful. The leadership model presented in the program was based on the concepts of shared responsibility and distributed leadership. Program content emphasized building trusting relationships and working on the subtleties of one's leadership style.

Unfortunately, leadership practices in Jack's family business, and indeed the entire industry in which it competed (nothing like banking, to be sure), were characterized by a lack of trust between labor and management. Order was kept through the use of ruthless and highly manipulative leadership practices.

Jack got something out of the program, though he was very concerned about his ability to put the ideas he had learned into practice. Returning to his family's business, he discussed what he had learned with other firm executives, who proceeded to ridicule him for some of the changes he proposed.

Not all leadership education programs are alike! The public seminar Jack attended is very well respected because it is excellent. However, if Jack, his father, and other executives at his company had stopped to reflect on what Jack really needed to learn, they might have chosen a very different course. Case 14.1 illustrates a very important point for all coaching managers and those they coach. Leveraging time and money spent in the classroom requires some advance thinking as to (a) what needs to be learned and (b) which, if any, classroom experiences will facilitate that learning.

If Jack, his father, the CEO, and the company's advisers had talked about what Jack needed to learn, they might have decided that negotiation skills, for example, were much more important than team leadership. They might have gone one step further and looked for a negotiations program that others in his industry had found to be effective. This advance work could have created the kind of alignment that would have ultimately rewarded Jack for his learning efforts, rather than leaving him feeling quite punished.

Some might reasonably argue that Jack needed to learn a new approach to leadership that was quite different from the one that had previously been successful in his business and industry. In some cases, that can be an appropriate course of action. Indeed, the classroom can provide new ideas that can help the learner challenge previously held assumptions and consider innovative approaches to old problems. The problem is that Jack would have had to transfer what he learned at the program to a hostile environment.

The coaching manager and the learner need to discuss such challenges in advance. They may agree that the employee's goal in participating in the classroom program is to bring back innovative and possibly controversial perspectives. Both need to acknowledge that transfer of learning to the workplace may face significant barriers. The employee may need the coaching manager's concrete assistance and support in addressing those barriers. Job designs may need to be altered. Compensation plans may need to change. Customer relationships may be affected. New information can be revolutionary; it is in that sense very exciting to go to the university or the industry conference and return with the latest ideas from across the globe. In the process of transferring those ideas into new practices, remember that it may be necessary for other employees or the entire business unit to go through the stages of unfreezing, change, and refreezing. This is really an organizational change problem. Classroom experiences alone are rarely sufficient to accomplish organizational change.

Case 14.2: Leadership Education That Helped

A worldwide real estate management company brought the heads of each of its local territories together for a series of classes on business strategy and leadership. Employees and managers throughout the company were made aware that a change in business conditions required local managers to assume more autonomous and strategic roles in the firm. Instead of relying on the regional vice presidents for building a local business strategy, the local managers would be expected to develop a business plan and execute it. As a result, the local

(Continued)

(Continued)

managers needed to build new business skills as well as develop new mind-sets about their work. They needed to learn to see themselves as leaders rather than as followers. Prior to the program, each local manager defined learning goals for the classroom portion of the change project with his or her regional vice president, as part of the formal (written) development planning process.

Every regional vice president attended the last 3 days of the classroom program. They talked with faculty, sat in on classes, and attended a half-day meeting with other regional vice presidents. The topic of that meeting was coaching. They talked about their local managers' development goals and discussed strategies for helping leverage the work that had taken place during the classroom period when the local managers returned to their home territories. They brainstormed ideas for follow-up to keep the learning process going. After the classroom program was completed, the regional vice presidents met weekly with local managers, in person or by phone, for developmental coaching sessions. They worked with redefined development goals that each local manager articulated at the close of the classroom experience. Some of their goals had shifted on the basis of input from class faculty and other program participants. The regional vice presidents and the local managers agreed that they all had to take responsibility for transferring what had been learned back to the workplace.

Case 14.2 is, of course, the kind of story that management educators love to hear. We suggest, however, that the real beneficiary of this kind of effort is the company. The company obviously believed that it was important to the business for its employees to develop new business competencies.

Learning goals were specifically defined for each participant. Note that it isn't possible to specifically design classroom program content or processes to meet those needs. The classroom experience can't meet the exact needs of every participant, because the class is taught to a group. However, if the content of the program was chosen with a degree of care, participants will emerge with some insights that are specifically relevant to their own learning needs. They will gain some serendipitous insights or perspectives that they may not have gone looking for but were worthwhile, nevertheless.

Individual coaching attention, before and after, can help the employee and the organization take the most relevant and useful insights or skills gained in the classroom and think through how they can be used in practice. One local manager who went through the classroom program described in this case faced some very specific challenges as we see in the next example.

Case 14.3: The Challenge of Becoming More Strategic

As a "hands-on" local manager, David was comfortable with tactics, managing existing accounts, and keeping clients happy. However, he missed important opportunities to expand his unit's portfolio of business. For instance, his geographical area had become home to a number of emerging companies, some of which had quickly become quite large. He did not immediately see the opportunity to put together a real estate management program for emerging technology companies or consider other strategies for proactively reaching this market. Several important potential accounts were lost to the competition. In his newly redefined role, he would need to think about potential business opportunities differently and instill a more proactive attitude in some of his direct reports as well. In the past, the corporation would have done most of this kind of marketing. Now it was up to the local team.

Given his hands-on management style, David knew that this would be a real challenge for him. In the classroom, he developed a clearer understanding of what strategic marketing really means, and through his discussions with other participants, he realized he'd have to spend at least 20% of his time scouting out other opportunities and less time monitoring current accounts. He proposed this shift in his own job description to his regional vice president, who heartily agreed. David felt he could handle the reallocation of his weekly schedule on his own, but he was still new at evaluating and responding to more strategic opportunities. Not being confident in this key aspect of his new role, he felt very unsure of his ability to communicate effectively to his own employees, who looked to him for direction. He and his regional vice president agreed that helping David learn more about evaluating business opportunities would be the focus of their work together, going forward. They also agreed that if David had a deeper understanding of how his group needed to assess and respond to business opportunities, he would be in a much better position to communicate the task more effectively to his team.

The classroom offers insight. The coaching manager works with the coachee to prepare for the classroom and to help the coachee apply what has been learned in practice. The examples in Cases 14.2 and 14.3 show an alignment of employee learning goals, business goals, classroom goals, and company goals in a large firm engaged in a major organizational change project.

To further enhance this alignment between classroom and workplace, companies are increasingly creating shared learning experiences for groups of employees that rely on "action learning" to facilitate learning transfer (Conger & Benjamin, 1999; Dotlich & Noel, 1998). Action learning projects involve teams of employees working together to address specially chosen, but very real, business challenges. Action learning team participants may be from a single business unit, but such teams more commonly involve employees from different units or geographies. Diverse team participation can promote the integration of learning across functions and areas through the building of relationships, a major challenge in most large companies. The shared interests of team members can create a coaching-friendly context that supports peer coaching even while the individuals and/or the team receive coaching from a manager, corporate team sponsor, or external coach. Classroom help is provided on a periodic basis and is usually targeted at the specific skills or concepts that team members need to fulfill their team's charter. What is learned in the classroom is then immediately relevant and directed squarely at learner goals and needs. Action learning and team coaching represent another thoughtful approach to effectively making use of what should be of great benefit to the employee and the business: time spent in an appropriate and helpful classroom learning experience.

Making the Most of Classroom Learning

We are now ready to draw out a series of simple but important practices that can help the coaching manager and employee get the most out of an investment in formal classroom education. These practices are described in Box 14.1. They address three overriding concerns: the need to properly define the learning goal or goals, choose an appropriate program, and follow up to ensure that the transfer of learning from the classroom to the workplace is facilitated.

BOX 14.1 | **Practices That Support the Transfer of Learning From the Classroom to the Workplace**

1. First, define the learning goal(s). Will a classroom experience be helpful? It is likely to be helpful in the following situations:
   - The employee has to learn new skills or concepts, particularly in a short period of time.
   - The employee is "stuck," and an educational intervention can address the specific problem that is causing this.
   - It would be particularly helpful for the employee to be working with others who are addressing similar learning needs.

---

2. Choose the right program:

- Make sure it is aligned with the employee's learning goals.
- Also consider whether or not the content of the program is aligned with the needs and culture of the business unit. If it is not, proactively address any barriers that may make transfer of learning more difficult.

3. Provide coaching follow-up to the employee on completion of the classroom experience:

- Immediately after the learner returns from the program set aside a 1- to 3-hour block of time during which you and the learner review the content of the program. Discuss what the learner thought, saw, and/or felt that might be relevant to his or her performance or the organization. It is likely that some of the content will be helpful and some will not. (Don't get bogged down in complaints about the program. For that individual, what is done is done. If there are legitimate complaints about a particular classroom experience, record those as data for use in decision making the next time the opportunity arises. Hold the learner responsible for getting the most out of the program.)
- Either at the end of this meeting or within the next day or two, ask the learner to describe one to three personal learning goals that emerged from his or her experience in the executive education program. (See Chapter 11 on goal setting and a further discussion of this topic below.)
- Help the learner define what effective performance would look like if he or she were successful in attaining the goal(s).
- Consider whether or not you are the best person to provide the learner with appropriate follow-up coaching. You will need some knowledge of the content area related to the learner's goals and some opportunity to gather performance data and provide the learner with balanced feedback. If you're not the right person, help the learner identify and solicit help from someone who is.
- Support the learner by helping make sure that he or she has meaningful work related to the learning goals the two of you have identified. Only by using the skills on the job will the learning "stick."
- Follow up with the learner on a regular basis to assess progress.
- If a group has attended a program, bring the employees together to discuss what they learned, jointly.
- Congratulate employees when they have achieved their goals.

Defining the Learning Goal

The practice of defining a learning goal or goals should be an outgrowth of the developmental coaching between manager and employee that has taken place prior to the program. In a coaching-friendly context, both are thinking about learning and progress toward the development of new skills. Classroom education may be appropriate when several different contingencies arise:

- *The employee has to learn a new set of concepts.* If an employee needs to learn something about which he or she knows very little, or if the employee has to learn a great deal in a short period of time, the classroom can be an effective means of addressing the learning need. A focus on learning with the aid of subject matter experts who are also skilled teachers allows for the presentation and digestion of a large amount of information in a short period of time.

- *The employee is "stuck" in his or her learning, and no one in the workplace is able to help that individual get "unstuck."* If an employee is having trouble dealing with a highly conflicted team and the coaching manager's feedback isn't being particularly helpful, taking the problem into the classroom can be useful. The employee can work on the situation with subject matter experts, gain perspective on his or her own approach through reflection and self-assessment, and develop concrete ideas for approaching the problem in a new way.

- *It could be useful for the employee to work directly with others who are addressing a similar set of issues.* The development of certain skills, corporate entrepreneurship or leadership, for example, can be aided by working with others engaged in the same task. The employee may be the only one on his or her team thinking about leading a new product development group. He or she may not be "stuck" but may still find that there is a great deal to be learned from others, particularly peers from other business units or companies.

These simple guidelines are meant to suggest only that it is useful, before deciding on a classroom experience, to consider whether or not such an approach is most appropriate for the particular learning goal of the employee. The classroom offers a great deal. However, it is inappropriate to expect it to be helpful in every case. The employee with a serious personal problem, for instance, will not become a more effective leader by attending a leadership class.

Choosing the Right Program

Cases 14.1 and 14.2 illustrate the importance of choosing the right program. The program should address the learning needs of the participant. The employee, with the coaching manager's help, needs to move beyond the "brand" of the educational institution offering the program, the program's title, or the glowing recommendations of previous participants. The employee should find out in advance whether or not the content is specifically related to his or her goals. In the case of external educational experiences, such as those offered by universities or consulting companies, the employee should carefully examine program brochures and Web sites and, if necessary, call the program faculty directly. (Most will be happy to hear from any potential participant.) Describe the learning goal and ask the faculty member how the content of the program will relate to the goal. It is in the interest of most faculty and trainers to have a realistic discussion about this issue because they are more likely to be successful if the appropriate participants are in their programs.

Following Up

Follow-up begins with setting aside a meaningful block of time shortly after the employee returns from the program and reviewing the employee's experience in relationship to his or her learning goals. We recommend that a follow-up meeting take place within 5 to 7 days of the employee's return. Check for any serendipitous learning that may have occurred as well. Participants in external programs may pick up an idea unrelated to their learning goals but very useful to the group.

The coaching manager should ask the employee to revisit those learning goals and choose several on which to focus for a time. If the employee has learned a new approach to negotiations, for instance, and thinks it will be helpful, discuss how the employee can use the new approach in his or her work. Ask the employee to consider what success would look like if the new approach to negotiation were to become part of his or her repertoire.

Finally, discuss what kind of coaching the employee needs going forward. Ideally, the coaching manager will be in the right position to provide follow-up, but this may not always be the case. For example, suppose an employee has learned a new software language, a language that others on her team, including the coaching manager, don't know. She may need to find a connection with another expert in the organization with whom to consult as she attempts to work with the new language. The coaching manager's role is to help her locate such a resource and support her efforts to build a relationship with that individual.

If an employee's efforts to put into practice part or all of what was learned in the classroom are likely to encounter serious barriers, more follow-up with the employee will be necessary. Remember that if refreezing does not occur, regression to actions that rely on previous learning will take place almost automatically. If the employee is really trying something new and different, follow-up support (as we describe it in Chapter 11) is essential.

The Classroom and the Coaching Manager

The process we have described should sound fairly simple. We believe that it is. Unfortunately, too many managers don't take such a direct interest in the impact of classroom learning (with the exception of technical skills training) on the employee and on the business. This may be a manifestation of the unaddressed split between learning and working that exists in most organizations. Most companies pay for at least some classroom training for their employees and then, strangely, do little with it back at the workplace. The coaching manager can lead the way in this regard and learn quite a bit in the process.

Epilogue

The Coaching Manager

The field of developmental coaching within organizations has changed a great deal over the decade since we began writing the first edition of *The Coaching Manager*. In preparing this second edition, we have been forced to think about the rise in new technologies and their impact on coaching, massive economic turbulence resulting in the loss of some of our most cherished business institutions, and continuing evolution of the demographic nature of the workforce. Yet, we continue to be told, wherever we go, that "our managers just don't do enough coaching." So much has changed, and yet, so little seems to have changed as well. Before closing we want to touch briefly on this compare-and-contrast situation with which we are confronted. First, what's changing?

Technology and Coaching

We had hoped to be able to present the definitive model for distance-based coaching in this second edition, but alas, that definitive model is still evolving. Without question, though, we've learned a great deal. Much of the core technology of coaching, it seems, can be "ported" to non-face-to-face contexts to good effect. Some executive coaches have been practicing their craft by telephone for many years. Follow-up reports indicate that it can be quite helpful under the right circumstances. Technology in particular seems to be helpful in its ability to enable coaching, to make it possible.

Technology can facilitate the creation of connections between people, and in doing so it can facilitate the development of coaching and mentoring relationships. Social networking sites, both those that are available "retail" and those that are company sponsored, make it possible for people with different learning needs to connect with those with the right kind of expertise.

This may in fact revolutionize the nature of company-sponsored mentoring programs (which are often quasi–peer coaching programs in fact). Such Web-based systems allow those involved to engage in a full range of mentoring activities to a degree that might have been quite surprising only a few years ago (Francis, 2007). These activities include defining development areas that are linked to organizationally sanctioned competency needs, articulating learning goals, and engaging in the creation of mentoring matches (one of the most time-consuming and costly aspects of corporate mentoring programs) via databases with appropriate coaches. The costs associated with facilitating such matches are greatly reduced, allowing programs to be highly democratic in their participation. Anyone can join in.

Participants can control their learning activities, a key feature of the developmental coaching process, and at the same time experience a host of side benefits, such as gaining knowledge about potential distant parts of the organization. This requires some rethinking about the nature of developmental relationships on the part of the participants, however. Learning and developmental relationships must be seen as coming from any direction. It also requires, obviously, that care be taken to create a coaching-friendly context that encourages candid conversations. Technology then can serve to connect and administrate coaching efforts. The core exchange, the coaching dialogue, remains the same.

One significant unanswered question remains. Will coaching and learning actually take place? The initial indicators are quite positive (Francis, 2007). However, we have to note that the success of such programs depends on the skill set of those involved. Do they know how to coach in an online environment? Basic coaching skills are required, but beyond that, facility in the skill set associated with online coaching and with being an online coachee is required as well. The latter is still poorly understood. As such, we have to conclude that the face-to-face or telephone-mediated coaching dialogue remains the gold standard in developmental coaching.

Can we make judicious use of that gold standard? We suggest that those who have been involved with the management of virtual teams can provide us insight as to what techniques are most appropriate to what particular need. Face-to-face or telephone is probably best for the most important, ambiguous, or difficult concerns in team management and in coaching (Katzenbach & Smith, 2001). Face-to-face and/or telephone is also of significant importance at the early stages of a coaching relationship. Information sharing and updates, however, can often be done by e-mail or through the use of other Web-based tools, with appropriate care (taking into account how easily people can misunderstand one another in the absence of audio or visual cues).

Changing Demographics

As we've already mentioned, the current generation (Gen Y, Millennials, etc.) of younger coachees is likely to have a very different set of expectations with regard to coaching. All the data at hand suggest they want more of it, and they want it to do more in the context of their work, informally (Kehrli & Sopp, 2006). This is probably a good thing for those of us interested in pushing more managers to coach. The demand will grow. Good managers, or those who wish to be good managers, will simply have to respond, or they will lose their talented associates.

We anticipate that this generation of coachees will also drive the continued exploration in the utilization of technology to mediate coaching. Their ability to communicate comfortably through texting, for instance, may make it easier for us to utilize written communications in our coaching efforts.

Coaching in Tough Times

As our work on the second edition of *The Coaching Manager* comes to a close, we are in the midst of a severe economic recession. The unemployment rate is very high, and all seems quiet along the fronts of the "war for talent." Training and development budgets have been cut in many, though by no means all, organizations. Short-term survival thinking seems to have a firm grasp on the leadership. This of course would be a decent description of the state of things during any significant recession. There's nothing new here, right? Perhaps, but perhaps not.

In fact, we've increasingly run across organizations that have decided not to let short-term survival–oriented thinking run the show. Yes, massive cuts have been made. Perhaps those cuts have been so massive in some organizations that a paradigm shift in how management views its task is under way. The old approach, whatever it is, in many businesses may really no longer be working. New ideas, innovation, and the leadership to drive that innovation may be absolutely essential. We've begun to run across executives who, while perhaps decreasing their expenditures on executive coaching, have decided not to eliminate their budgets for leadership development.

However, they are becoming far more cost conscious, and as such, they are looking for their managers to do more coaching. The trend of developmental coaching may in fact be receiving a massive boost from these difficult times. At a workplace summit on "The Future of Learning and Development" with thought leaders such as Howard Gardner and Noel Tichy, held in 2007, several trends were apparent (Laff, 2007). First, there is a significant need to move more toward the use of leaders in teaching and coaching roles. The rationale is obvious. Coaching managers know the company and the industry, and they know the jobs. If they can learn to coach and to teach, they are much better positioned to provide a crisp understanding of the requirements for performance success and career advancement than learning and development specialists.

The second trend is even more challenging. Historically, we used to absorb a great deal of learning in the first two or three decades of life and then leverage that to a significant degree in the remainder of our careers. That's no longer a tenable approach. Lifelong learning will differentiate those who are more likely to succeed. Yet, too many employees don't know how to sustain lifelong learning, and too many managers don't know how to provide support. So we circle back again to the imperative need for developmental coaching that supports experiential learning, yet we need more of it than we have available. An effective coaching manager creates a context in which employees learn to be lifelong learners. If we are to sustain learning through difficult periods, we need to be less dependent on "experts" and more able to help one another, and help ourselves.

The Relationship With the Coaching Manager Is the Key

Whether augmented by technology or other innovative tactics, the employee's relationship with his or her manager sets the tone for how the employee feels about the work and the organization. The power of that relationship is not to be underestimated. We're saying here not that the employee is solely dependent on the manager but that, ideally, when the two work together to create learning, exciting things can happen (Hymowitz, 2007). The power of this relationship goes well beyond its ability to facilitate learning. It facilitates engagement, and it supports our humanity.

In light of that, what should organizations do? Most of the answers to this question are well-known and have been explored here: Create an open and honest culture in which people can talk freely, without fear of reprisal. Encourage people to take manageable risks. Don't punish innovative failures—reward them. Show interest in new ideas. Stay current as a firm. Make sure all levels of management are paying attention to their industry, community, and the larger business world. In other words, show that you value learning in general. Make sure that compensation practices don't discourage learning. But beyond that, pay attention to the value of relationships. Relationships make learning possible, but they also support leadership, innovation, and communications.

With regard to coaching itself, remember that coaching is a skill. Most managers don't know how to coach. They will need quality training to get a basic sense of what coaching is and how to do it. Most organizations are capable of providing the basic training for their managers. However, as in most adult learning, on-the-job learning is what counts the most. Coaches in our training programs have consistently found that the ability to work and talk with other coaches is probably the most helpful thing they do. Coaching is not a conceptually complex task. It is a complex task in execution. Each coaching encounter is different, just as each relationship between manager and employee is different. The learning for coaching managers comes from thinking about the specifics of each case: What can I learn from this effort to help this specific employee?

Coaching managers can help each other with this kind of reflection, simply by drawing on a rudimentary knowledge of coaching and a basic knowledge of people and the business. It is a common practice for the senior management of some companies to spend a few hours each quarter talking about how the top 50 or so people (or, in small firms, the top 3 or 4) below their level in the organization are doing. They review the assignments of the "high potentials," what they are learning, what they will be ready for next, and what kind of help they need along the way. (If management doesn't do this, it should.) Consider the implications of driving such a process all the way down the organization: bringing groups of managers together who work in related areas to reflect on and talk about their talent, how these people are doing, and what they need to learn to prepare for whatever is coming next. Would such a discussion be worthwhile? We suspect that it would. We propose that creating such a process is likely to be one of the most important steps that an organization can take to create a coaching-friendly context.

A Final Word for Our Coaches, Old and New

The implications for you of this last discussion are that you should never forget your own need to learn. You are probably coaching because you enjoy the processes of helping and of discovery. Those who teach generally like to learn. Coaching managers like to receive coaching. Find others who share your interest and spend some time reflecting on your good works and what you need to do to keep on going..

Appendix

The following represent descriptions of effective leadership, teamwork, decision-making, oral communications, and listening behaviors. These descriptions are likely to be useful when coaching others. Remember that whatever definition of a behavior and its effectiveness you use as a coach, both the coach and the learner should understand that definition.

These competencies are described in relation to three levels of personal effectiveness: highly effective, moderately effective, and needs development. Examples are then given of the kinds of behaviors or attitudes that are likely to be associated with each level of expression of the competency. This is not intended to be an all-inclusive checklist. Remember that our effectiveness, for the most part, will be determined by patterns of our behavior, not individual instances. As a coach, you should keep an eye out for specific behavioral incidents, but then consider how those incidents fit into any observable pattern.

Leadership Competency

LEADERSHIP: Effectiveness in influencing others to accomplish a task and in getting ideas accepted without incurring hostility.

The following are some of the behaviors that can be observed when an individual is displaying a high level of effectiveness in a formal or informal leadership role:

___ Helps self and others understand goals or tasks to be achieved.

___ Consistently keeps group focused on its task and tracks progress.

___ Draws ideas and suggestions from others.

___ Encourages a focus on both the task and group harmony.

___ Group members don't usually react to this individual's efforts with hostility.

___ Rarely dominates or overpowers the group.

___ Demonstrates sensitivity to group progress and process.
___ Shows enthusiasm for the task.
___ Effectively uses a variety of influence strategies.
___ Demonstrates an awareness of cultural diversity in efforts to influence others.

The following are some of the behaviors that can be observed when an individual is displaying moderate effectiveness in a formal or informal leadership role:

___ Generally attempts to move group toward goal, although may occasionally get off track.
___ Sometimes encourages the involvement of other group members.
___ Sometimes commands or dominates others, though not all the time.
___ Shows moderate sensitivity to group progress and process.
___ Shows some enthusiasm for the task.
___ Tends to use only one or two influence strategies with mixed results.

The following are some of the behaviors that can be observed when an individual is displaying a low level of effectiveness in a formal or informal leadership role:

___ Shows little or no desire to influence the group, or tries too hard to force the group into his or her way of thinking.
___ Demonstrates little awareness of group process issues.
___ Often strongly states opinions with little attempt to draw upon the ideas of others.
___ May make a point and then withdraw.
___ Uses influence strategies ineffectively.
___ Group members react to influence efforts with hostility.
___ Shows little or no enthusiasm for the task or the group.
___ Demonstrates little or no awareness of cultural diversity in efforts to influence others.

Teamwork Competency

TEAMWORK: The ability to work effectively with others.

The following are some of the behaviors that can be observed when an individual is highly effective as a participant in the work of his or her team:

___ Helps team members address and resolve issues together.
___ Treats team members with respect.

___ Works collaboratively with others.

___ Shows concern about maintaining or enhancing team spirit.

___ Displays sensitivity to the needs of the group as much or more than to his or her own needs.

___ Frequently considers the implications of decisions on the team.

___ Demonstrates an awareness of cultural diversity when working collaboratively with others.

The following are some of the behaviors that can be observed when a team member is moderately effective as a participant in the work of his or her team:

___ Generally tries to promote a team feeling.

___ Usually treats people with respect.

___ Focuses sometimes on the group's needs and sometimes on her or his own.

___ Generally considers the implications of decisions on the team.

The following are some of the behaviors that can be observed when a team member is not effectively participating in the work of his or her team:

___ Rarely shows any concern about the team or its members.

___ Rarely works effectively in collaboration with others.

___ Does not encourage or help team members address and resolve problems.

___ Does not show respect to others.

___ Does not consider the implications of decisions on the team.

___ Behaves in a fashion that encourages divisiveness among team members.

___ Demonstrates little awareness of the impact of cultural diversity when working with others.

Decision-Making Competency

DECISION MAKING: The ability to analyze problems and to decide on an appropriate course of action in a timely fashion.

The following are some of the behaviors that can be observed when an individual is involved in a highly effective decision-making process:

___ Gathers and uses appropriate information before taking action.

___ Weighs the advantages and disadvantages of several options before deciding.

___ Makes decisions that support the needs of individuals and groups.

___ Shows an understanding of the need to make decisions based on facts.

___ Works to gain acceptance of others involved in the decision or its impact.

___ Encourages the team to search for creative or novel solutions.

___ Contributes novel or creative ideas willingly.

___ Considers ethical issues before deciding.

___ Typically considers the impact of cultural diversity before deciding.

The following are some of the behaviors that can be observed when an individual is involved in a moderately effective decision-making process:

___ Generally considers appropriate information before taking action.

___ Usually weighs courses of action.

___ Shows some understanding of the need to make decisions based on facts.

___ Shows some awareness of the need to address the impact of a decision on those involved.

___ Open to creative or novel solutions.

___ Occasionally offers novel or creative ideas.

___ Shows some concern about ethical issues before deciding.

___ Occasionally raises concerns about the impact of cultural diversity before deciding.

The following are some of the behaviors that can be observed when an individual is involved in an ineffective decision-making process:

___ Makes decisions without gathering the necessary information.

___ Does not weigh the consequences of decisions.

___ Rarely considers how decisions will impact individuals and groups.

___ Discourages group members from considering creative or novel solutions.

___ Does not offer creative or novel ideas.

___ Does not consider the ethical implications of decisions.

___ Does not consider the impact of cultural diversity before deciding, even when such issues are relevant.

Listening Competency

LISTENING SKILL: The ability to focus on and understand what is being said, in individual or group situations.

The following are some of the behaviors that can be observed when an individual is listening in a highly effective manner:

___ Demonstrates good listening skills by clarifying, restating, and summarizing important points or issues made by others.

___ Makes good eye contact, nodding to indicate understanding.

___ Follows up on another's conversation as opposed to abruptly changing topic.

___ Reflects on what others have said.

___ Rarely cuts others off while they are speaking.

___ Demonstrates an awareness of cultural diversity when attempting to understand the communications of others.

The following are some of the behaviors that can be observed when an individual is listening in a moderately effective manner:

___ Generally listens to others, but may cut others off to interject his or her own thoughts.

___ Occasionally asks follow-up questions, clarifies, restates, and summarizes.

___ Makes some eye contact.

___ Does not usually change the subject inappropriately.

The following are some of the behaviors that can be observed when an individual is listening in an ineffective manner:

___ Does not allow others to finish sentences; often interrupts.

___ Seldom clarifies, restates, or summarizes input from others.

___ Often changes topic.

___ Shows interest in only own ideas and suggestions.

___ Seldom nods or demonstrates good eye contact.

___ Does not demonstrate an awareness of cultural diversity when attempting to understand the communications of others.

Oral Communications Competency

ORAL COMMUNICATIONS: Effectiveness of expression in individual or group situations.

The following are some of the behaviors that can be observed when an individual is engaging in highly effective oral communications:

___ Clear and concise expression of thoughts.

___ Articulate, correct use of language, expressive.

___ Makes good eye contact with others while speaking.

___ Well-organized presentation of thoughts.
___ Consistently holds the attention of others.
___ Demonstrates an awareness of cultural diversity when presenting ideas to others.

The following are some of the behaviors that can be observed when an individual is engaging in moderately effective oral communications:

___ Generally gets points across although not necessarily smoothly.
___ Holds some eye contact.
___ Generally uses language correctly; moderately expressive.
___ Thoughts are fairly well tied together and presented.
___ Able to get the attention of others on occasion.

The following are some of the behaviors that can be observed when an individual is displaying ineffective oral communications:

___ Has difficulty getting point across to others.
___ May ramble, talk around the point, or get "lost."
___ May switch topics without rationale.
___ Frequently says "ah."
___ Demonstrates low frequency of eye contact.
___ May appear to be unsure of what he or she is trying to say.
___ Unable to get the attention of others in most instances.
___ Does not demonstrate an awareness of cultural diversity when presenting ideas to others.

References

Altman, B., & Post, J. (1986). Beyond the social contract. In D. T. Hall and Associates (Eds.), *The career is dead, long live the career* (pp. 47–71). San Francisco: Jossey-Bass.

Antonioni, D. (1996, Autumn). Designing an effective 360-degree appraisal feedback process. *Organizational Dynamics*, pp. 24–38.

Argyris, C., Putnam, R., & Smith, D. (1985). *Action science*. San Francisco: Jossey-Bass.

Argyris, C., & Schon, D. (1978). *Organizational learning: A theory of action perspective*. Reading, MA: Addison-Wesley.

Ashford, S. (1986). Feedback-seeking in individual adaptation: A resource perspective. *Academy of Management Journal, 29*(3), 465–487.

Baird, L., & Kram, K. (1984). Career dynamics: Managing the superior/subordinate relationship. *Organizational Dynamics, 12*(4), 46–64.

Beer, M. (1997). *Conducting a performance appraisal interview* (Case No. 9-497-058). Cambridge, MA: Harvard Business School Press.

Benner, P. (2001). *From novice to expert: Excellence and power in clinical nursing practice*. Upper Saddle River, NJ: Prentice-Hall.

Bingham, T. (2009, August). Informal learning. *T&D*, pp. 56–63.

Bolles, R. (2009). *What color is your parachute?* New York: Ten Speed Press.

Boyatzis, R. (1982). *The competent manager: A model for effective performance*. New York: Wiley-Interscience.

Boyatzis, R., Smith, M., & Blaize, N. (2006). Developing sustainable leaders through coaching and compassion. *Academy of Management Learning and Education, 5*(1), 8–24.

Bradford, D., & Cohen, A. (1998). *Power up*. New York: Wiley.

Bray, D., Campbell, R., & Grant, D. (1977). *Formative years in business*. Huntington, NY: Kreager.

Briscoe, J., & Hall, D. (1999, Autumn). Grooming and picking leaders using competency frameworks: Do they work? An alternative approach and new guidelines for practice. *Organizational Dynamics*, pp. 37–51.

Buckingham, M., & Clifton, D. (2001). *Now, discover your strengths*. New York: Free Press.

Buckingham, M., & Coffman, C. (1999). *First break all the rules*. New York: Simon & Schuster.

Buron, R., & McDonald-Mann, D. (1999). *Giving feedback to subordinates.* Greensboro, NC: Center for Creative Leadership.

Butler, T., & Waldroop, J. (1999, September). Job sculpting: The art of retaining your best people. *Harvard Business Review,* pp. 144–152.

Clardy, A. (2000). Learning on their own: Vocationally oriented self-directed learning projects. *Human Resource Development Quarterly, 11*(2), 105–125.

Clark, K., & Clark, M. (1996). *Choosing to lead* (2nd ed.). Greensboro, NC: Center for Creative Leadership.

Collins, J. (2001). *Good to great.* New York: Harper Business.

Conger, J., & Benjamin, B. (1999). *Building leadership: How successful companies develop the next generation.* San Francisco: Jossey-Bass.

Daudelin, M. (1996, Winter). Learning from experience through reflection. *Organizational Dynamics, 36–48.*

DeRue, S., & Wellman, N. (2009). Developing leaders by experience: The role of developmental challenge, learning orientation and feedback availability. *Journal of Applied Psychology, 94*(4), 859–875.

Dessler, G. (1999). *Essentials of human resource management.* New York: Prentice-Hall.

Donnellon, A. (2000). *Note on action planning.* Babson Park, MA: Babson College.

Dotlich, D., & Noel, J. (1998). *Action learning: How the world's top companies are re-creating their leaders and themselves.* San Francisco: Jossey-Bass.

Drath, W. (1993). *Why managers have trouble empowering.* Greensboro, NC: Center for Creative Leadership.

Dreyfus, H. L., & Dreyfus, S. E. (1986). *Mind over machine: The power of human intuition and expertise in the era of the computer.* New York: Free Press.

Edmondson, A. (1996). Learning from mistakes is easier said than done: Group and organizational influences on the detection and correction of human error. *Journal of Applied Behavioral Sciences, 32*(1), 5–28.

Edmondson, A. (1999). Psychological safety and learning behavior in work teams. *Administrative Science Quarterly, 44*(2), 350–383.

Eichinger, B. (2007). Is "build on your strengths" the best advice? *Human Resource Planning, 30*(4), 6–8.

Ellinger, A., Watkins, K., & Bostrom, R. (1999). Managers as facilitators of learning in learning organizations. *Human Resource Development Quarterly, 10*(2), 105–134.

Epperheimer, J. (2000, Fall). A different view from business. *Career Planning and Adult Development Journal,* 93–97.

Ericsson, K., Prietula, M., & Cokely, E. (2007, July/August). The making of an expert. *Harvard Business Review,* 115–121.

Evered, R., & Selman, J. (1989). Coaching and the art of management. *Organizational Dynamics, 18,* 16–32.

Fernandez-Araoz, C. (1999, July/August). Hiring without firing. *Harvard Business Review,* pp. 109–120.

Fernandez-Araoz, C. (2007). *Great people decisions: Why they matter so much, why they are hard, and how you can master them.* San Francisco: Wiley.

Francis, L. (2007, July). Mentoring makeover. *T&D, 53–57.*

Garvin, D. (2000). *Learning in action.* Cambridge, MA: Harvard Business School Press.

General Electric Corporation. (2000, June). *GE annual report.* Fairfield, CT: Author.

Goleman, D. (1998). *Working with emotional intelligence.* New York: Bantam.

Goleman, D. (2000, March/April). Leadership that gets results. *Harvard Business Review,* pp. 78–90.

Goodman, J., & Wood, R. (2004). Feedback specificity, learning opportunities and learning. *Journal of Applied Psychology, 89*(5), 809–821.

Goodman, J., Wood, R., & Hendricks, M. (2004). Feedback specificity, exploration and learning. *Journal of Applied Psychology, 89*(2), 248–262.

Greenleaf, R. (1998). *The power of servant leadership.* San Francisco: Berrett-Koehler.

Hall, D. T. (1986). Breaking career routines: Mid-career choice and identity development. In D. T. Hall (Ed.), *Career development in organizations* (pp. 120–159). San Francisco: Jossey-Bass.

Hall, D. T. (1996). Protean careers of the 21st century. *Academy of Management Executive, 1*(4), 8–16.

Hicks, M., & Peterson, D. (1997). Just enough to be dangerous: The rest of what you need to know about development. *Consulting Psychology Journal, 49*(3), 171–193.

Higgins, M., & Kram, K. (2001). Reconceptualizing mentoring at work: A developmental perspective. *Academy of Management Review, 26*(2), 264–288.

Hofstede, G. (1993). Cultural constraints in management theories. *Academy of Management Executive, 7*(1), 81–91.

Holland, J. (1992). *Making vocational choices.* Odessa, FL: Psychological Assessment Resources.

Hunt, J. (1994). *The impact of work group culture on work and family stress.* Unpublished doctoral dissertation, Boston University.

Hunt, J. (2004). Successful executive coaching from the consumer's perspective: Adaptive and developmental learning. In A. Buono (Ed.), *Creative consulting: Innovative perspectives on management consulting* (pp. 165–200). Greenwich, CT: Information Age.

Hunt, J., & Weintraub, J. (2007). *The coaching organization: A strategy for developing leaders.* Thousand Oaks, CA: Sage.

Hurst, D. (2002, July/August). The swing of things: Keys to learning golf and management. *Leadership in Action,* pp. 8–11.

Hymowitz, C. (2007, March 19). Managers lose talent when they neglect to coaching their staffs. *Wall Street Journal.* Retrieved March 20, 2007, from http://online.wsj.com/article/SB117426316483240982.html

Ibarra, H., & Hunter, M. (2007, January). How leaders create and use networks. *Harvard Business Review,* pp. 40–47.

Inkson, K., & Arthur, M. (2001). How to be a successful career capitalist. *Organizational Dynamics, 30*(1), 48–61.

Kaiser, R. (2009, March). Too good to be true. *Chief Learning Officer Magazine.* Retrieved August 30, 2009, from www.clomedia.com

Kaplan, R. (2008, July/August). Reaching your potential. *Harvard Business Review,* pp. 45–49.

Kaplan, R., Drath, W., & Kofodimos, J. (1991). *Beyond ambition: How driven managers can lead better and live better.* San Francisco: Jossey-Bass.

Katzenbach, J., & Smith, D. (2001, Fall). The discipline of virtual teams. *Leader to Leader,* 16–25.

Kehrli, S., & Sopp, T. (2006, May). Managing Generation Y. *HR Magazine,* pp. 113–119.

Kluger, A., & DeNisi, A. (1996). The effects of feedback interventions on performance: A historical review, a meta-analysis and a preliminary feedback intervention theory. *Psychological Bulletin, 119*(2), 254–284.

Knowles, M., Holton, E., & Swanson, R. (1998). *The adult learner.* Houston, TX: Gulf Publishing.

Kram, K. (1985). *Mentoring at work.* Glenview, IL: Scott Foresman.

Kram, K. (1986). Mentoring in the workplace. In D. T. Hall (Ed.), *Career development in organizations* (pp. 160–200). San Francisco: Jossey-Bass.

Kram, K., & Bragar, M. (1992). Development through mentoring: A strategic approach. In D. Montross & C. Schinckman (Eds.), *Career development theory and practice* (pp. 221–254). Springfield, IL: Charles C Thomas.

Laff, M. (2007, December). The future of learning and work. *T&D,* 40–44.

Levinson, H. (1978, May/June). The abrasive personality. *Harvard Business Review,* pp. 86–90.

Levinson, H. (1986). *Ready, fire, aim: Avoiding management by impulse.* Cambridge, MA: The Levinson Institute.

Livingston, J. (1988, September/October). Pygmalion in management. *Harvard Business Review,* pp. 121–130.

Locke, E., & Latham, G. (1990). *A theory of goal setting and task performance.* Englewood Cliffs, NJ: Prentice-Hall.

Locke, E., Latham, G., & Erez, M. (1988). The determinants of goal commitment. *Academy of Management Review, 13*(1), 23–39.

Lombardo, M., & Eichinger, R. (2001). *The leadership machine.* Minneapolis, MN: Lominger.

London, M. (1997). *Job feedback.* Mahwah, NJ: Lawrence Erlbaum.

Ludeman, K., & Erlandson, E. (2004). Coaching the alpha male. *Harvard Business Review, 82*(5), 58–67.

Manzoni, J., & Barsoux, J. (1998, March/April). The set-up-to-fail syndrome. *Harvard Business Review,* pp. 101–114.

McCall, M. (1998). *High flyers: Developing the next generation of leaders.* Cambridge, MA: Harvard Business School Press.

McCall, M., Lombardo, M., & Morrison, A. (1988). *The lessons of experience: How successful executives develop on the job.* New York: Lexington Books.

McClelland, D., & Burnham, D. (1995, January). Power is the great motivator. *Harvard Business Review,* pp. 126–135.

McGregor, D. (1960). *The human side of enterprise.* New York: McGraw-Hill.

McGregor, D. (1985). *The human side of enterprise* (25th-anniversary printing). New York: McGraw-Hill.

McGuire, G. (1999). Do race and sex affect employees' access to help from mentors? Insights from the study of a large corporation. In A. Murrell, F. Crosby, & R. Ely (Eds.), *Mentoring dilemmas* (pp. 105–120). Mahwah, NJ: Lawrence Erlbaum.

Milliman, J., Taylor, S., & Czaplewski, A. (2002). Cross cultural performance feedback in multinational enterprises: Opportunity for organizational learning. *Human Resource Planning, 25*(3), 29–43.

Nannus, B. (1992). *Visionary leadership.* San Francisco: Jossey-Bass.

Noe, R. (1999). *Employee training and development.* New York: McGraw-Hill.

O'Reilly, C., & Pfeffer, J. (2000). *Hidden value.* Cambridge, MA: Harvard Business School Press.

Peter F. Drucker Foundation for Nonprofit Management. (1998). *Lessons in leadership* [Videotape, featuring Peter F. Drucker]. San Francisco: Jossey-Bass.

Pfeffer, J. (1998). *The human equation: Building profits by putting people first.* Cambridge, MA: Harvard Business School Press.

Pfeffer, J. (2000). *Hidden value: How great companies achieve results with ordinary people.* Cambridge, MA: Harvard Business School Press.

Pfeffer, J. (2001, October). Economic cure all: Take care of your clients. *Consulting,* pp. 38–40.

Phillips, K. (1998, March). The Achilles' heel of coaching. *T&D,* 41–43.

Ragins, B., & Kram, K. (2007). *The handbook of mentoring at work: Theory, research and practice.* Thousand Oaks, CA: Sage.

Reingold, J. (2001, September). Teacher in chief. *Fast Company Magazine,* pp. 66–68.

Ritz-Carlton Hotel Company. (2009). *Service values: I am proud to be Ritz-Carlton.* Retrieved November 29, 2009, from http://corporate.ritzcarlton.com/en/about/goldstandards.htm#steps

Rosier, R. (Ed.). (1994). *The competency model handbook.* Lexington, MA: Linkage, Inc.

Ross, R. (1994). The ladder of inference. In P. Senge, R. Ross, B. Smith, C. Roberts, & A. Kleiner (Eds.), *The fifth discipline fieldbook.* New York: Currency Doubleday.

Rossett, A. (1997, July). That was a great class but. *T&D,* pp. 19–24.

Sanders, L. (2001, October 18). *Southwest weathers tough quarter.* Retrieved October 20, 2001, from www.CBSMarketwatch.com

Schein, E. (1979). Personal change through interpersonal relationships. In W. Bennis, J. Van Maanen, E. Schein, & F. Steele (Eds.), *Essays in interpersonal dynamics* (pp. 129–162). Homewood, IL: Dorsey.

Schein, E. (1996). Career anchors revisited: Implications for career development in the 21st century. *Academy of Management Executive, 10*(4), 80–88.

Schein, E. (2006). *Career anchors self-assessment.* San Diego, CA: Pfeiffer.

Schlender, B. (2000, May). The odd couple. *Fortune,* pp. 106–126.

Schmuckler, J. (2001). Cross-cultural performance feedback. *OD Practitioner, 33*(1), 15–20.

Schu, J. (2001, October). Even in hard times, SAS keeps its culture intact. *Workforce,* p. 21.

Schwab, G. (1999, December 18). Woody Hayes: TKO vs. Clemson. *The Charlotte Observer.* Retrieved August 14, 2001, from www.Charlotte.com

Seibert, K. (1999, Winter). Tools for cultivating on-the-job learning conditions. *Organizational Dynamics, 1,* 54–65.

Senge, P. (1990). *The fifth discipline.* New York: Doubleday.

Senge, P., Ross, R., Smith, B., Roberts, C., & Kleiner, A. (1994). *The fifth discipline fieldbook.* New York: Doubleday.

Spencer, L., McClelland, D., & Spencer, D. (1994). *Competency assessment methods: History and state of the art.* Boston: Hay/McBer.

Sperry, L. (1993). *Psychiatric consultation in the workplace.* Washington, DC: American Psychiatric Press.

Steinberg, M. (2001, September 23). *Master violinist Isaac Stern dead at 81.* Associated Press State and Local Wire. Lexis-Nexis® Academic Universe Document. Retrieved November 18, 2009, from http://www.lexisnexis.com.ezproxy.babson.edu/us/lnacademic/results/docview/

Sugrue, B., & Kim, K. (2004). *State of the industry: ASTD's annual review of trends in workplace learning and performance.* Alexandria, VA: American Society for Training and Development.

Tapscott, D. (2008). *Growing up digital: How the net generation is changing your world.* New York: McGraw-Hill.

Tichy, N. (1997). *The leadership engine: How winning companies build leaders at every level.* New York: Harper Business Press.

Underwood, S. (2001, August). The nurturing bond. *Consulting,* pp. 42–47.

Vaccaro, B. (1991). *Depression, corporate experiences and innovations.* Washington, DC: Washington Business Group on Health.

Vancouver, J., & Tischner, E. (2004). The effect of feedback sign on task performance depends on self-concept discrepancies. *Journal of Applied Psychology, 86*(6), 1092–1098.

Van Velsor, E., McCauly, C., & Moxley, R. (1998). Our view of leadership development. In C. McCauley, R. Moxley, & E. Van Velsor (Eds.), *Handbook of leadership development* (pp. 1–23). San Francisco: Jossey-Bass.

Vincola, A. (2001, June). Helping employees balance work/life issues. *Workspan,* pp. 26–33.

Waldroop, J., & Butler, T. (1996, November/December). The executive as coach. *Harvard Business Review,* pp. 111–117.

Waterman, R., Waterman, J., & Collard, B. (1994, July). Toward a career-resilient workforce. *Harvard Business Review,* pp. 87–95.

Weeks, H. (2001, July/August). Taking the stress out of stressful conversations. *Harvard Business Review,* pp. 113–119.

Weintraub, J. (1996). *The success manual.* Wellesley, MA: Organizational Dimensions.

Whetten, D., & Cameron, K. (1998). *Developing management skills.* Reading, MA: Addison-Wesley.

Witherspoon, R., & White, R. (1997). *Four essential ways that coaching can help executives.* Greensboro, NC: Center for Creative Leadership.

Wolfe, D., & Kolb, D. (1984). Career development, personal growth, and experiential learning. In D. Kolb, I. Rubin, & J. McIntyre (Eds.), *Organizational psychology* (4th ed., pp. 124–152). New York: Prentice Hall.

Yammarino, F., & Atwater, L. (1997). Do managers see themselves as others see them? Implications of self-other rating agreement for human resources management. *Organizational Dynamics, 25*(4), 35–44.

Index

About the Authors

Dr. James M. Hunt is an associate professor of management and the Charles Barton Term Chair Holder at Babson College, in Wellesley, Massachusetts. He teaches management, talent development, and leadership. He is also a faculty member of the Leadership and Influence program at Babson Executive Education. James has consulted to numerous business and health care organizations on the development of an organizational coaching capability, executive coaching, and talent development by managers. He designed the Babson College Managerial Assessment and Development course in the MBA program, which utilizes talent management and coaching concepts in an innovative blended learning environment. He was also a founder and former faculty codirector of the Babson College Coaching for Leadership and Teamwork Program and a founder and former faculty codirector of the Babson Executive Education Coaching Inside the Organization program, designed for organizational development and human resource professionals. James is coauthor of the book *The Coaching Organization: A Strategy for Developing Leaders*, a groundbreaking study of best practice companies and coaching, published by Sage (2007).

Dr. Hunt graduated from the Massachusetts Institute of Technology with a bachelor's of science degree and received a doctorate in business administration from Boston University Graduate School of Management, where he studied career and leadership development and work/life balance.

Dr. Joseph R. Weintraub is a professor of management and is the Charles Barton Term Chair Holder at Babson College, in Wellesley, Massachusetts. He is an organizational psychologist who focuses in the areas of individual and organizational effectiveness. He teaches and consults in the areas of leadership development, coaching, team effectiveness, human resources, and performance management. Dr. Weintraub is the founder and faculty codirector of the Babson Coaching for Leadership and Teamwork Program. His work on coaching has received several awards, including the "Management Development Paper of the Year" from the Academy of Management. He is the coauthor (with Dr. James Hunt) of *The Coaching Organization: A Strategy for Developing Leaders* (Sage, 2007).

Dr. Weintraub serves as Faculty Director at Babson Executive Education, where he is the codirector of Coaching Inside the Organization, an innovative certification program for internal executive coaches. In addition to his work at Babson, Dr. Weintraub is also president of Organizational Dimensions, a management consulting and assessment firm based in Wellesley. His clients have included General Electric, Bose, Fidelity Investments, Serono, and the Los Angeles Dodgers.